SPECIAL EDUCATION SERIES
Peter Knoblock, *Editor*

WHOLE-SCHOOL SUCCESS AND INCLUSIVE EDUCATION

*Building Partnerships for Learning,
Achievement, and Accountability*

EDITED BY WAYNE SAILOR

Teachers College, Columbia University
New York and London

#48098535

Published by Teachers College Press, 1234 Amsterdam Avenue, New York, NY 10027

Library of Congress Cataloging-in-Publication Data

Whole-school success and inclusive education : building partnerships for learning,
    achievement, and accountability / edited by Wayne Sailor.
        p. cm. — (Special education series)
    Includes bibliographical references and index.
    ISBN 0-8077-4178-7 (cloth : alk. paper) — ISBN 0-8077-4177-9 (pbk. : alk. paper)
    1. Inclusive education—United States. 2. Community and school—United States.
    I. Sailor, Wayne. II. Special education series (New York, N.Y.)
    LC1201 .W54 2002
    371.9'046—dc21   2001052282

ISBN 0-8077-4177-9 (paper)
ISBN 0-8077-4178-7 (cloth)

Printed on acid-free paper

Manufactured in the United States of America

09 08 07 06 05 04 03 02   8 7 6 5 4 3 2 1

Contents

Strengthening Democracy, Promoting Caring School Communities, and Expanding The Boundaries of School Reform

Democracy is a political system that accommodates differences of opinion. It encourages the formation of competing interest groups. Interest groups such as professional-disciplinary communities and political parties form around specialized concerns; promote their religious, secular, and professional ideologies; and compete with each other to gain political power, authority, and legitimacy in support of their respective agendas. Democracy, viewed in this light, is the politics of compromise, consensus building, accommodation, and coalition development. Another way of defining democracy is to call it a political system in which *people actively attend to what is significant* (Bellah, Madsen, Sullivan, Swindler, & Tipton, 1991, p. 273, emphasis added).

Children and youth hold the promise for a better future. As a group, they must be enduring, *significant* concerns for our democracy. They depend on healthy, supportive families, good schools, and vibrant, safe, and secure neighborhood communities. In other words, children and youth, families, schools, and their neighborhoods are interdependent. Planning for one must incorporate planning for the others, and this planning must be grounded in a unity of purpose. Indices of individual and social well being guide planning and promote unity of purpose and interdependence:

- Safe, secure, neighborhood communities are developed in which children are safe and healthy.
- Children and youth are successful in school as evidenced in high graduation rates, low social promotion rates, and low dropout rates.
- Full employment is prioritized, especially meaningful employment for parents.
- Families' basic needs are met: housing, food, clean air, drinkable water, social service provision, and health care.
- Social supports are provided through person-to-person and family-to-family networks.
- Citizens of all ages are engaged in issues affecting them, their schools, and their local neighborhood communities.
- Children and their families benefit from, and contribute to, vibrant communal associations for play, health enhancement, spirituality, politics, and economics.

- Socioeconomic inequalities are within an acceptable tolerance range, promoting social health and preventing violent conflicts and social marginalization (e.g., Wilkinson, 1996).
- Community collaboratives, schools, and governments rely on well-being indicators to plan, advocate, evaluate, learn, and improve.

When well-being is low, vicious cycles develop, and they are self-reinforcing. Indices of vicious cycles include ineffective schools, unhealthy children and youth, unsafe neighborhoods, toxic social and physical environments, destabilized family systems, high levels of unemployment, and clusters of co-occurring social problems such as substance abuse, domestic violence, delinquency, and child abuse and neglect.

By contrast, virtuous cycles benefit schools, children, families, and neighborhood communities. These "good news cycles" comprise a significant success formula for a strong democracy. In turn, strong democracy reinforces virtuous cycles.

This book by Wayne Sailor and his colleagues is intended to promote virtuous cycles. Sailor and his colleagues' agenda is to persuade you to think and act differently in relation to special needs children and public schools. This book will be controversial to some educators, researchers, parents, and policy-makers who, as members of civic and professional interest groups, have competing agendas. Advocates for these competing agendas entertain different views of special needs children, youth, families, and schools. Compromises may be required.

These contrasting views raise basic, important questions. How does a public school promote democracy? How will public schools meet the needs of special children and youth? Their families?

Simply said, different people have different views of schools. Senge (1990), a leader in promoting organizational learning, development, and change, calls these different ways of thinking "mental models." Changing these mental models is critical to improved planning, learning and performance at all levels—individual, group, organization, system, and cross-system.

A dominant mental model for school endures. Democratic dialogue in the behalf of special needs children, their families, and the professionals who serve them can be facilitated by examining mental models (e.g., Lawson, 1999a, 1999b).

Today's dominant mental model is informed by the generative metaphor of the factory, the assembly line and machine. No wonder. Schools and agencies were constructed and constituted to reflect and advance an emergent industrial society. Today's specialized professions, schools, and agencies continue to carve out one or two components of human wants, needs, and problems. They have established professional boundaries and jurisdictions. For example, schooling for children and youth belongs to the educators; families and communities belong to social workers. In this industrialized calculus, social workers dare not tread upon teachers' work and responsibilities, and vice versa.

Although everyone knows that schools are influenced by their surrounding ecologies, in this mental model schools continue to be viewed in many places as "stand-alone institutions" connected only with children's learning and academic achievement. Today's school reform proposals can be framed and evaluated against this dominant mental model. When the reform dictates are identified and combined, the equivalent of a success formula can be derived. This success formula can be examined for its validity, along with its social–moral justifications and authority.

Here are some of the success theories (Lawson, 1999b). Ensure that children enter school ready and able to learn. Add teachers and reduce class size. Enhance computer and video technologies. Change management styles and decision-making structures. Link social and health services to schools. Add after-school programs. Increase parent involvement. Buy better textbooks. Improve teacher education and, in turn, instructional practices. Add more workshops. Promote collaboration among teachers. Support mentor teachers as they help beginning and ineffective teachers. Build teachers' leadership for authentic teaching–learning strategies and their correlates. Professionalize teaching, and give teachers the power and authority physicians wield. Together, these claims-as-theories comprise one success formula. My evaluation of this formula and its component claims leads to two conclusions.

The first conclusion: *This success formula reflects and reinforces the dominant mental model for a public school.* Unfortunately, this mental model is part of the problem. The second conclusion: *This school reform success formula is not wrong; it is limited and incomplete.* It needs to be amended.

Imagine what schools would look like, and do, if planners began with this fundamental premise: *Every child is special and deserves a special education.* Imagine the alternative mental models for schooling that might derive from this fundamental premise and the companion premises, which follow.

Every child is gifted and talented. Each is unique. Every child needs, wants, and deserves opportunities for continuing learning, healthy development, and success in school. Despite their differences, teachers, parents, and other professionals who work with children are committed to these core premises. Every caring adult has the responsibility to advocate for diverse and special needs children. These adults provide family supports and, at the same time, allow every child to learn in ways that are impossible without their presence. In this sense, *the children of any school community are everybody's children.*

The challenge for caring adults is to help identify each child's gifts and talents; learn about children's and their parents' aspirations, hopes, and dreams; and build upon those things. In this kind of special education, no child is permanently "pulled out" or "pushed out" of classrooms. No child is labeled "learning disabled." No child experiences the shame along with the loss of efficacy and self-esteem, which stem from unpleasant and unsuccessful experiences in school. Every family feels supports from the school and offers supports in return.

These caring adults collaborate in designing, implementing, and evaluating optimal teaching–learning and service strategies in a safe and nurturing environment. Teachers no longer work alone. Parents, especially parent paraprofessionals, work alongside them and providers of social and health services. Each school has a parent and family resource center. Teamwork is the norm. Parents, service providers, and teachers collaborate in determining effective strategies for children. Teaching–learning, counseling, and social service strategies are integrated and tailored to meet each child's needs. Learning communities are evident throughout the school community.

Like schools, no family can be an island unto itself. Insecurities and stresses associated with the basic necessities of family support—employment, housing, safety, social trust networks, and food—are like cracks in the foundations of child development. Barriers to children's healthy development and learning arise when families are insecure, stressed, and destabilized. No school can compensate for all of these barriers because schools are not designed for comprehensive family support, and teachers are not prepared for it. However, schools will not be effective if families are not strong and supported. School reform must encompass family support strategies.

Because strong schools require strong, supported families living in safe, vibrant neighborhood communities, new partnerships are needed among them. Schools alone cannot give families all they want and need. Community collaboratives form, and as they do, the boundaries of school reform expand. New school–community partnerships, facilitated by these collaboratives, provide the foundation for the healthy development and continuing learning of children. As these partnerships are implemented, the dominant mental model for school and school reform expands (Lawson, 1999b).

From this perspective, readers can evaluate this important book by Sailor and his colleagues. Ask yourself questions like these: To what extent does this book reflect and reinforce the dominant mental model for the school? What changes are proposed? What evidence is there in support of these changes as "success formulas"? Are there missing components? Do the proposals depend on important preconditions and resources? Will these proposals work anywhere, any time? Does this book's primary value reside in its "enlightenment effects"—that is, in sensitizing readers and helping them to think differently so that they act more prudently and effectively? Is this book written for professionals, or should every concerned citizen benefit from it? In my view, the issues raised by Sailor and his colleagues are essential for strong democracy and for promoting virtuous cycles.

The agenda is urgent and important, and it requires moral courage and effective mobilization for collective action. Complexity, ambiguity, uncertainty, and criticism are constant companions for persons undertaking this work. As usual, politicians and concerned citizens want "magic bullets." The basic idea of public schooling is being attacked by some interest groups. Popular buzzwords add to the challenges. Systems change, service integration, full-service schools, community schools, school reform and restructuring, school-linked and -based services, and interprofessional case management mean different things even in the same settings. The need for more clarity and precision is apparent, as is the need for dialogue and action planning that are focused upon improved outcomes and accountability. Plans for collaboration among professionals, and partnerships among organizations, are important preconditions for improvements, but they are insufficient and inadequate by themselves.

In short, today's unmet needs and problems break the mold. Significant improvements are called for in schools and community health and social service agencies, as well as in the daily practices of the helping professionals—teachers, social workers, nurses, principals, school psychologists, counselors, and others. It is clear that the boundaries for school reform must be expanded. Educators simply cannot provide all that children and families need. Educators need help with how children spend their time during the nonschool hours, and so do families. Unity of purpose must be a priority. Other changes may follow, which eventually may transform school community relationships, service delivery systems, family support strategies, and community development agendas.

I appreciate the work of Wayne Sailor and his distinguished colleagues because they understand that a much broader agenda surrounds theirs. This agenda is about the future of children, along with the professions and institutions that serve them and their families. These improvements are part of a new agenda for child welfare, an agenda that prioritizes the welfare of children so that democracy is strengthened and all of us fare well (Lawson, 1995).

Read this engaging book with this larger agenda in mind. As you read, ask yourself these questions. What are the consequences of not doing anything more, or less, than we do today? What are the consequences of perpetuating the dominant mental model for schooling?

Clearly, my questions are rhetorical. The answers may be obvious, but they are no less significant for our children, their families, the schools that serve them, and our democracy. Sailor's book is a significant work because it promotes democratic dialogue focused on these questions and the well-being of children, families, and communities.

Hal A. Lawson, Ph.D.

REFERENCES

Bellah, R., Madsen, R., Sullivan W., Swindler, A., & Tipton, S. (1991). *The good society*. New York: Vintage.

Lawson, H. (1999a). Two frameworks for analyzing relationships among school communities, teacher education, and interprofessional education and training programs. *Teacher Education Quarterly, 26*(4), 9–30.

Lawson, H. (1999b). Two new mental models for schools and their implications for principals' roles, responsibilities, and preparation. *National Association of Secondary School Principals' Bulletin, 83*(611), 8–27.

Senge, P. (1990). *The fifth discipline: The art and practice of the learning organization.* New York: Currency Doubleday.

Wilkinson, R. (1996). *Unhealthy societies: The affilictions of inequality.* New York and London: Routledge.

Introduction

This book is about including students with disabilities in the broader context and mainstream of general education. But it is more than just that. It is a book about going beyond inclusive practices into an examination of the basis for school reform in general. It looks at current trends in the provision of community-based services to all children and families who require special assistance for any reason, and asks the question: Are there common threads that link all of these reform efforts? For if such common threads can be identified, and if we can deduce meaning or common themes in these seemingly disparate areas of human endeavor, then there is the possibility of arranging mutually facilitative systems by bringing these various reform measures into juxtaposition with one another.

To do so is to make an important assumption—that these various reform efforts are inherently good and that the lives of people with special needs as well as people in general will benefit from them. To make such an assumption is to enter a realm about which little is known with certainty. In Chapter 1 on shifts in federal policy in human services that can be grouped under the rubric "New Federalism," I argue the following points:

- New Federalism devolves public funds, responsibility, and a measure of accountability to the states (i.e., block grants).
- States, ill equipped to recreate federal bureaucracies to administer block programs, seek ways to further devolve to communities (i.e., more local arrangements).
- Communities respond to these policy shifts by seeking linkages across systems through the sanctioning of partnership arrangements.
- Formation of partnerships requires overcoming obstacles that arise from categorization and separate funding streams, to achieve coordinated planning and integrated service delivery mechanisms.
- Within schools, this process implies inclusion as the chief way to harness resources from special education and other categorical programs in the interests of schoolwide benefits from all categorical supports
- All of these processes have in common a general trend away from sole reliance on representative democracy and toward participatory democracy with its themes of voice and direct participation.

Thus there are many indications that these dramatic changes in human services arrangements are inherently good and that there are grounds for optimism in the downstream effects on lifestyles and opportunities not just for children with disabilities but for all children. Certainly, many will disagree. Those who believe that a strong central government is essential to protect vulnerable citizens will not favor devolution policy. Those who embrace a medical model for human services will not favor decategorization schemes and will seek to maintain the separateness and stability of discrete programs. And, certainly, those who support categorical services within special education based on diagnosis and labeling of various disabilities will not favor inclusion and unified educational resources policy. So this book may be fairly classified as advocacy for particular reform policy in a panoply of contrasting viewpoints. As such, it stands as a kind of hypothesis, yet to be tested. The hypothesis is that the lives of children will be better—and that children will respond more positively to efforts to teach them—in inclusive schools that have active and vigorous partnership arrangements: first within and across categorical programs inside schools, second with community-based supports and services, and third with the families of the students who attend the school. It is to these new arrangements, what Hal Lawson and others call "Community Schools," that this book is dedicated in the hope that this general hypothesis can be put to the test of time and with positive educational outcomes for all.

The book is arranged to provide a closer examination of the relationships of inclusion as a special case of school reform to the formation of productive school/community partnership arrangements. The text is divided into four parts. Part One examines inclusion and partnership formation from the perspective of public policy. Chapters in this section examine federal devolution policies and welfare reform implications for inclusive school reform; the Goals 2000 and subsequent federal legislation in the light of school reform and partnerships; and the implications of Part C of the reauthorized IDEA for these issues.

Part Two provides a closer look at the processes impelling the formation of collaborative partnerships. Issues in strengthening families through integrating services, the future of service integration efforts, and the formation of partnerships for transition from school to work are examined. Finally, Kentucky's School Reform Act is discussed as an example of sweeping reform at a comprehensive, systems change level.

Part Three focuses on inclusive teaching practices with an examination of constructivist methods, mixed-ability groups (of teachers), and collaborative teaching models that cut across general and special education, paraprofessionals, and related services personnel. The chapters in this part reveal some of the approaches that schools are taking to restructure teaching as well as curriculum to respond to inclusive, unified resource policy.

Finally, Part Four presents a glimpse of future practices in two important areas of new partnerships development, fiscal incentive models and professional preparation at the university level. New funding formulas for special education are examined that hold portent for merging special education more effectively into general education as both an outgrowth of, as well as a stimulus for, inclusion. University partnerships for training as still another component in the movement to more local, more collaborative, and ultimately more democratic partnership arrangements are examined with the University of South Florida as a case study in progress.

PART I

Inclusive Education in a Context of Emerging Partnerships

In Part One, we examine aspects of social policy that illustrate the theme of inclusion as a particular case of school reform that is closely aligned with evolving policy in a variety of public education programs. In Chapter 1, Wayne Sailor lays out the case for the general theme of the text. The chapter examines implications for inclusive educational practices of the accelerating federal block-grant and welfare reform strategy. As the federal government provides funds and program responsibilities to the states, sometimes with large cuts as in recent welfare reform legislation, these, in turn, are increasingly devolving to more localized governance arrangements through school/community partnerships. These developments have significant implications for schoolwide reform, the unification of school programs, and school linkages with other community support systems for children and families, together with business and industry. Inclusion, as a key element in special education reform, both contributes to and benefits from the emergence of these new partnerships.

In Chapter 2, Jeannie Kleinhammer-Tramill and Karen Gallagher consider inclusion from the perspective of general education policy. The Goals 2000: Educate America Act and Improving America's Schools Act both reflect the spirit of "third wave" educational reform. Both acknowledge that America's schools can improve only to the extent that all students, including those with disabilities and other significant risks for educational failure, have access to challenging curriculum and excellent instruction. Both acknowledge that in order for all students to access education fully, schools, families, and communities must collaborate in new ways to support every child's education. These policies also encourage development or enhancement of partnerships among schools, universities, and businesses to enrich local curriculum, to ensure that teachers have a coordinated system of opportunities for preservice education and professional growth, and to encourage collaborative research aimed toward solving real problems in the daily lives of children. Likewise, both policies expressly provide for coordination and integration of the full range of child health and social services necessary to ensure that every child can access education. This chapter provides an analysis of how the Goals 2000: Educate America Act is envisioned by federal policy-makers as the centerpiece for educational policy and how related policies at the state and federal level, mirror the inclusive intent of Goals 2000. Within the Goals 2000 framework, states and local schools are the focal point of systemic improvement. Thus the chapter provides examples of one state's attempts to align educational systems to enhance education for all students.

Finally, in Chapter 3, Pat Gallagher and Jim Tramill focus on the implications for inclusive education of the early childhood programs, particularly Part C of the reauthorized Individuals With Disabilities Education Act (IDEA). Intervention services available to young children at risk for or identified with disabilities and their families have expanded dramatically in the last three decades of the 20th century. The energy that propelled this growth can be attributed to several sources at the federal, state, and local levels. These factors have resulted in the expansion of existing agencies and the formation of new ones, each addressing pressing problems of children and their families. In spite of these well-intentioned efforts to provide services, a cumbersome, fragmented, and sometimes competitive system has evolved that reduces access to those who have the greatest need. To change the outcome for these families, successful service delivery must include agencies representing health, social services, and education who work together and establish linkages in a cooperative fashion. The purpose of this chapter is to address the current state of intervention for young children and their families and includes the following: (a) an appraisal of the legislation that has provided our current structure; (b) identification of the roles played by each of three agency-level components; (c) discussion of how collaboration among agencies can facilitate shared goals to improve the child's and the family's outcome; and (d) an examination of current models for interagency collaboration.

CHAPTER 1

Devolution, School/Community/Family Partnerships, and Inclusive Education

Wayne Sailor

The purpose of this chapter is to take a close look at the implications of the "devolution revolution" for a particular aspect of public assistance, namely, progress toward inclusive education as federal policy. The term "devolution revolution" refers to the recent shift in federal policy to increasingly turn fiscal resources and responsibilities over to the states for the administration of human services programs. The chapter begins with an examination of inclusion as a policy reform agenda, its origins in special education, and its present focus in general education. Next, the chapter examines the implications of the devolution revolution. It then reviews school/community partnership models and how these models affect, and in turn are affected by, devolution policies. The chapter then examines current issues in school reform and educational reform in general, in terms of how these policy changes interact with devolution, and considers how these various policy reform agendas come together to form the beginnings of a new framework for the provision of child and family assistance and support. Finally, the role of, and implications for, inclusive education in these transformational policy reform efforts are considered, including the future of university-based, special education and other professional training programs.

The concept of inclusion in education has its origins in efforts that began in about 1973 to integrate education of students with severe disabilities within a broader context of general education (Sontag, Burke, & York, 1973). Efforts to create inclusive programs began with a values-based premise; the belief that students with disabilities should not be segregated for their education but should have access to friendships and interactive relationships with nondisabled peers—a civil rights argument (Stainback & Stainback, 1990). When the civil rights/values-based argument came up against the reality of public schools, professionals and parents aligned themselves with disability-rights lawyers and exercised due process as allowed for in the amendments to the Education of the Handicapped Act, now known as the Individuals With Disabilities Education Act (IDEA). Hearings often escalated into litigation (Turnbull & Turnbull, 1997), and several landmark decisions resulted at the level of appellate courts and the Supreme Court (Lipsky & Gartner, 1997). In one case, Holland vs. Sacramento USD, a school district spent over a million dollars to prevent a single little girl, Rachel Holland, who had moderate disabilities, from being included in a general education classroom. The district lost, and, in fact, the tenor of virtually all of the significant court cases on the topic have seemed to impel the principle of inclusive education.

Meanwhile, impressive amounts of published research have appeared in the literature of special education, funded through federal policy expressed by the IDEA discretionary grants program. Virtually all of these studies supported further progress toward inclusive education (Halvorsen & Sailor, 1990; Sailor et al., 1989; Sailor, Gee, & Karasoff, 1993). After nearly two decades of special education efforts at policy reform in the direction of inclusive education, the corner has finally been turned and the question has shifted from "should we do it?" to "how do we do it?" Thus the history of inclusion passed through three distinct phases: (a) the civil rights argument; (b) enforcement litigation; and (c) federal, research-driven policy implementation.

The fourth major phase in the history of inclusion, which is now in its inception and promises to be a key element in implementation of the reauthorized IDEA (Egnor, 1996), is best characterized as school-driven (as opposed to driven by family/professional, legal, and scientific forces, in that order). It is the central thesis of this chapter and, ultimately, this book that this change of circumstances reflects the growing emergence of localized, democratic processes in the allocation and distribution of tax-supported resources in the human services systems (Sailor & Skrtic, 1996; Skrtic, Sailor, & Gee, 1996). Also, these processes are augmented, if not accelerated, by the devolution policies of the New Federalist political agenda. Although special education, as a field, drove policy reform in the first three phases, general education and, to some extent, health and social services systems are now in the driver's seat. Inclusion is now viewed as part of the broader agenda to unify school resources and integrate programs in ways that benefit all students (Miles & Darling-Hammond, 1998). The reauthorized version of IDEA contains language on "incidental benefits" that, for the first time, places this perspective into the special education statute (Egnor, 1996). The language on incidental benefits refers to the intent of Congress to direct IDEA funds to children in special education for whom Individualized Educational Plans (IEPs) have been developed. If, however, under circumstances of inclusive education, general education students receive some "incidental" benefits from the application of special education supports and services, so much the better (Egnor, 2000). Finally, the challenges of implementing inclusive educational programs are driving as well as benefiting from the emergence of collaborative partnership arrangements of the school, the community, and the family.

THE DEVOLUTION REVOLUTION

Not since the time of John Randolph, John C. Calhoun, and Andrew Jackson (c. 1820) has federal policy so clearly advanced an agenda favoring the rights and powers of the individual states. As with "Jacksonian democracy," the rhetoric of the New Federalism implies a ringing endorsement of the principles of democracy and, in particular, the idea that the best government is local government. Thus we have, at the end of the 20th century, "devolution: the delegation or surrender of powers formerly held by a central government to regional or local authorities" (*Webster's Third New International Dictionary*, 1986, p. 620).

In 1960, states raised, altogether, less than half of the sum of taxation revenue raised by the federal government. By 1993 states collectively raised 95 cents to every federal tax dollar, and today the lines have crossed for the first time in two centuries; the states now tax more than does the central government. A century of centralized welfare state ended in 1997 with the signature of President Clinton, thus ending the open-ended policy of federal guaranteed income support for needy children and their families. Now, through block grants from the federal government, the states are coming to have the authority and the responsibility to transform welfare into something more like a temporary transitional support to job training and work (Broder, 1997).

These changes in federal and corresponding state policy are very significant in terms of their implications for children and families who need special assistance and support. The Individuals With Disabilities Act (IDEA) of 1990 (P.L. 101–476) is a case in point. Congress has regularly reauthorized this cornerstone of federal education legislation since its inception in 1975 as P.L. 94–142 and has provided incremental increases in levels of support to the states for its administration—that is, until the 104th Congress took up debate on its renewal in 1995 and 1996, and failed to pass its reauthorization. IDEA was finally reauthorized by the 105th Congress after extended and rancorous debate in 1997 and signed by President Clinton. The principal stumbling blocks that had to be overcome by skillful political maneuvering were disciplinary suspension and expulsion, and lawyers' fees. Both issues are targets of concern of the National Governors' Association and are primarily general education—rather than special education—issues.

As the federal government devolves funding and responsibility to the states consistent with New Federalism, so do the states, in turn, scramble to seek ways to further devolve responsibilities to regional and local authorities, as depicted in Figure 1.1. As much as states have sought to get the federal government off of their backs with calls for ending "unfunded mandates," and so on, so do these same states find themselves ill-prepared to administer large, centralized support programs (Council of Governors' Policy Advisors, 1996; U.S. General Accounting Office, 1995). All of this strain is, of course, greatly exacerbated by passage of the Personal Responsibility and Work Opportunity Reconciliation Act of 1996. This welfare reform blockbuster, coupled with devolution policy, will over the next few years

Figure 1.1. "Pass-It-Along Politics", © 1997 by Herblock in *The Washington Post*. Used with permission.

quite substantially alter the landscape of how supports and services, including education, are provided to children and families who require special assistance (Chapter 4).

The term "devolution revolution" began to appear in policy literature in 1995 and described much of the agenda being advanced by the activist, Republican-dominated 104th Congress. Although New Federalism had its origins in the Nixon administration and was a cornerstone in the rhetoric of the Reagan–Bush administrations, it took a decade before new federalist policies began to take form and to be implemented in earnest at the state level. The period from 1995 to the present has witnessed an acceleration of new federalist policies, partly in response to the approach of the second millennium marker on the Christian calendar (i.e., Goals 2000, Healthy Children 2000, etc.) and partly in reaction to the passage of the welfare reform legislation. As Gerry (Chapter 4) points out, the welfare reform act significantly devolves welfare responsibility to the states through the block-grant mechanism. In addition to the Child Care and Development Block Grant, after cuts at the federal level representing a transfer of about $16 billion, states now anticipate a near-term transfer of up to $90 billion for Medicaid and about $7 billion for employment and training programs (Stanfield, 1995).

States are reacting to the accelerated neofederalist policy in two principal ways: first, with significant efforts to restructure state government through consolidation and realignment of programs to fit the immediate and anticipated block-grant authorities; and second, with attempts to strengthen the capacity of local communities to implement a more coordinated and decentralized array of programs. Massachusetts, Idaho, Minnesota, Michigan, North Dakota, Rhode Island, and Nebraska, for example, have instituted major state restructuring initiatives to consolidate programs and integrate services (Council of Governors' Policy Advisors, 1996). New York is preparing to launch a system of block grants from the state to local communities. Kansas has recently begun large-scale efforts to privatize much of its child–family public welfare support system, and this effort has run into trouble (Legislative Post-Audit Committee, State of Kansas, November, 1998). Florida has begun a program of organizing and establishing community management boards. Iowa has created nine separate "clusters" at the state level, each organized to respond to a real or potential federal block-grant program. These Iowa clusters meet regularly to create a state and local capacity to decategorize funds (Council of Governors' Policy Advisors, 1996).

For educators, the new federalist policies of devolution offer a mixed bag of news: good in the form of new opportunities to combine formerly disparate and isolated programs, and bad in the form of fewer funds in most cases with which to administer existing programs. Opportunities to link schools and communities together in common planning and resource management efforts are coming about at a rapid pace. How schools and community services systems respond to these opportunities will depend on their capacities and desires to create new ways of doing things.

Some of the emerging models of school restructuring and school-linked services integration (SLSI) that respond to these challenges are examined in the following sections of this chapter. First, however, let us examine the issue of "inclusion" and where it fits into the broader picture of systems change to accommodate new federalist policies.

INCLUSION

Defining Inclusion

As a field, special education experienced its "great leap forward" in 1975, with passage of P.L. 94–142, the Education of the Handicapped Amendments. With this passage, all children with disabilities who met certain eligibility requirements were enfranchised for a free, public education. The real beneficiaries were those with the most severe disabilities, most of whom had been previously excluded from public education. Since 1975, the dominant theme of policy reform in special education has been concerned with the nature of special education efforts and the extent of their proximity to general education practices. Viewed conversely, special education reform has been concerned with the extent to which students are isolated, grouped, and otherwise "segregated" for the purposes of meeting their educational requirements.

The policy reform thrust in this area, which continues today, has generally dealt with three issues: mainstreaming, integration, and, most recently, inclusion. Each of these three concepts refers to a discrete set of assumptions and practices and each has had its cluster of local policy guidelines for implementation, fair hearing findings, court cases, instructional practices, curricular recommendations, and assessment procedures. Each of the three has its own history and differs in many ways from the other two. For these reasons, it is important to distinguish among them and not to use the terms interchangeably.

Mainstreaming is the older of the three concepts and has been primarily concerned with the amount of time and specific circumstances under which students with mild or moderate disabilities would simply be in a general education classroom (Filler, 1996; Sailor, Kleinhammer-Tramill, Skrtic, & Oas, 1996). Where mainstreaming referred to the specific times that a child with an IEP would not be pulled out for specialized supports and services—for example, to participate in a resource room—the other two concepts are more focused on the extent to which specialized supports and services would be provided in immediate proximity to same-age, general education peers.

Integration as a term grew out of published research findings beginning about 1980 that drew attention to the growing extent to which students with severe disabilities were clustered for their educational day in environments such as special schools, development centers, institutions, and other placement situations far removed from contact with general education peers. As a policy reform effort, integration dominated much of the research, teaching, and policy literature of special education that applied to severe disability for most of the decade of the 1980s (Halvorsen & Sailor, 1990; Sailor et al., 1989). The primary thrust of the integration movement in reform policy was to educate students with severe disabilities in proximity to their general education peers with opportunities to interact with them, share experiences, and so on. No assumptions were made concerning placement in general education classrooms under the rubric of integration. For the most part, placement in special classes located in regular public schools with time together at lunch, recess, and special occasions were desired outcomes of integrated education (Sailor, 1991).

The term *inclusion* began to appear about 1990 and referred specifically to placing students with disabilities of all ranges and types in general education classrooms with appropriate services and supports provided primarily in that context (Filler, 1996). Where integration had principally to do with proximity and opportunities for social interaction, inclusion has to do with full membership and conjoint participation with peers at all levels of education. Each of these three policy thrusts, beginning with mainstreaming, then later integration, and now inclusion, has represented incremental progress toward gradual realization of a common theme: participation. As will be discussed later in this chapter, this theme of participation and its embedded idea of membership has its counterparts in virtually all human services policy reform literature, including all branches of health service delivery (e.g., "family-centered care"), social services (e.g., "person-centered planning"), judicial programs (e.g., "family preservation"), and so on. Collectively, these themes can be viewed as representative of a gradual emergence of localized democratic processes in the use of tax distributive resources (Skrtic, 1995).

Each of these three concepts engendered much controversy before giving way to the next iteration of the common theme. Arguments against integration focused on the "fragility" of the population of persons with severe disabilities and the need to protect them from harm while imparting educational benefits (Haywood, 1981). Arguments against inclusion have been marshaled more against the difficulty of providing "appropriate" special education practices in the general education classroom (Fuchs & Fuchs, 1994). With each new thrust, however, the person with disabilities comes to be viewed as more like everyone else and less in need of shelter, protection, and otherwise seemingly patronizing ways to provide assistance.

Sailor (1991) attempted a specific six-point definition of inclusion that was further developed and elaborated upon in Turnbull, Turnbull, Shank, and Leal (1995). The six points are:

1. All students receive education in the school that they would attend if they had no disability.
2. A natural proportion (i.e., representative of the school district at large) of students with disabilities occurs at each school site.

3. A zero-reject philosophy exists so that typically no student will be excluded on the basis of type or extent of disability.
4. School and general education placements are age- and grade-appropriate so that no self-contained special education classes will exist.
5. Cooperative learning and peer instruction are the preferred instructional methods.
6. Special education supports exist within the general education class and in other integrated environments.

Lipsky and Gartner (1997) reviewed some 21 state policies, from an assortment of states, that address inclusion. They concluded that they share a "number of common features in the movement toward inclusion: the importance of leadership, collaboration across the lines of general and special education, the need for changes in pedagogy and school staffing, and financial issues" (p. 113).

It is clear from reviewing the literature on definitions of, and approaches to, inclusive education that the focus has shifted away from special education concerns to whole school concerns. The debate has shifted from how to best apply special education supports and services in the general education classroom to how to align special education with all other school-based resources, including general education, in a manner that most effectively and efficiently imparts a quality education to all of the students at the school. Nowhere has this palpable shift in public policy been more forcefully revealed than in the debate that has occurred in both the 104th and 105th Congresses over reauthorization of IDEA. In previous reauthorizations of IDEA—for example, 1990—debate was focused exclusively on special education concerns. Organizations with a primary focus on general education issues and concerns, such as the National School Boards Association, contributed little to the debate. By contrast, the debate in the 104th and 105th Congresses, leading to the 1997 reauthorization, was largely dominated by the general education organizations, particularly over the issue of removal from placement for reasons of discipline (Egnor, 2000).

SCHOOL/COMMUNITY PARTNERSHIPS

School-linked Services Integration

In a nutshell, SLSI brings school resources and processes into a broader planning context for the allocation and distribution of available community resources to accomplish a forward-looking risk-prevention agenda for children and families. Readers interested in a scholarly review of the history of efforts to integrate human services and link services to schools should see Crowson and Boyd (1993), Gerry (1999; Chapter 4), and Kagan and Neville (1993). Although the space limitations of this chapter prevent a detailed explication of various service integration models, such can be found in Calfee, Wittwer & Meredith (1998), Melaville and Blank (1991), and Melaville, Blank, and Asayesh (1993).

As an approach to the formation of school/community/family partnerships, SLSI models typically occur in one of two forms: school-based service integration, and school-linked, community-based service integration. A third form, discussed in Gerry (1999), integrates services in the community but has no particular ties to schools and thus is of no interest here.

School-based Models

Perhaps the best examples of school-based versions of SLSI can be found in implementation of the *full service schools* concept (Calfee, et al., 1998; Dryfoos, 1994; Dryfoos, Brindis, & Kaplan, 1996). As Gerry (1997; Chapter 4) points out, in the school-based strategy, the school becomes a kind of comprehensive children's center, providing a wide range of psychological, health, social, recreational, and other treatment modalities in addition to traditional educational functions. These "one-stop shops" seek to provide support services to all children in the context of a quality education (Sailor, 1994a, 1994b; Sailor et al., 1996). Such models require a full-time coordinator or program director; a team of culturally sensitive, perhaps bilingual, cross-professional staff (and perhaps family and community members); a designated space for meetings and clinic functions; and, finally, a coordinated means of linking families and all services and supports to the child with the child's educational program (Turnbull & Turnbull, 1997, pp. 17, 252–257).

School-linked Models

Other state initiatives that promote school/community SLSI partnerships call for family resource centers, which may or may not include health clinic facilities, to be established in neighborhoods in close proximity to schools, but not on the school campus. In Iowa, for example, family resource centers linked to schools are associated with the state's Child Welfare Decategorization Program. Locally operated "decat" programs are designed to implement services that are "family-focused, community-based and reduce reliance on out-of-home and out-of-community care" (Bennett, 1994). Thus Iowa's SLSI program is stimulated by the Department of Human Services, which oversees all welfare and juvenile justice authorities. Linkages to the schools are left to local policy rather than mandated at the state level. The Iowa program is largely a pooled funding stream effort but contains a unique feature that makes it a very interesting SLSI model in terms of its long-range prevention potential. If prevention works, investments made in the interests of young children and their families should result in downstream savings. Those very much more expensive programs (i.e., substance abuse, teen pregnancy) that address problems of teenagers, for example, theoretically would not be activated if young children at risk for these problems were successfully treated through a risk prevention strategy (Schorr, 1997). Counties participating in the "decat" program are monitored to determine the financial impact of their total service structure when the investment is made in the prevention agenda represented by the "decat" program. Those counties that realize a savings under this yearly evaluation are allowed to reinvest that savings in an expanded and restructured system of prevention supports and services.

A common theme that emerges in the descriptions of all of these school/community/family partnership arrangements is that of building "*social capital*" (Stone & Wehlage, 1992). Social capital is "the product of social and organizational relationships among people and is a resource for creating collective action" (Corbett, Wilson, & Webb, 1996, p. 47). When democratic processes are set into motion at a *local* level—say, in forming a school/community/family partnership to implement SLSI—the energy, enthusiasm, and time invested by stakeholders, especially family members from high-risk populations, contribute to the formation of social capital, a process that at once empowers the participant and at the same time provides needed resources to the developing structure. American human services systems have failed historically to recognize the value of social capital, preferring instead to lay responsibility for the provision of assistance in the hands of professionals who, from their agency standpoints, are expected to solve the social problems of others (Sailor & Skrtic, 1995).

Collaboration

Detailed analyses and examples of SLSI initiatives can be found in Rigsby, Reynolds, and Wang (1995), who focus primarily on applications in urban settings, and in Kagan, Goffin, Golub, and Pritchard (1995), who examine state initiatives to accomplish SLSI in Colorado, Indiana, Florida, and Oregon. Finally, the Harvard Family Research Project (1996) reported results-based evaluative data from SLSI programs in some 16 states. All school-linked or school-based service integration systems require an enhanced degree of cooperation among diverse service provider systems. Under traditional community services structures, no real coordination or cooperation was required. It was up to the consumer to seek out each agency, fill out forms for each, and be entered into various databases with various "case managers," and so on. One of the significant virtues of SLSI models is at least the promise, if not the reality, of a single-entry, coordinated planning mechanism. To make such a "seamless" system work requires both inter- and intra-agency planning and systems change. People such as directors of large agencies, whose budgets often compete for scarce state or local resources, must work together. The speed and efficiency of systems change as well as the extent to which the vision for the outcome is realized may well depend on the nature and structure of these planning efforts.

Crowson and Boyd (1993, 1996) have contributed much to the study of cooperation/collaboration. As they point out, the term *case management* is rapidly becoming pejorative. Informed consumers of human services and supports are disinclined to be considered "a case" and would prefer to manage, at least in part, their own assistance plans. Terms like *planners* and *facilitators* or *family advocates* are replacing *case managers* in these arrangements in SLSI systems. Crowson and Boyd (1996) in turn recognize the extensive contributions of Barbara Gray and her colleagues on the nature and practice of institutional models of collaboration (Gray, 1991; Gray & Wood, 1991).

School-linked Services Integration and Inclusive Education

Again, what do these seemingly disparate areas of systems change have in common? Schools can provide inclusive programs for students with disabilities without participating in an SLSI model. There are plenty of SLSI models around that do not exhibit inclusive educational programs. But the processes that establish and characterize each have many common elements. Can these common elements serve to facilitate the reciprocal development of one or the other if brought into tandem relationship? In our introduction to the September 1996 Special Issue of *Remedial and Special Education*, Tom Skrtic and I argued that such a scenario, although untested, appears likely, at least in theory (Sailor & Skrtic, 1996). Whereas traditional bureaucratic interdependence is hierarchical and monological (top-down discourse), problem-solving entities created to decentralize authority and to disburse resources in a shared modality require organizational structures that are holistic and constructivist. Skrtic (1991) argues that the postindustrial age increasingly requires that products and services be personalized to the particular needs of those who will consume them. This personalization is, in turn, dependent upon collaboration between organizations and their consumers (Reich, 1983, 1990). Postindustrial organizational analysis thus offers a theory of change that is applicable to school reform, to inclusive educational processes, and to community services systems change. Partnerships among consumers and providers to achieve new forms of organization impel movement from cooperation to more personalized forms of collaboration (Gray, 1996). One can hypothesize from such a theory that more efficient and effective forms of inclusive education—with more dramatic educational outcomes for students—will result when democratic planning processes involve family members (consumers) rather than just professionals on the problem-solving team. Similarly, SLSI models will be stronger and will produce better outcomes when their governance structures include consumers.

Kirst and Kelley (1995) make the argument that it is not enough to create SLSI systems without directly linking those efforts to school restructuring and, by this mechanism, to academic outcomes. Their vision for restructured schools mirrors the postindustrial organizational themes delineated by Skrtic (1991).

SCHOOL REFORM AND SCHOOL/COMMUNITY/FAMILY PARTNERSHIPS

School Unification

A summary of findings from the 5-year study of school reform by the Center on Organization and Restructuring of Schools at the University of Wisconsin (Newmann, King, & Rigdon, 1997) reported the results of a study of 24 elementary, middle, and high schools that had undergone restructuring to improve pupil progress in 16 states. The study was designed to examine the relationship of accountability (strong vs. weak) on student outcomes. What they found was that the relationship was completely compromised by several other intervening factors. The most significant of these were the organizational capacity of the schools and the presence of an internal accountability system (i.e., progress indicators specific to the school) in the absence of a strong external system (i.e., progress indicators set by the district or state) of accountability.

Thus school reformers, of an earlier generation, having built specialized, highly concentrated enclaves within schools such as special education and Title I programs, now argue for unified, integrated resources with a high degree of local autonomy (i.e., decentralization). The same conclusion has been reached by Howard Adelman, Linda Taylor, and their associates at the UCLA-based National Center for Mental Health in Schools (Adelman & Taylor, 1996, pp. 14–15).

I published an article in 1991 that contained the statement, "Sufficient parallels exist between the general and special education reform agendas to suggest that the time may be at hand for a shared educational agenda" (Sailor, 1991, p. 8). I went on to argue that the rights, protections, and specialized funding afforded through IDEA should be maintained, but only in an integrated, programmatic structure that will use IDEA resources to improve outcomes for children with disabilities in ways that also have a positive impact on children who have not been tagged for special education. The newly reauthorized IDEA bill contains "incidental benefit" language to that effect. This theme was also picked up by Paul and Rosselli (1995) and by Miles and Darling-Hammond (1998).

Site-based Management

One element of contemporary school reform that readily lends itself to an agenda of school unification and integration of resources is decentralized management, or site-based decision making (Sage & Burrello, 1994). Site management councils, sometimes called school improvement committees when part of comprehensive school improvement processes, are most effective when they have shared budget authority with the school administration (Darling-Hammond, 1990). Where schools have site management councils in place to ensure equitable and cognizant distribution of available resources, a school unification agenda can prescribe how resources for integration can be harnessed (McLaughlin & Warren, 1992, 1994). A model for implementing a form of unified school resources was described by Burello and Lashley (1992). Finally, I provided a broader discussion of the relationship of site-based management, as a school restructuring issue, to school unification policy and inclusive education (see Sailor, 1996).

School and the Family

One of the most salient features of emerging school/community partnerships is the "coming of age" of substantive family involvement in the life of the school. Family/school participation arrangements are being enhanced by recent federal law.

The Goals 2000: Educate America Act of 1994, for example, set new standards for student, family, and school performance (Moles, 1996). The law included a new national goal that was systematically tracked by studies on educational performance. This goal read: "Every school will promote partnerships that will increase parental involvement and participation in promoting the social, emotional and academic growth of children" (National Education Goals Panel, 1994). One of the objectives listed for the goal directs schools to help parents strengthen home learning experiences and to bring parents into active roles in school governance and decision making (Moles, 1996).

Another aspect of the voice/participation manifestation in school reform is the renewed interest in the students' role in partnership arrangements. Without question, the father of participatory education in the modern age was John Dewey. In *The School and Society* (1899) and *The Child and the Curriculum* (1902) (both reprinted in Dewey, 1990), Dewey argued that the educational process must begin with, and expand upon, the interests of the child. The school should be organized as a "virtual community" with the teacher as a guide, alternating as a coworker with the students. Through this interactive participation, with mutual discovery and problem solving, students will become literate, numerate, democratic citizens through the process of learning by participating. Of course, all of this was lost in the industrial expansion that occurred in what has come to be called the "modern era," with specialization and school organization mirroring "machine bureaucracies" (Skrtic, 1995). Bronfenbrenner (1979) has carried these ideas of Dewey forward by consistently arguing for a relationship between development in children and power sharing as a precursor to the acceptance of responsibility. Epstein (1996) reinforces this view and summarizes some of the recent research in student participation in family/school partnerships.

In her summaries of the research of the National Center on Families, Communities, Schools and Children's Learning especially, Epstein suggests a number of key points for intervention that may be effective to stimulate school/family partnership arrangements: (a) Increase opportunities for and encouragement of parents' volunteer activities at school; (b) increase extent of family participation in homework and school projects; (c) increase parent inclusion on school governance councils and problem-solving teams; and (d) increase the extent of school/community partnerships at large (Epstein, 1996: Bierman, 1996).

IMPLICATIONS FOR INCLUSIVE EDUCATION

The perspective that inclusion is embedded in the bigger set of change issues is well represented in the recent monograph by Hal Lawson and Katherine Briar-Lawson (1997), now at the State University of New York at Albany. Lawson and Briar-Lawson discuss four change initiatives that they see as both interactive and interdependent: school reform (including school reorganization to unify and integrate resources), parent involvement, school-linked services, and community schools. In their analysis, the distinction between school-based models of service integration, such as full-service schools (Dryfoos, 1996), and school-linked, family resource center models should best be viewed as separate initiatives rather than as versions of a single initiative, as in the special-education-focused model delineated by Sailor (1996) and Skrtic, Sailor, and Gee (1996). The fourth component in the Lawson model, "community schools," is envisioned as a modern-day representation of Dewey's concept (circa 1902) of the school as a social center (Benson & Harkavy, 1997). Such community schools today would be education-focused community centers for children and families, possibly operating around the clock and offering programs on a year-round basis. Such schools would become key components in plans to rebuild and revitalize inner-city neighborhoods and in the restoration of democratic traditions and processes. Community schools would offer such programs as adult and family literacy classes; homework and other "latch-key" clubs; classes for students suspended or expelled from the regular program; sports programs; arts and crafts programs; microenterprise and small business development for youth, parents, and families (Lawson & Sailor, 2000).

Citing the work of Adelman and Taylor (1996) and Moore (1992), Lawson and Briar-Lawson (1997) use the term *educational reform* to describe the intersection of the four initiatives they delineate. Educational reform differs from *school reform* by placing policy analysis in a larger context, the school as part of a changing and evolving community system of services and supports for children and families. This concept is consistent with the tripartite analysis advanced in this chapter and published under the rubric "New Community School" (Sailor, 1996).

CONCLUSION

"Other People's Children"

Asa Hilliard in his 1995 keynote address to the TASH Conference developed the theme of "other people's children." According to Hilliard, the welfare state in America was constructed for "them" and is not applicable to "us." If we wish to procure a house, we secure a real estate agent. If they need a house, they are referred to a housing service. We use money or credit cards to buy food. They use food stamps (the welfare reform act notwithstanding). We get around with cars, buses, and taxis. They use a transportation service. The distinctions are numerous. Hilliard pointed out that it is, at times, hard to discern whether the systems evolved by Americans to support those who need special assistance were designed primarily to benefit the providers (i.e., professionals) or the consumers. Can we as a nation, Hilliard argued, continue to increase tax expenditures that primarily support "professionals, bureaucrats, and gatekeepers" while situations in the streets, in deteriorating communities, and in low-achieving schools continue to worsen? Clearly, the answer is no, and many of the change processes that have been addressed in this chapter and elsewhere in the book can be linked to this critical issue. See also Delpit (1998) for a thorough analysis of the theme of "other people's children."

To summarize, I set out in this chapter to examine inclusion first as a work-in-progress in special education reform and next as a metaphor for broad-based systems-change processes in all of the human services professions and their respective service arenas. The history of inclusive education, is now in its fourth stage of progression, a stage in which it has moved from being a concern for the field of special education to becoming, more rightfully, that of general education and schoolwide reform processes. Processes impelling inclusive education are being accelerated, first by the millennium change date (the years 2000–2001) but, more important, by significant economic forces associated with devolution policies at the federal level.

Community services reform processes that include school-linked or school-based service integration (SLSI) models are possible sources of support and development of inclusive education programs. However, for SLSI models to interact successfully with inclusive school practices, other outcomes of transformation associated with school restructuring must be in place. Again, these broader-based school reform processes demand democratic practices of voice, participation, and collaboration that seem to be present in all human services reform efforts. These themes, which may be described in terms of postmodern social theory or, more conservatively perhaps, in terms of postindustrial organizational realignments in corporate America in the age of advanced communication technologies, afford the potential for each reform process to inform as well as contribute to each of the other two processes, so that they advance as a unit through a combination of school/community/family partnership arrangements.

Inclusion, then, is best viewed within this argument as a necessary cog in a bigger and better wheel. All of these substantive transformations have many implications for how kids, families, service providers, professionals, teachers, administrators, and others go about their various roles in the process. Perhaps we are finally winding down our efforts to do something about other people's children. Perhaps we are reinventing government in a sense, creating new structures that reduce the importance of differences among us and seek to meet all of our needs in a common marketplace.

REFERENCES

Adelman, H. S., & Taylor, L. (1996, October). *Policies and practices for addressing barriers to student learning: Current status and new directions* (CMHS Policy Rep.). Los Angeles: UCLA Center for Mental Health in Schools, Department of Psychology.

Bennett, B. (1994). *Iowa Child Welfare Decategorization Project: A model of collaboration.* Unpublished manuscript.

Benson, L., & Harkavy, I. (1997). School and community in the global society: A neo-Deweyan theory of community problem-solving schools and cosmopolitan neighborly communities and a neo-Deweyan "manifesto" to dynamically connect school and community. *Universities and community schools, 5*(1/2), 11–69.

Bierman, K. L. (1996). Family–school links: An overview. In A. Booth & J. F. Dunn (Eds.), *Family–school links: How do they affect educational outcomes?* (pp. 275–287). Mahwah, NJ: Lawrence Erlbaum.

Broder, D. S. (1997), (February 2). Ready or not, governors, here comes the devolution. *The Washington Post,* p. C-2.

Bronfenbrenner, U. (1979). *The ecology of human development.* Cambridge, MA: Harvard University Press.

Burello L., & Lashley, C. (1992). On organizing for the future: The destiny of special education. In K. Waldron, A. Riester, & J. Moore (Eds.), *Special education: The challenge of the future* (pp. 64–95). San Francisco: Edwin Mehlen Press.

Calfee, C., Wittwer, F., & Meredith, M. (1998). *Building a full service school: A step-by-step guide.* San Francisco: Jossey-Bass.

Corbett, H. D., Wilson, B., & Webb, J. (1996). Visible differences and unseen commonalities: Viewing students as the connections between schools and communities. In J. G. Cibulka & W. J. Kritek (Eds.), *Coordination among schools, families, and communities: Prospects for educational reform* (pp. 27–48). Albany: State University of New York Press.

Council of Governors' Policy Advisors. (1996). *The states forge ahead despite the federal impasse: CGPA's January 1996 survey of states on the "devolution revolution."* Washington, DC: Author.

Crowson, R. L., & Boyd, W. L. (1993). Coordinated services for children: Designing arks for storms and seas unknown. *American Journal of Education, 101*(2), 140–179.

Crowson, R. L., & Boyd, W. L. (1996). Structure and strategies: Toward an understanding of alternative models for coordinated children's services. In J. G. Cibulka & W. J. Kritek (Eds.), *Coordination among schools, families, and communities: Prospects for educational reform* (pp. 137–170). Albany: State University of New York Press.

Darling-Hammond, L. (1990). Teachers and teaching: Signs of a changing profession. In R. Houston, M. Haberman, & J. Sikula (Eds.), *Handbook of research on teacher education* (pp. 267–290). New York: Macmillan.

Delpit, L. (1998). *Other people's children: Cultural conflict in the classroom.* New York: The New Press.

Dewey, J. (1990). *The school and society and the child and the curriculum.* Chicago: University of Chicago Press.

Dryfoos, J. G. (1994). *Full-service schools: A revolution in health and social services for children, youth, and families.* San Francisco: Jossey-Bass.

Dryfoos, J. G., Brindis, C., & Kaplan, D. (1996). Evaluation of school-based health clinics. In L. Juszak & M. Fisher (Eds.), *Adolescent medicine: State of the art health care in schools* (pp. 221–286). Philadelphia: Hanley and Belfus.

Egnor, D. (1996). *Individuals With Disabilities Education Act Amendments of 1996: Overview of the U.S. Senate Bill (S.1578).* Unpublished manuscript, U.S. Senate Subcommittee on Disability Policy.

Egnor, D. (2000). *Idea reauthorization and issue of student discipline: A case study of crisis policymaking in the U.S. Congress.* Unpublished doctoral dissertation, University of Kansas.

Epstein, J. L. (1996). Perspectives and previews on research and policy for school, family, and community partnerships. In A. Booth & J. F. Dunn (Eds.), *Family–school links: How do they affect educational outcomes?* (pp. 209–246). Mahwah, NJ: Lawrence Erlbaum.

Filler, J. (1996). A comment on inclusion: Research and social policy. *Social Policy Report,* X(2/3), 31–32.

Fuchs, D., & Fuchs, L. (1994). Inclusive schools movement and the radicalization of special education reform. *Exceptional Children, 60*(4), 294–310.

Gerry, M. (1999). Service integration and beyond: Implications for lawyers and their training. In J. Heubert (Ed.), *Law and school reform: Six strategies for promoting educational equity* (pp. 244–305). New Haven, CT: Yale University Press.

Gray, B. (1991). *Collaborating: Finding common ground for multiparty problems.* San Francisco: Jossey-Bass.

Gray, B. (1996). Obstacles to success in educational collaborations. In L. C. Rigsby, M. C. Reynolds, & M. C. Wang (Eds.), *School-community connections: Exploring issues for research and practice* (pp. 71–100). San Francisco: Jossey-Bass.

Gray, B., & Wood, D. J. (1991). Toward a comprehensive theory of collaboration. *Journal of Applied Behavioral Science, 29*(2), 95–114.

Halvorsen, A., & Sailor, W. (1990). Integration of students with severe and profound disabilities: A review of research. In R. Gaylord-Ross (Ed.), *Issues and research in special education* (pp. 110–172). New York: Teachers College Press.

Harvard Family Research Project (1996). *Resource guide of result-based accountability efforts: Profiles of selected states.* Cambridge, MA: Author.

Haywood, H. (1981). Reducing social vulnerability is the challenge of the eighties (AAMD presidential address). *Mental Retardation, 19*(4), 190–195.

Hilliard, A. (1995). *Other people's children.* Presentation to the TASH International Conference, San Franscisco.

Kagan, S. L., Goffin, S. G., Golub, S. A., & Pritchard, E. (1995). *Toward systemic reform: Service integration for young children and their families.* Falls Church, VA: National Center for Service Integration.

Kagan, S. L., & Neville, P. (1993). *Integrating services for children and families.* New Haven, CT: Yale University Press.

Kansas Legislative Division of Post-Audit. (1998). Performance audit report. Assessing how well the foster care program in Kansas is working. Parts I & II. Topeka, KS: Author.

Kirst, M. W., & Kelley, C. (1995). Collaboration to improve education and children's services: Politics and policy making. In L. C. Rigsby, M. C. Reynolds, & M. C. Wang (Eds.), *School-community connections: Exploring issues for research and practice* (pp. 21–44). San Francisco: Jossey-Bass.

Lawson, H. A., & Briar-Lawson, K. (1997). *Connecting the dots: Progress toward the integration of school reform, school-linked services, parent involvement and community schools.* Oxford, OH: Institute for Educational Renewal.

Lawson, H., & Sailor, W. (2000). Integrating services, collaborating, and developing connections with schools. *Focus on Exceptional Children, 33* (2), 1–22.

Lipsky, D. K., & Gartner, A. (1997). *Inclusion and school reform: Transforming America's classrooms.* Baltimore: Paul H. Brookes.

McLaughlin, M. J., & Warren, S. H. (1992). Outcomes assessments for students with disabilities: Will it be accountability or continued failure? *Preventing School Failure, 36*(4), 29–33.

McLaughlin, M. J., & Warren, S. H. (1994, June). *Resource implications of inclusion: Impressions of special education administrators at selected sites* (Policy Paper No. 1). Palo Alto, CA: Center for Special Education Finance.

Melaville, A. I., & Blank, M. J. (1991). *What it takes: Structuring interagency partnerships to connect children and families with comprehensive services.* Washington, DC: Educational and Human Services Consortium.

Melaville, A. I., Blank, M. J., & Asayesh, G. (1993). *Together we can: A guide for crafting a profamily system of education and human services.* Washington, DC: U.S. Government Printing Office.

Miles, K. H., & Darling-Hammond, L. (1998). Rethinking the allocation of teaching resources: Some lessons from high performing schools. *Educational Evolution and Policy Analysis, (2)*1, 9–29.

Moles, O. C. (1996). New national directions in research and policy. In A. Booth & J. F. Dunn (Eds.), *Family-school links: How do they affect educational outcomes?* (pp. 247–254). Mahwah, NJ: Lawrence Erlbaum.

Moore, D. (1992). The case for parent and community involvement. In G. Hess (Ed.), *Empowering teachers and parents: School restructuring through the eyes of anthropologists* (pp. 131–156). Westport, CT: Bergin & Garvey.

National Education Goals Panel. (1994). *The national education goals report: Building a nation of learners.* Washington, DC: U.S. Government Printing Office.

Newmann, F. M., King, M. B., & Rigdon, M. (1997). Accountability and school performance: Implications from restructuring schools. *Harvard Educational Review, 67*(1), 41–74.

Paul, J. L., & Rosselli, H. (1995). Integrating the parallel reforms in general and special education. In J. L. Paul, H. Rosselli, & D. Evans (Eds.), *Integrating school restructuring and special education reform* (pp. 188–213). Ft. Worth, TX: Harcourt Brace College Publishers.

Reich, R. B. (1983). *The next American frontier.* New York: Times Books.

Reich R. B. (1990). Education and the next economy. In S. B. Bacharach (Ed.), *Education reform: Making sense of it all* (pp. 194–212). Boston: Allyn and Bacon.

Rigsby, L. C., Reynolds, M. C., & Wang, M. C. (Eds.). (1995). *School-community connections: Exploring issues for research and practice.* San Francisco: Jossey-Bass.

Sage, D. D., & Burrello, L. C. (1994). *Leadership in educational reform: An administrator's guide to changes in special education.* Baltimore: Paul H. Brookes.

Sailor, W. (1991). Special education in the restructured school. *Remedial & Special Education, 12*(6), 8–22.

Sailor, W. (1994a). New community schools: Issues for families in three streams of reform. *Coalition Quarterly, 11*(3), 4–7.

Sailor, W. (1994b). Services integration: Parent empowerment through school/community partnerships. *Coalition Quarterly, 11*(3), 11–13.

Sailor, W. (1996). New structures and systems change for comprehensive positive behavioral support. In L. K. Koegel, R. L. Koegel, & G. Dunlap (Eds.), *Positive behavioral support: Including people with difficult behavior in the community* (pp. 163–206). Baltimore: Paul H. Brookes.

Sailor, W., Anderson, J., Halvorsen, A., Doering, K. F., Filler, J., & Goetz, L. (1989). *The comprehensive local school: Regular education for all students with disabilities.* Baltimore: Paul H. Brookes.

Sailor, W., Gee, K., & Karasoff, P. (1993). Full inclusion and school restructuring. In M. E. Snell (Ed.), *Instruction of students with severe disabilities* (4th ed., pp. 1–30). New York: Charles Merrill.

Sailor, W., Kleinhammer-Tramill, J., Skrtic, T., & Oas, B. K. (1996). Family participation in New Community Schools. In G. H. S. Singer, L. E. Powers, & A. L. Olson (Eds.), *Redefining family support: Innovations in public–private partnerships* (pp. 313–332). Baltimore: Paul H. Brookes.

Sailor, W., & Skrtic, T. (1995). American education in the postmodern era. In J. L. Paul, H. Rosselli, & D. Evans (Eds.), *Integrating school restructuring and special education reform* (pp. 418–432). Ft. Worth, TX: Harcourt Brace College Publishers.

Sailor, W., & Skrtic, T. M. (Eds.). (1996). School/community partnerships and educational reform (Special issue). *Remedial and Special Education, 17*(5).

Schorr, L. (1997). *Common purpose: Strengthening families and neighborhoods to rebuild America.* New York: Anchor Books.

Skrtic, T. M. (1991). *Behind special education: A critical analysis of professional culture and school organization.* Denver, CO: Love.

Skrtic, T. M. (1995). The organizational context of special education and school reform. In E. Meyen & T. Skrtic (Eds.), *Special education and student disability: Traditional, emerging and alternative perspectives.* Denver, CO: Love.

Skrtic, T. M. (Ed.). (1995). *Disability and democracy: Reconstructing (special) education for postmodernity.* New York: Teachers College Press.

Skrtic, T. M., Sailor, W., & Gee, K. (1996). Voice, collaboration, and inclusion: Democratic themes in educational and social reform initiatives. *Remedial and Special Education, 17,* 142–157.

Sontag, E., Burke, P., & York, R. (1973). Considerations for serving the severely handicapped in the public schools. *Education and Training of the Mentally Retarded, 8,* 20–26.

Stainback, W., & Stainback, S. (Eds.). (1990). *Support networks for inclusive schooling: Interdependent integrated education.* Baltimore: Paul H. Brookes.

Stanfield, R. L. (1995, September 9). Holding the bag? *National Journal,* p. 2206.

Stone, C., & Wehlage, G. (1992). *Community collaboration and the structuring of schools.* Madison, WI: Center on Organization and Restructuring of Schools.

Turnbull, A. P., & Turnbull, H. R. (1997). *Families, professionals, and exceptionality: A special partnership* (3rd ed.). Englewood Cliffs, NJ: Merrill.

Turnbull, A. P., Turnbull, H. R., Shank, M., & Leal, D. (1995). *Exceptional lives: Special education in today's schools.* Englewood Cliffs, NJ: Merrill.

U.S. General Accounting Office. (1995, May). *Welfare programs: Opportunities to consolidate and increase program efficiencies* (GAO/HEHS-95-139). Washington, DC: Author

Webster's third new international dictionary of the English language unabridged. (1986, p. 620). Springfield, MA: Merriam-Webster.

CHAPTER 2

The Implications of Goals 2000 for Inclusive Education

P. Jeannie Kleinhammer-Tramill and Karen Symms Gallagher

On March 31, 1994, President Bill Clinton signed the Goals 2000: Educate America Act into law. For 2 years, Goals 2000 legislation enjoyed a special status as the linchpin of the Clinton administration's education policy plan, the framework to which other legislation was later added—the reauthorization of the Elementary and Secondary Education Act, especially Title I, and the School-to-Work Opportunities Act. The Goals 2000 legislation focused all efforts on building aligned systems of standards, assessment, and accountability, or "standards-based reform."

In the presidential politics of 1996, Goals 2000 survived the budget battle in Congress, but it was stripped of several of its initial provisions. Subsequently, the Clinton administration shifted public attention away from the legislation and toward its component parts under the general rubric of standards-based reform (e.g., Riley, 1998, 1999). Nonetheless, Goals 2000 remained a political policy strategy that called for improving all facets of the education system to support better outcomes. What has been the impact of the Goals 2000 policy on other educational policies? Has it provided the basis for accomplishing the types of improvement necessary to reduce the risks the nation faces as it approaches the 21st century, and, in the context of this book, did Goals 2000 provide a window of opportunity for education to finally become inclusive and equitable? How did Goals 2000 legislation impact reauthorization of the Individuals With Disabilities Education Act (IDEA)? And, perhaps most important, can public interest and political energy for improving education be sustained after the era of reforms that failed to address what former Secretary of Education Terrance Bell referred to as the core technology of schooling?

We argue in this chapter that the Goals 2000: Educate America Act held the potential to address many of the shortcomings of earlier efforts to develop educational policy. Goals 2000 provided a coherent framework for federal, state, and local educational policy. Most important in the context of this book on inclusive education, Goals 2000 as legislation fully embraced the concept that all students must achieve at higher levels, and it provided resources to assure that the lowest achieving students, students with limited English proficiency, students who live in poverty, and students with disabilities can access challenging curriculum and instruction. Chapters 9 and 11 of this book describe the types of support mechanisms that must be available if students with disabilities are to be included in neighborhood schools and general education classrooms. Goals 2000 acknowledged that these support mechanisms—accountability tied to standards and assessments, service integration, empowerment of families and teachers, flexible use of resources, and site-based management—are indeed critical to the success of all students including those with disabilities and other educational risks, and encouraged their availability. Thus Goals 2000 offered a highly promising policy environment for the realization of inclusive practices described.

Reauthorization of the Elementary and Secondary Education Act as the 1994 Improving America's Schools Act (IASA) provided a model for how education policy can be transformed and aligned with the broader Goals 2000 framework. Through the reauthorization process, IASA has become a vehicle for promoting school improvement and infusion of resources to promote inclusive education and standards-based accountability for student progress. Now, the reauthorized IDEA of 1997 (P.L. 105–17) extends the promise of Goals 2000 to promote higher expectations by including students with disabilities in standards-based reform. However, this promise can be fully realized only to the extent that the implementation of IDEA provides for alignment with other ongoing educational reform, becomes more flexible and less compliance-driven, and provides incentives and mechanisms for building supports for all children. Thus although Goals 2000 provided a historic opportunity for the ideals of inclusive education to be realized, we believe that the culture, practice, and policies of special education must change for inclusive practice to be implemented.

In the section to follow, we describe the components of Goals 2000 and the promise of the Goals 2000 framework for achieving coherence in both policies and practices for serving all students including those with disabilities and other educational risks.

THE PROMISE OF GOALS 2000: EDUCATE AMERICA ACT

In describing the purpose of Goals 2000: Educate America Act, U.S. Secretary of Education Richard Riley spoke of the urgent need for ending the tyranny of low expectations that prevent many American students from achieving to their fullest potential (Riley, 1995). The national goals described what education would be like if the nation's schools succeeded in developing high expectations for all students by the year 2000. Table 2.1 lays out the national goals.

Table 2.1. The National Education Goals

By the year 2000:

- All children in America will start school ready to learn.

- The high school graduation rate will increase to at least 90 percent.

- American students will leave grades 4, 8, and 12 having demonstrated competency in challenging subject matter including English, mathematics, science, foreign languages, civics and government, economics, arts, history, and geography, and prepared for responsible citizenship, further learning, and productive employment.

- The nation's teaching force will have access to programs for the continued improvement of their professional skills and the opportunity to acquire the knowledge and skills needed to prepare students for the next century.

- U.S. students will be first in the world in science and mathematics achievement.

- Every adult American will be literate and will possess the knowledge and skills necessary to compete in a global economy and exercise the rights and responsibilities of citizenship.

- Every school in America will be free of drugs, violence, and the unauthorized presence of firearms and alcohol and will offer a disciplined environment conducive to learning.

- Every school will promote partnerships that will increase parental involvement and participation in promoting the social, emotional, and academic growth of children.

The Goals 2000: Educate America Act consists of five components. Title I of the act describes the national goals. Title II provided a system for accountability for progress toward meeting the national goals. The accountability system included a National Education Goals Panel that was responsible for reporting on national progress toward meeting the goals, for providing information to the public and building public support, and for reviewing national standards. The accountability system was also to include a National Education Standards and Improvement Council to certify voluntary state and national standards [U.S. Department of Education (USDE), 1994]. Although Goals 2000 included provisions for development of national standards that would be adopted voluntarily by states, the development of national standards has remained controversial. However, most states have developed standards and assessment systems that are designed to align with standards of one or more national professional associations or learned societies [Council of Chief State School Officers (CCSSO), 1989].

Title III supported community and state efforts to improve education and outlined strategies for meeting the national goals. This portion of Goals 2000 reflected a significant step toward building coherent educational policy. It acknowledged that education is a state and local responsibility but provided for development of mutual support systems and shared responsibilities between federal, state, and local units of government to improve education. Strategies were recommended for alignment of all the resources that make up the education system so that states and local schools could meet the national goals. The first steps in the process recommended by Goals 2000 included gaining broad citizen involvement in development of a state's improvement plan for education through representative participation in a Goals 2000 panel and development of a plan for how the states and local schools would work together to meet the national goals.

Table 2.2 lists the strategies for improving education that Goals 2000 challenged states to undertake. It is important to note that the seven strategies listed in Table 2.2 comprised a set of recommendations, not mandates; however, Title III of Goals 2000 appropriated incentive funds to assist states in accomplishing the goals of their educational improvement plans and allowed states and local schools to waive certain federal requirements to assure that they would have the flexibility they needed to accomplish their goals.

Title IV of the Goals 2000: Educate America Act supported the partnership development strategy described above through creation of parental information and resource centers. Title V of the act provided for development of a National Skill Standards Board to stimulate the development and implementation of voluntary occupational skill standards and certification. The U.S. Department of Education (1994) indicated that, "This Board will serve as a cornerstone of the national strategy to

Table 2.2. Goals 2000 Legislation Suggestions

- Development or adoption of high standards for the content of education and for student performance.

- Development of assessment systems that provide for authentic measures of student progress toward meeting the standards.

- Improvement of teacher development systems.

- Development or improvement of the technological infrastructure for schools.

- Development of school/community partnerships.

- Development of equitable systems for financing education.

- Development of strategies to meet the needs of students who have dropped out of school.

enhance workforce skills" (p. 11). Goals 2000 served as a milestone in the history of educational policy—bridging the federalism vs. local control gap.

When the Goals 2000: Educate America Act was signed into legislation on March 31, 1994, it became the first legislation to provide for general aid to education. The new legislation enjoyed widespread support from the National Governors Association, whose members, during the previous decade, had built major political agendas around educational policy development in their states as well as at the federal level with the first-round development of national goals through America 2000 (P.L. 103-227) (Mazzoni, 1995). Moreover, as Mazzoni points out, governors' agendas received further support from business, which helped to fund and promote the message that economic viability depends on a well-educated work force. The governors were direct beneficiaries of the "devolution revolution," described by Sailor in Chapter 1. Growing to some extent from the Reagan administration's press to devolve responsibility for education to the states, the governors were more effective than the administration in ending an era of progressive federalism in that America 2000, later to become Goals 2000, provided great autonomy to states in renewing educational systems and acknowledged states, localities, and individual schools as the units of change for educational improvement.

At the national level, Goals 2000 provided a policy framework for improving education at local and state levels. The U.S. Department of Education (1994) states, "The Goals 2000 Act provides resources to states and communities to develop and implement comprehensive education reforms aimed at helping students reach challenging academic standards" (p. 8).

Implementation of Goals 2000 was overtly aimed at changing the federal and state relationship in education. The U.S. Department of Education (1994) states:

> The Act recognizes that there is no simple or cookie cutter approach to improving education. It supports a wide array of state and local approaches to raise academic achievement, and to provide a safe, disciplined learning environment for all children. The Goals 2000 Act reaffirms that the responsibility for control of education is reserved to the states and local school systems.

Under Goals 2000, the focus of government shifted away from rules and compliance, and toward flexibility and support for student achievement of high standards and accountability for results. Moreover, Goals 2000 provided support for communities and states to tailor improvement efforts to meet their own needs. The 2-page Goals 2000 application and the absence of any regulations associated with the Goals 2000 plans were important—and unprecedented—manifestations of this new partnership.

The requirements for state participation in Goals 2000 were indeed minimal compared to those of other federal education programs. States were encouraged to develop an educational panel representing a broad cross-section of educational stakeholders; they were also encouraged to submit a plan for state improvement and capacity development aligned with the general provisions of the act and to participate in an on-site review of their efforts.

In return for deciding to participate in Goals 2000, states received funds appropriated on the basis of population for use in stimulating both educational reforms at the level of local schools or districts and partnership development between schools and institutions of higher education to improve teacher development systems. The inclusive aim of Goals 2000 was explicit in the portions of the act that authorized distribution of funds to stimulate local reform and preservice/professional development partnerships. The act required each state educational agency to award subgrants with priority given to a local educational agency or consortium serving a high number of disadvantaged students; a local education agency or consortium that has partnerships with collegiate educators to establish professional development sites; or a local education agency or consortium that focuses on upgrading teachers' knowledge of content areas or targets preparation and continued professional development of teachers of students with limited English proficiency and students with disabilities.

Overall, the Goals 2000 policy framework sought to promote coherence in state and local efforts to improve education. Although the act offered specific suggestions for the processes that might lead to improvement, implementation of these was left to the discretion of the states and local school districts.

GOALS 2000 AS BALANCE IN EXCELLENCE VS. EQUITY

As noted at the beginning of this chapter, the current standards-based reform initiative grew from realization that the educational system could not improve until the lowest achieving students begin to learn. An examination of the core technology of schooling over the past two decades produced the realization that the United States has institutionalized low expectations, minimalist common curricula, and, thus, low achievement for a sizeable proportion of children in schools (Bell, 1993; Robinson, 1995). Many of these children could realize more benefit from education if their hunger, poverty, and health care needs were addressed in a systematic fashion; however, both the child service system and the education system suffer from incoherent policies that produce fragmented practices (Fuhrman, 1993; Kirst, 1992). The situation is particularly urgent because changing work-force demands make it likely that poorly prepared children will have difficulty finding and maintaining employment when they graduate from high school. On a more optimistic note, a few particularly effective schools produce high outcomes by exposing students with the greatest educational risks to challenging curriculum, excellent instruction, and high expectations.

In 1989, the CCSSO adopted the position that curricular changes must proceed from the basic assumption that all children can respond successfully to appropriate and excellent instruction. In other words, improvement of curriculum and instruction was the key to addressing the needs of a more demographically diverse student population rather than "dumbing down" the process to accommodate an increasing proportion of students who were failing to achieve (Honig, 1987). The CCSSO and others took the position that efforts to improve mathematics and reading by stressing basic skills (rote learning) relative to higher order, critical thinking and reasoning skills were not effective for pupils with educational risks. Rather, combinations of "effective schools" teaching methodologies, using cooperative groups (e.g., Johnson & Johnson, 1990; Schlechty, 1989; Slavin, Karweit, & Madden, 1989), peer instructional methods (e.g., Clark, 1989; Montero, 1990), heterogeneous grouping strategies at the school site (e.g., Boyer, 1990; Slavin, Karweit, & Madden, 1989), challenging curriculum and higher order thinking skills (e.g., Jones & Idol, 1990; Pressley & Harris, 1990), and high expectations for student learning (e.g., Brophy & Good, 1986; Robinson, 1995; Wittrock, 1986) were found to be powerfully linked to positive outcomes for all students, including those at risk for dropping out of school (CCSSO, 1989). Goals 2000 encouraged states to embed these concepts in standards and assessments; thus this shift in approach to educating students with educational risks lay at the heart of Goals 2000.

Goals 2000 represented the most significant departure from previous educational legislation such as IDEA and Chapter I in its focus on setting high standards and assessing student progress toward meeting those standards. In contrast to the remedial or compensatory approaches embodied in IDEA and in the ESEA and IDEA prior to reauthorization, Goals 2000 attempted to end the polarization of excellence and equity by arguing that application of "effective schools" principles would produce improvements in how all students learn, including students with the greatest risks for educational failure. Smith and Scoll (1995) capture the essence of this philosophical shift when they state,

> New understandings of how children learn has forced us to reexamine our ideas about the capacity of children and the nature of intelligence, and how we exhibit it. A rich body of research in the area of cognitive science and dozens of "existence proofs" . . . have shown us the power of high expectations and hard work to elicit remarkable student performance, and have demonstrated that all children can learn to far higher academic levels than we previously expected. (p. 394)

Goals 2000 was explicit in its inclusive intent that *all* students should have access to challenging curriculum and instruction aligned with high standards and that *all* students should be included in assessment processes to ensure that schools are meeting their responsibilities. The National Education Goals Panel, for example, was explicitly authorized to review standards and assessment data relevant to the National Goals to ensure that they applied to students with disabilities (Hocutt & McKinney, 1995). It directed the National Center on Educational Outcomes at the University of Minnesota to "increase the likelihood of making valid, reliable, fair and nondiscriminatory assessments about the extent to which education works for all students, including students with disabilities" (p. 25, quoted in Hocutt & McKinney, 1995). Finally, the report explicitly stated that the assessment systems should encourage and not discourage local educators to include students with disabilities in the general education program.

In response, the Minnesota center recommended that school districts make an up-front commitment to include all students in their system of accountability for outcomes and student performance; promote inclusion of all students in assessments through reasonable accommodations; be broad when setting up their standards; and build efforts on existing data collection (Shriner, Ysseldyke, Thurlow, & Honetschlager, 1994, p.38). These recommendations are reflected in the IDEA's new requirements for including students with disabilities in state standards, assessments, and accountability systems [P.L. 105–17, Sec. 612(A)(16)(A–D)].

Goals 2000 also addressed Verstegen's (1996) argument that development of new systems for school finance is, perhaps, the most important step in assuring both equity and excellence in education. Acknowledging the disparity in funding levels between states and within states, Verstegen argues that the current school finance system in many states effectively denies many students in inner-city urban schools as well as in impoverished rural schools access to good teachers, adequate curricula and materials for instruction, and technology. The Goals 2000: Educate America Act, thus, suggested that states examine their school finance systems to assure that they provide equitable support for all schools to meet the states' standards for education (see also Chapter 13).

Several sections of Goals 2000 addressed the need for schools to collaborate with other child service systems to assure that children who live with hunger, poverty, violence, and disabilities have the supports they need to fully access challenging standards, curriculum, and instruction. For example, provisions for Goals 2000 State Improvement Plans [sec. 306 (f) (2)] indicated that states' plans should describe strategies for increasing the access of all students to social services, health care, nutrition, related services, and child care services, and locating such services in schools, cooperating agencies, community-based centers, or other convenient sites designed to provide "one-stop shopping" for parents and students.

Likewise, the recommendation that State Improvement Plans address strategies for extending education to students who have dropped out of school should promote a coordinated approach to adolescent services. The goals for school readiness; adult literacy; safe, disciplined, and alcohol- and drug-free schools; and parent participation all implied the need for development of school and community partnerships to support children in accessing high-quality education. Goals 2000 also made the commitment to inclusive education apparent in the priorities for distribution of Goals 2000 subgrants at the state level. Subgrants could be awarded to school districts or consortia that target the "preparation and continued professional development of teachers of students with limited English proficiency and students with disabilities" [sec. 309 (6)(1)(B)(ii)]. Thus Goals 2000 offered supports to states and local education agencies in upgrading their ability to provide inclusive education.

Goals 2000 as the Basis for Systemic Improvement

Fullan and his colleagues (Fullan, 1991, 1994; Fullan & Miles, 1992) suggest that sustained improvement in education necessitates coordinated top-down and bottom-up efforts. Local initiatives in the form of grass-roots collaboration and/ or innovation to solve problems are essential, but they must be accompanied and supported by coherent policy directions from the top. The Goals 2000: Educate America Act provided a policy basis that is internally coherent and that offered the possibility for lending coherence to the range of existing educational policies. The internal coherence of Goals 2000 was represented by the emphasis on alignment of educational systems at the local, state, and federal levels to improve education. Simultaneously, Goals 2000 policy encouraged grass-roots initiatives to improve education by stressing flexibility in state and local approaches to educational improvement.

Goals 2000 also provided for alignment of policies. Richard Riley, secretary of the U.S. Department of Education, saw the Goals 2000: Educate America Act as the "prism" through which all other education legislation can be viewed (Riley, 1995). Riley thus challenged both educators and policy-makers to end the fragmentation and incoherence that led to Clune's (1993) observation that U.S. education policy is the least effective in the world. The 1994 reauthorization of the ESEA as the IASA and the 1997 reauthorization of IDEA offer evidence that we may, as a nation, be able to meet this challenge.

IASA programs focus on ensuring that all children, especially those in high-poverty areas, limited-English-proficient, migrant children, children with disabilities, and others in need of extra educational supports are taught the same content and to the same standards as all other children in the state. Resources from ESEA supported professional development, safer school environments, and other key elements of educational improvement to buttress the Goals 2000 reforms. Flexibility in program administration and implementation provided further support for state and local reform efforts.

The key provisions of IASA are included in 14 Title programs. The changes in Title I (formerly Chapter I) for helping disadvantaged children to meet high standards are particularly important here. Under the IASA, Title I requires states, LEAs, and schools to align all curriculum, instruction, and assessment practices with the state's standards and to show how Title I programs fit with other components of their education reform agendas. Students served through Title I were expected to meet the same state standards developed under Goals 2000. Changes in Title I also allow more schools to develop schoolwide programs by lowering the minimum poverty level that determines eligibility and by encouraging schools to use Title I as a catalyst for integrating their programs, strategies, and resources. The new Title I is prescriptive with regard to quality of curriculum and instruction and alignment with standards. The U.S. Department of Education (1994) states, "Title

I programs that rely on drill and practice or fail to increase the quality and amount of instructional time will no longer meet the requirements of the law" (p. 2).

Title II of the Eisenhower Professional Development program continues to support professional development in the areas of mathematics and sciences but expands the program to support professional development in other areas as well. Five percent of Title II funds are reserved by the federal government to support activities such as development of a national clearinghouse on math and science, local and national professional development networks for teachers and administrators, and teaching standards and activities of the National Board for Professional Teaching Standards. Title II also requires that states draw up plans outlining long-term strategies for providing and sustaining the high-quality professional development needed to improve teaching and learning.

Title III supports use of technology in education and addresses the need to develop and align state and local technological capacity to support students in meeting the states' standards. Title IV, safe and drug-free schools, adds violence prevention, continues to require states and local education agencies (LEAs) to develop community-wide strategies for prevention, and authorizes development of coordinated services arrangements focused on prevention. Title V promoted equity by providing assistance to local education agencies that want to start magnet school programs, by requiring that magnet school programs were aligned with Goals 2000 plans, and by supporting strategies to improve equity for women. Title VI supports innovative education program strategies that represent the types of grassroots efforts that are a critical part of the systemic improvement process. Title VII for bilingual education, education enhancement, and language acquisition programs simplifies the program structure and activities by building local capacity and adds support to LEAs, which have experienced increases in immigrant populations, to develop transition services and better coordination with regular education programs. Title VIII of the IASA restructures and simplifies the impact aid formula. Title IX assures Native American children equal opportunities to learn at a level that is up to challenging state standards and supports adult education and professional development. Title X coordinates several programs, including the Fund for the Improvement of Education, the Javits Gifted and Talented Education program, the Public Charter Schools program, a new authority for arts in education, and provides for capacity building in civic education. Title XI allows local education agencies, schools, and consortia of schools to use up to 5% of their ESEA funds to develop, implement, or expand coordinated services to increase child and family access to social, health, and education services. Title XII addresses the need to improve school buildings that are badly in need of repair by providing grants for school construction to LEAs. Title XIII funds the technical assistance network. Finally, Title XIV authorizes consolidated applications for ESEA participation and allows states to grant waivers of federal ESEA requirements to enhance flexibility in approaches to improving education at the local level.

Implications of Goals 2000 for IDEA

Congressional activity and discussions among special education advocacy groups regarding attempts to reauthorize IDEA during the 1996 Congressional session suggested that special education policy-making would, likewise, capture the promise of systemic improvement offered by Goals 2000. Both the U.S. House of Representatives and the Senate appeared to recognize the need to move from compliance and quantity of services under IDEA to quality of programs for students with disabilities, and both the initial Senate and House reauthorization bills provided more flexibility to state and local education agencies in implementation of IDEA.

In 1994, Tom Hehir, director of the Office of Special Education Programs for the U.S. Department of Education, drafted recommendations for the reauthorization of IDEA and provided the following description of how IDEA might be aligned with Goals 2000 and IASA:

> We envision an education system that would set higher expectations for all students, give all students the opportunity to learn to challenging standards, and take responsibility and be accountable for the success of all children. To the extent appropriate, students with disabilities would have access to the same curricula aligned with the state's content standards that other students are receiving and, with reasonable accommodations, be included in state and local assessments. The needs of students with disabilities would be considered as part of state and local planning. (p. 5)

Accordingly, the 1997 amendments to IDEA include several important changes that prompted alignment of special education services with Goals 2000 and standards-based reform. Part B of IDEA [sec. 612(a)(16)(A–D)] requires states to establish performance goals for children with disabilities that are "consistent to the maximum extent appropriate, with other goals and standards for children established by the State." States and/or local education agencies must also include children with disabilities in general state and district-wide assessments and develop alternate assessments for children who cannot participate in the regular assessments [sec. 612(a)(17)(A)(I–ii)]. These requirements also apply to Individualized Education Programs [sec. 614(d)(1)(A)]. IDEA also allows more flexibility in state and local implementation. The new State Improvement Plan and grant provisions under Part D give states the opportunity to develop plans that are coordinated with other federal programs including IASA and provides states with incentive grants to align special education systems for accountability and personnel development with the state's standards-based reform initiatives. The Congressional Findings and Purpose for these provisions state: "An effective educational system now and in the future must maintain high academic standards and clear performance goals for children with disabilities, consistent with the standards and expectations for all students in the educational system, and provide for appropriate and effective strategies and methods to ensure that students who are children with disabilities have maximum opportunities to achieve these standards and goals" [sec. 651(a)(6)(A)].

Although these changes pose immense challenges to traditional special education practices, they offer a unique and important opportunity for recognition and integration of special education into the broader policy context surrounding education in the United States. Moreover, while reconciliation of standards-based reform with traditional IEP processes is not easily accomplished (McDonnell & McLaughlin, 1997), it also holds the promise of making traditionally fragmented general education curricula more accessible to students with disabilities.

CONCLUSION

The reauthorization of IDEA in 1997 heralds a major policy shift toward alignment of services for students with disabilities with broader education reforms such as those embodied in the Goals 2000: Educate America Act. Although the Goals 2000 legislation has now ended, its emphasis on standards-based reform and alignment of educational systems and services has had a visible impact in virtually all states (CCSSO, 1998). The consistency of the reauthorized IDEA with the Goals 2000 policy framework likewise attests to the impact that Goals 2000 has had on education in the United States. A recent evaluation of the impact of federal legislation enacted in 1994 indicates that children in the United States are achieving at higher levels and that dropout rates have been reduced since 1994 (USDE, 1999). Consistent with a continuous improvement framework, the report points out that we must set new performance targets and continue the progress.

The concept of policy maturation introduced by McDonnell and McLaughlin (1997) in an early report on implementation of Title I and the Education of All Handicapped Children Act of 1975 (P.L. 94–142) would appear to be particularly useful in considering how the policy shifts in IDEA are bringing about alignment of special education systems and services to create more coherent education for all children.

McDonnell and McLaughlin (1997) describe policy maturation in the following:

> "Federal policies implicitly assume that compliance is a necessary and positive first step in state-level implementation of federal policy goals. However, this assumption may not always be correct, particularly in states that have invested heavily in their own program development. Federal regulations often assume "worst case" conditions or attempt to prescribe a minimum response. Such regulations may promote appropriate organizational arrangements in states that have *not* already addressed a particular program concern without federal prompting. But worst case regulations can be counterproductive in states that have developed their own program and moved beyond a simple compliance response." (pp. 11–12)

In addition, McDonnell and McLaughlin (1997) note in the case of new policies (the EHA had been in effect for only 7 years when they completed their evaluation), tight regulations are probably helpful at the federal, state, and local levels because they provide guidelines for how a program should work. Later, however, as the policy "matures," it is natural for state and local education agencies that have developed sophistication in implementing the program at a procedural level to shift their attention to issues of program quality.

In this chapter we have argued that policy development can have a direct impact on how children are educated and that children who have disabilities, who have limited English proficiency, or who live in poverty have, historically, been placed at risk by educational policies that lead to low expectations and fragmentation of curricula and programs. The nature of the system risks to which we have exposed many of America's children is described by Howard (1995) in the following:

> American educators are not in the business of preparing all children for the twenty-first century. Instead, they are paid to decide who can learn at high levels, and who cannot.... Many children face serious social and economic obstacles outside the classroom, too, but our schools, instead of offering haven and hope, exacerbate the problem with pervasive labeling and exclusion. The failures we deplore are directly attributable to the instructional practices we support. (pp. 85–86)

Pugach (1988) argues that the existence of a separate system offers prima facie evidence that the need exists for such a system whether it be special education, compensatory education for children in poverty, specialized classes for those who have limited English proficiency, or what have you; and the existence of specialist roles as they are currently defined serves as a reminder to mainstream teachers that they lack the skills and competencies to work effectively with students for whom specialized services are available. Thus, when educators are faced with the challenge of educating students with diverse needs and a system for addressing those needs, the existence of the other system for those children suggests that referrals to that system are rational and correct (Pugach, 1988; Skrtic, 1991).

We have argued in this chapter that the Goals 2000: Educate America Act offered a policy framework that, for the first time in U.S. history, ensured equity while promoting excellence and provided a coherent national vision and resources to support state and local education agencies in their efforts to improve education. Moreover, we would predict that any educational policy that emerges through the early years of the 21st century will contain many of the elements of Goals 2000 if not the centralization of policy support for systemic improvement.

As described in other chapters in the book, current attempts to transform the organization of schools so that the boundaries of control are more permeable to stakeholders are evident in a variety of movements including site-based management within restructured public schools, charter schools, private schools, and home schools (Sailor, Kleinhammer-Tramill, Skrtic, & Oas, 1996). Each of these attempts to reorganize education appears to be spurred by stakeholder demands for empowerment and voice. Indeed, the traditional notion that responsibility for education should be handed over to a professional bureaucracy (Conley, 1993) has been usurped by growing demands from parents, teachers, business leaders, and other community members to participate in the governance of education and by a growing realization that schools cannot accomplish their tasks without more universal support systems in place for families and children. Goals 2000 acknowledged the multiple constituencies involved in the educational enterprise and provided a basis for public agenda-building.

The role of policy in shaping educational programs is critical. Goals 2000 offered the promise of encouraging states and communities to build education capacity through partnership development and through systemic improvements that could lead the entire education enterprise to focus on helping all students to access challenging curriculum and excellent instruction.

REFERENCES

Bell, T. H. (1993). Reflections one decade after A Nation at Risk. *Phi Delta Kappan, 74,* 592–604.

Boyer, E. (1990). *The basic school.* New York: Harper & Row.

Brophy, J., & Good, T. (1986). Teacher behavior and student achievement. In M. Wittrock (Ed.), *Handbook of research on teaching* (pp. 328–375). New York: Macmillan.

Clark, R. M. (1989). *The role of parents in assuring education success in restructuring efforts.* Washington, DC: Council of Chief State School Officers.

Clune, W. H. (1993). System change educational policy: A conceptual framework. In S. H. Fuhrman (Ed.), *Designing coherent education policy: Improving the system* (pp. 125–140). San Francisco: Jossey-Bass.

Conley, D. T. (1993). *Roadmap to restructuring: Policies, practices and the emerging visions of schooling.* Eugene, OR: Eric Clearinghouse on Educational Management.

Council of Chief State School Officers. (1989). Success for all in a new century: A report by the Council of Chief State School Officers on restructuring education. Washington, DC: Author.

Council of Chief State School Officers. (1998). State education accountability reports and indicator reports: Status of reports across the states for 1998 results of a 50-state survey by the CCSSO State Education Assessment Center. Washington, DC: Author

Education of All Handicapped Children Act of 1975. Public Law 94-142.

Elementary and Secondary Education Act of 1965. Public Law 89-10.

Fuhrman, S. H. (Ed.). (1993). *Designing coherent educational policy: Improving the system.* San Francisco: Jossey-Bass.

Fullan, M. G. (1991). *The new meaning of educational change.* New York: Teachers College Press.

Fullan, M. G. (1994). Coordinating top-down and bottom-up strategies for educational reform. In R. J. Anson (Ed.), *System reform: Perspectives on personalizing education* (pp. 7–24). Washington, DC: U.S. Government Printing Office.

Fullan, M. G., & Miles, M. B. (1992). Getting reform right: What works and what doesn't. *Phi Delta Kappan,* 745–752.

Hehir, T. (1994). Improving the Individuals With Disabilities Education Act: IDEA reauthorization. Unpublished manuscript. Washington, DC: United States Department of Education, Office of Special Education Programs.

Hocutt, A. M., & McKinney, J. D. (1995). Moving beyond the Regular Education Initiative: National reform in special education. In J. Paul, D. Evans, & H. Rosselli (Eds.), *Integrating school restructuring and special education reform* (pp. 43–62). Ft. Worth, TX: Harcourt Brace College Publishers.

Honig, W. (1987, April). Honig Advisory Committee Meeting. Sacramento, CA.

Howard, J. (1995). You can't get there from here: The need for a new logic in education reform. *Daedalus: Journal of the American Academy of Arts and Sciences, 124*(4), 85–92.

Improving America's Schools Act of 1994. Public Law 103-382.

Individuals With Disabilities Education Act of 1997. Public Law 105-17.

Johnson, D. W., & Johnson, R. T. (1990). Social skills for successful group work. *Educational Leadership, 47*(4), 29–33.

Jones, B. F., & Idol, L. (Eds.). (1990). *Dimensions of thinking and cognitive instruction.* Hillsdale, NJ: Lawrence Erlbaum.

Kirst, M. W. (1992). Financing school-linked services (Policy Brief No. 7). Los Angeles: Center for Research in Education Finance, University of Southern California.

Mazzoni, T. L. (1995). State policymaking and school reform: Influences and influentials. In J. D. Scribner & D. H. Layton (Eds.), *The study of educational politics: The 1994 commemorative yearbook of the Politics of Education Association (1969–1994)* (pp. 53–74). Washington, DC: Falmer Press.

McDonnell, L. M., & McLaughlin, M. J. (1997). *Educating one and all: Students with disabilities and standards-based reform.* Washington, DC: National Academy Press.

Montero, M. (1990). Ideology and psychosocial research in third world contexts. *Journal of Social Issues, 46,* 43–55.

Pressley, M., & Harris, K. R. (1990). What we really know about strategy instruction. *Educational Leadership, 48*(1), 31–34.

Pugach, M. (1988). Special education as a constraint on teacher education reform. *Journal of Teacher Education, 39*(3), 52–59.

Riley, R. W. (1995). Reflections on Goals 2000. *Teachers College Record, 96*(3), 380–388.

Riley, R. W. (February 17, 1998). Remarks as prepared for delivery by U.S. Secretary of Education Richard W. Riley. Education first: Building America's future. The fifth annual State of American Education Speech, Seattle, Washington.

Riley, R. W. (February 16, 1999). Remarks as prepared for delivery by U.S. Secretary of Education Richard W. Riley. New challenges, new resolve: Moving American eduation into the 21st century. The sixth annual State of American Education Speech, California State University, Long Beach, California.

Robinson, S. P. (1995). Life, literacy, and the pursuit of challenges. *Daedalus: Journal of the American Academy of Arts and Sciences, 124*(4), 135–142.

Sailor, W., Kleinhammer-Tramill, J., Skrtic, T., & Oas, B. K. (1996). Family participation in New Community Schools. In G. H. S. Singer, L. E. Powers, & A. L. Olson, *Redefining family support: Innovations in public–private partnerships* (pp. 313–332). Baltimore: Paul H. Brookes.

Schlechty, P. (1989). Creating the infrastructure for reform. Washington, DC: Council of Chief State School Officers.

School-to-Work Opportunities Act of 1994. Public Law 103-239.

Shriner, J. G., Ysseldyke, J. E., Thurlow, M. L., & Honetschlager, D. (1994). "All" means "all." *Educational Leadership, 51*(6), 38–43.

Skrtic, T. M. (1991). *Behind special education: A critical analysis of professional culture and school organization.* Denver, CO: Love.

Slavin, R. E., Karweit, N. L., & Madden, N. A. (Eds.). (1989). *Effective programs for students at risk.* Boston: Allyn and Bacon.

Smith, M. S., & Scoll, B. W. (1995). The Clinton human capital agenda. *Teachers College Record, 96*(3), 389–404.

U.S. Department of Education. (1994). Sixteenth annual report to Congress on implementation of the Individuals With Disabilities Education Act. Washington, DC: Author.

U.S. Department of Education. (1999, April 8). Federal education legislation enacted in 1994: An evaluation of implementation and impact, executive summary. Washington, DC: United States Department of Education, Planning and Evaluation Service, Office of the Under Secretary.

Verstegen, D. A. (1996). Reforming American education policy for the 21st century. In J. G. Cibulka & W. J. Kritek (Eds.), *Coordination among schools, families, and communities.* Albany: State University of New York Press.

Wittrock, M. (Ed.). (1986). *Handbook of research on teaching.* New York: Macmillan.

CHAPTER 3

Early Childhood Legislation: Formation of Collaborative, School/Community Partnerships for Serving Families of Young Children with Disabilities

R. J. Pat Gallagher and James L. Tramill

Intervention services available to young children at risk for, or identified with, disabilities and their families have expanded dramatically in the last four decades of the 20th century. Much of the energy that propelled this growth can be attributed to legislative and financial efforts at the federal, state, and local levels. These factors have resulted in the expansion of existing agencies and the formation of new ones to address pressing problems of children and their families. In spite of these well-intentioned efforts, the support system that includes health, education, and social services has evolved into a cumbersome, fragmented, and sometimes competitive system that reduces access to those who have the greatest need. This problem is most apparent with children and families who have complex medical, educational, and social service needs. To improve the outcomes for these families, a successful service delivery system must include agencies such as health, social services, and education working together and establishing linkages in a cooperative fashion.

In this section, we provide a brief review of the federal legislation that, in part, structures and provides educational intervention services for young children with disabilities and their families. In the next section, we examine the implications of specific provisions of this legislation for the youngest children; those from birth through 2 years of age. These very young children are covered under the Part C provision of the 1997 reauthorization of IDEA (P.L. 105-17). This portion of the law, although voluntary across states, impacts the delivery of services to infants and toddlers with disabilities, those who are at risk for disabilities, and the families to which these children belong. The final section of the chapter provides an overview of the current state of intervention for these very young children and their families. It identifies the roles played by federal, state, and local levels of government in implementing the mandates of this and other important legislation; describes how collaboration between levels of government and agencies can facilitate shared goals to improve child and family outcomes; and examines current models for interagency collaboration.

The risks to overall development, health, and well-being for many children born in the United States are reaching crisis dimensions, with many children facing difficulties few envisioned even a few decades ago. Young children live in increasingly hostile surroundings with more than 50% of them residing in neighborhoods in which they will witness or suffer the consequences of violence (Osofsky, 1995; Taylor, Zuckerman, Harik, & Groves, 1994). Approximately 400,000 children, 5 years old or younger, are abused or neglected each year (U.S. Department of Health and Human Services, 1995). Nearly 25% of children less than 6 years of age are born into poverty (Children's Defense Fund, 1996; Huston, McLoyd, & Garcia Coll, 1994). One important factor contributing to this condition is the birth of approximately 500,000 children to young, unprepared parents each year, most of whom are adolescents without appropriate parenting skills or supports (Osofsky, Hann, & Peebles, 1993). Another factor of concern for young children is adversity that interrupts their lives. For example, about twice as many preschool-age as school-age children will endure the animosity and stress associated with a broken family (Garmezy & Masten, 1994). Other families that present conditions of considerable developmental risk for children are those in which mothers have identified cognitive disabilities (Keltner & Tymchuk, 1992). Without necessary educational and social supports many of these parents experience serious child-rearing difficulties (Kelly, Morisset, Barnard, & Patterson, 1995).

Many children are born prematurely and at low birth weight; in the United States each year, approximately 300,000 babies are born weighing less than 2500 grams. With technological advances, more of these children are surviving, but frequently they experience increased vulnerability to a wide range of developmental obstacles (McCormick, Workman-Daniels, & Brooks-Gunn, 1996). For example, 20% of the children born at 750 grams or less who survive to school age can expect to obtain intelligence test scores in the mentally retarded range. An additional 25% will need special educational services for less severe cognitive difficulties and will require educationally related supports in positioning and movement, communication, perception, and behavior (Hack et al., 1994). Approximately 2, out of 10, newborns are exposed prenatally to illegal drugs and/or alcohol (Brooks-Gunn, McCarton, & Hawley, 1994). In addition, nearly 1.7 million preschool-age children are exposed to lead at levels that threaten their development (Brody et al., 1994).

Prevalence estimates suggest that at least 800,000 children, age 5 or under meet eligibility criteria to receive services under current federal legislation for early intervention (Bowe, 1995). However, this is considered a conservative figure for children with established disabilities (i.e., diagnosed disabilities and/or assessed developmental delays) because of the difficulties in diagnosing developmental delays in young children, policy and practice issues in early identification, and lack of developmental awareness among parents (First & Palfrey, 1994).

The incidence of multiple problems, both for children at biological and environmental risk and for those with established disabilities, is well documented (Guralnick, 1995). For example, poverty frequently predicts the existence of many other risk factors that further compromise a child's development to a striking degree. Children with established developmental disabilities are also vulnerable to multiple problems. Many disabilities co-occur, so that children with cognitive delays must frequently deal with motor impairments, language problems, or sensory difficulties (Boyle, Decouflé, & Yeargin-Allsopp, 1994).

LEGISLATIVE UNDERPINNINGS OF THE CURRENT STRUCTURE

As Americans, we have completed the fourth decade of actively providing services to children with disabilities. We have come a long way since the passage of P.L. 85-926 in 1958, which provided financial support for those interested in teaching children with mental retardation, to the 1997 reauthorization of IDEA. However, the needs of our children and their families have not abated. Modest early federal and state mandates helped establish funding of programs serving children who were disabled. Legislation at the federal level provided support for training professionals to staff these programs. Moreover, accompanying these early efforts was the arrival of parent-driven advocacy groups. These groups spawned debates that dramatically affected public policy and the development of services for individuals with disabilities and their families. By the early 1970s, the number of special education programs in the public schools rapidly increased in number throughout the country (Gallagher & Gallagher, 1992). The decade of the 1970s experienced a nearly threefold increase in school-based programs and community-based intervention services for children with disabilities. This rapid growth was supported using a combination of federal, state, and local dollars and represented a tangible demonstration of America's commitment to the education of children with disabilities (Gallagher, 1984). The growth of programs for very young children with disabilities continued through the 1990s and into the current decade. Smith and McKenna (1994) report that fewer than 30,000 infants were served by states in 1986 as compared with nearly 250,000 by 1991. In spite of this continuing growth of programs, there remains considerable variation in the availability, quality, and variety of services from state to state, and overall we are serving only a portion of the infants and toddlers who qualify for services (Gallagher, 2000).

In 1975 Congress directly addressed the inequities in educational services available for school-age children with disabilities across states with the passage of P.L. 94-142, the Education for All Handicapped Children Act. This law changed the public debate and the reality of public school services for children with dis-abilities and their families forever. Although the law made available limited fed-eral funding to offset part of the total cost of meeting the intent of the mandates for these programs, state and local school districts absorbed most of the costs.

The primary focus of P.L. 94-142 was school-age children and their educa-tional needs; however, there were inducements in the legislation that conveyed commitment to addressing the needs of preschool children. Although voluntary, such programs were required to meet the mandates of P.L. 94-142 for this younger population of children once states established them (Gallagher & Gallagher, 1992). The effect of this legislation on educational services for young children and fami-lies was immediate and dramatic. Preschool programs were established across states, and by the middle 1980s, 50% of the states were serving a portion of the qualified population of preschool children with disabilities. However, there were consider-able service inequities within and across states. In 1984 Congress attempted to address these service inequalities by passing P.L. 98-199, an act that furnished fed-eral funds to help states develop and implement comprehensive services for chil-dren from birth through 5 years of age who are identified with disabilities or at risk for developmental disabilities. These funds were made available under an ex-panded Handicapped Children's Early Education Program (HCEEP, now known as the Early Education Program for Children With Disabilities, or EEPCD). These new federal dollars, along with earlier mandated financial set-asides to support the inclusion of children with disabilities into Head Start programs, provided the im-petus for the early childhood amendments to P.L. 94-142 (P.L. 99-457) in 1986.

The P.L. 99-457 amendments mandated educational services for qualified children with disabilities beginning at age 3 (Part B) and established cost-share incentives with the states to develop services for infants and toddlers under Part H. In 1990, P.L. 94-142 was reauthorized and renamed the Individuals With Dis-abilities Education Act (IDEA, P.L. 101-476). The Part H mandates of IDEA were reauthorized again in 1991, but in 1997's reauthorization Part H's mandates were retitled Part C. Under Part C this federal legislation continues a mandate for states to establish and maintain a continuum of permissive, family-oriented interven-tion services for children from birth to 3 years of age. This moved the country another step toward providing expanded services for all children with disabilities regardless of age. By the end of the 1990s, all states and territories had provisions for serving qualified children under the age of 6, and are committed to implement-ing their state plans for serving children under the Part C mandates (Gallagher, 1993; 2000; NEC*TAS, 1999; Smith & McKenna, 1994). The historical sequence of legislation leading up to the present Part C program is summarized in Table 3.1.

Part C: Its Provisions

The reauthorization of IDEA in 1997 continued to provide states latitude in deter-mining their own structures and funding patterns for establishing services to in-

Table 3.1. Milestones in Federal Legislation

Year	Legislation Description	Public Law
1958	Provided grants for preparing teachers in the education of handicapped children, related to education of children who are mentally retarded.	P. L. 85–926
1963	Maternal and child health program expanded.	P. L. 88–156
	Authorized funds for research and demonstration projects in the education of the handicapped.	P. L. 88–164
1964	Head Start program established.	P. L. 88–452
1965	Elementary and Secondary Education Act. Title III authorized assistance to handicapped children in state-operated and state-supported private day and residential schools.	P. L. 89–10
	Elementary and Secondary Education Act (ESEA) amended to allow for grants to state-operated or state-supported facilities serving children with disabilities, ages birth to 21 years.	P. L. 89–313
1967	Amendments to P.L. 88-164. Provided funds for personnel training to care for individuals who are mentally retarded and the inclusion of individuals with neurologic conditions related to mental retardation.	P. L. 90–170
	Early and Periodic Screening, Diagnosis, and Treatment (EPSDT) program added to Medicaid program.	P. L. 90–248
1968	Amendments to P.L. 89-10. Provided regional resource centers for the improvement of education of children with handicaps.	P. L. 90–247
	Handicapped Children's Early Education Program provided grants to develop and implement experimental programs in early education for children with handicaps, birth to age 6.	P. L. 90–538
1969	Amendments to P.L. 89-10. Title VI consolidated into one act—Education of the Handicapped Act (EHA)—the previous enactments relating to children with handicaps (HCEEP) folded into Part C of EHA.	P. L. 91–230

Table 3.1. *(continued)*

1972	Economic Opportunity Amendments. Required that not less than 10% of Head Start enrollment opportunities be available to children with disabilities.	P. L. 92–424
1974	Amended and expanded Education of the Handicapped Act in response to right-to-education mandates. Required states to establish goal of providing full educational opportunity for all children with handicaps, from birth to 21 years.	P. L. 93–380
1975	EHA amended to create the Education for All Handicapped Children Act. Required states to provide a free appropriate education for all handicapped children between the ages of 6 and 21.	P. L. 94–142
	Expanded services to preschool children with handicaps ages 3 through 5 years with the provision of preschool incentive grants.	P. L. 94–142 (sec. 619)
1983	EHA amended to allow use of funds for services to children with disabilities from birth and provide funding to states for systems planning.	P. L. 98–199
1986	EHA amended to extend mandated services to children from 3 years and create early intervention (Part H) programs for infants and toddlers and their families.	P. L. 99–457
1990	EHA amended and renamed the Individuals With Disabilities Education Act (IDEA).	P. L. 101–476
1991	Part H of IDEA reauthorized and amended.	P. L. 102–119
1996	Debate on reauthorization of IDEA Personal Responsibility and Work Opportunity Reconciliation Act of 1996: Federal welfare reform budget action that reduces federally funded programs that support the medical, nutritional, and income needs of poor families and their children.	no action
1997	IDEA reauthorization.	P. L. 105–17

fants and toddlers with special needs and their families. Part C allows states to define who is eligible to receive services (Trohanis, 1989; NEC*TAS, 1999). The primary foci for the legislation remain: (a) to enhance development; (b) to reduce educational costs and reduce the need for educational support services when children reach school age; (c) to increase opportunities for citizens with disabilities to lead independent lives as adults; (d) to enhance families' abilities to meet the needs of their young children; and (e) to help states to develop the capacity to meet the needs of infants and toddlers with disabilities and their families.

States varied in their responses to this legislation in their selections of the lead agencies to oversee the services (NEC*TAS, 1998), the structure and form of their interagency commitments, their eligibility formulas, and their patterns for service delivery. Each state and territory still require multiagency participation in decision making (NEC*TAS, 1999). The legislation created horizontal structures within states to encourage interagency cooperation to meet the diverse needs of infants, toddlers, and their families. Within each state, agencies with histories of limited collaboration, and often extensive histories of competition for limited resources, have been compelled to work together to create and implement services. The legal imperatives of the legislation continue as before to promote this kind of interagency collaboration. In some cases, however, these efforts have resulted in little more than a system for handing off responsibilities from one agency to another. In other instances there has been more systemic change, and interagency agreements have promoted blending of funds and coordination of services to meet consumer needs more efficiently and effectively. Typically, the state pattern of interagency cooperation is replicated at the local level. Without question, multiagency involvement with shared decision making and broad-based comprehensive intervention services for infants and toddlers and their families are a desired outcome of the legislation. Cross-agency collaboration and cooperation have impacted traditional notions of stand-alone agencies and interagency competition and have raised new questions about the structure of social agencies and schools in America (Hanson & Lynch, 1995; Peterson, 1991).

Funding services for infants and toddlers at the state and local levels continues to be a crucial issue. To persuade states to provide initial resources for such programs incentive funds were provided with the passage of P.L. 99-458 amendments. The plan that each state submits under the law requires it to address the multiple needs of children and their families. It was recognized early on that providing for very young children demanded that, "effective interventions . . . required involvement by many professional disciplines and services that crossed the jurisdictions and legislated program responsibilities of several agencies" (Peterson, 1991, p. 89). This inclusive approach nudged the system ever closer to developing multidisciplinary, comprehensive, interagency-focused, collaborative intervention programs.

Each state's governor authorizes a lead agency to coordinate Part C planning and implementation. As states wrestle with this complex service delivery problem, several questions in designing programs for this group of children and their families have emerged. Who needs to be involved in the planning? What state agency should be selected to take the lead in such an effort? Who is eligible to participate in the services? How will eligibility be determined? How will these interagency, collaborative programs be implemented at the local level?

From the outset, the notion of collaboration among service providers was an important aspect of any effort. Within the first 2 years after P.L. 99-457 was enacted, all 50 states complied with the procedural guidelines of the law. Each state selected the lead agency, usually either departments of health or education. They established state-level Interagency Coordinating Councils (ICC) comprised of representatives from groups including the state's legislature, service providers, personnel preparation programs, and consumers. The ICCs were intended to be working collaborations among the essential stakeholders involved in providing services to very young children and their families. The planning process also mandated each state to (a) define eligibility requirements, (b) develop a state directory of services and resources, (c) create a plan for personnel development, (d) initiate a system for compiling data on Early Intervention (EI) programs, (e) develop provisions for the Individualized Family Service Plan, and, (f) develop state assurances that a system was available for all eligible children in the state.

P.L. 99-457 left several questions about how states were to implement the permissive requirements. In the beginning ICCs struggled with multiple issues, including how to fund services, definitions for who qualifies for services, and operationalizing an interagency collaborative model. These issues continue to complicate service efforts, and states still face questions as to how individuals and agencies can provide expanded services to an increasing population in a climate of shrinking resources.

As stated earlier, the legislation did not specify eligibility criteria but left this important decision to the individual states. Ideally, program eligibility would be based on multiple factors that account for the complex, multidimensional, and interdependent view of overall development for children (Sameroff, 1982, 1983; Sameroff & Chandler, 1975; Sameroff & Fiese, 1991). Incorporating such a model requires that eligibility must include information related to the child and the child's family. Shonkoff and Meisels (1991) state that to meet the developmental needs of the child, the family must be directly involved in planning service providers to assure that the needs of both the child and family are met. This latter condition is not only "best practice" (Bredekamp, 1987; Bredekamp & Rosegrant, 1992; Wolery & Bredekamp, 1994) but also a legal mandate of the IDEA Part C itself. Many states answered this call by moving toward a multiple-risk model for determining eligibility, by adopting a family focus, and by encouraging active family involvement in the intervention process (Shonkoff & Marshall, 1991). Thus, instead of employing unreliable and incomplete single predictors as criteria for eligibility, states adopted a risk model in acknowledgment of the fact that child outcomes are multidimensional and complex.

Federal guidelines acknowledge this shift from child-focused criteria to multiple-risk-based criteria by outlining three broad conditions for eligibility under

Part C including Established Risk, Biological Risk, and Environmental Risk. Definitions for each of these categories include the following:

Established Risk

refers to children whose early developmental disabilities are related to diagnosed medical disorders. Examples of such disorders include Down syndrome, inborn errors of metabolism (e.g., untreated PKU and other disorders of the body's chemical system), multiple congenital anomalies (e.g., spina bifida), and morphological anomalies (e.g., cleft palate).

Biological Risk

refers to children who have a history of biological factors during their prenatal, neonatal, or postnatal periods that could have developmental sequelae. Such factors include metabolic disease and nutritional deficiencies in the mother, obstetrical complications, low birth weight, anoxia, and prematurity, among many others.

Environmental Risk

refers to children whose experiences are significantly limited during early childhood in areas of maternal attachment, family organization, health care, nutrition, and opportunities for physical, social, and adaptive stimulation. Such factors are highly correlated with probability of delayed development (Meisels & Wasik, 1990).

This multiple-risk, family-focused orientation attends to the needs of both the child and the family. Instead of focusing on a specific set of intervention strategies to be applied to the child only, this model uses *risk* as a "best fit" set of factors that allows the child entry into the intervention system. Intervention strategies within this model focus on the transactional needs of the child within the broader context of the family and community (Lewis & Lee-Painter, 1974; Meisels & Wasik, 1990; Sameroff, 1982, 1983; Sameroff & Chandler, 1975).

Effective, multidimensional, early intervention strategies involve collaboration among family members, professionals, and the agencies they represent. This intervention approach views the family as having a different role. Instead of a passive recipient of services, the family unit is viewed as a primary service delivery resource. Implementing such a model depends on collaboration among service providers with the family as an active participant. Individual families and their children bring to this process different sets of needs that range from comprehensive to episodic and that require varying levels of attention and time. There is no predetermined set of strategies that can be applied to a child on the basis of presumed attributes of a particular disability. Shonkoff and Meisels (1991) discuss the flexible arrangement such services necessitate when they state,

> Thus, a family whose child has an established diagnosis and whose internal family resources and external support networks are strong might be served best by the simple provision of educational materials, periodic reevaluation, and comprehensive pediatric care. Another family, whose personal resources for nurturing a young child are extremely limited and whose support network is highly tenuous, may have a relatively healthy infant whose need for extensive prevention services is great. (p. 24)

This approach is clearly different from the two previous intervention models. As described by Kleinhammer-Tramill and Gallagher in Chapter 2, earlier models were often based on a particular set of child attributes thought to characterize children with a particular disability. Eligibility for special education as well as for educational placements and curricular decisions was then based on these attributes. Inclusion of the family in this model was minimal, usually as one of several stakeholders who were signers of the IFSP. These two different approaches to entry into the special education and early intervention system had differential impacts on how services were planned and implemented. One was programmatically indeterminate and family-focused, in which the family entered a collaborative relationship with service providers who negotiated the best array of services to meet the needs of the child and the family. The services identified would ideally suit both the needs of the child and family and the service system's capacity. The key to this approach was the collaborative arrangement established between the family and professionals and based on working agreements among all the primary stakeholders. The other approach was program-focused and was prescribed by an agency on the basis of presumed aptitude/treatment interactions. Children with particular disabilities were presumed to benefit from particular curricular and instructional approaches. Families were provided entry into the program, but their participation was often limited to agreeing to predetermined strategies to ameliorate specific disabling conditions or characteristics.

Part C: A Case for Collaboration

A key component to fulfilling the promise of Part C is the opportunity for parties interested in the intervention efforts to work together in planning and implementing programs to impact the lives of children and families. How will such a program work? Who are the primary players or stakeholders in the process? What are the caveats to which attention must be paid to support this collaborative effort? The first part of this section addresses the concept of collaboration and its role in planning and implementing services for young children and their families. The second part provides a model for collaboration and partnership formation that could become a framework for establishing inclusive collaborative teams that can address the multidimensional and dynamic needs of families and young children.

Although the field of early intervention has witnessed dramatic evolution, this change is particularly evident when examining the change in roles for the child and family in the process. Reflecting our changing understanding of child development, and our understanding of best practices, active participation of the family increases the effectiveness of intervention efforts. Decades ago, when child development research was intent on describing the child and factors that a child possessed, research and intervention in disabilities were child-focused. In spite of the growing recognition of the importance of the family in improving child outcomes, the field, until recently, continued to be child-focused. Beginning in the 1960s and 1970s, research into the dynamics of the child with his or her care giver changed this child-focused emphasis and thus helped to transform our models for intervention (Field, 1979; Sameroff & Chandler, 1975; Sander, 1962).

Bronfenbrenner (1979) nudged the field of early intervention even farther when he adapted an ecological model for viewing development using a systems perspective. Typical development of children thus forms the basis for a template for intervention efforts with children who have disabilities or are at risk for disabilities. Children are viewed in this model as products of a complex, dynamic, interdependent environment in which everyone plays a part (Bronfenbrenner, 1979; Sameroff & Chandler, 1975). As paradigms for research in child development, became increasingly complex, education and early intervention witnessed similar changes. Reflecting this understanding of child development, we have systematically moved from child-focused intervention models, through strategies that acknowledge the importance of the family, to family-centered interventions where the care giver and the child are active partners in successful intervention plans. As active participants in a family-centered intervention model, care giver(s) play critical roles as team collaborators (planners and evaluators) in determining the outcomes for their child.

The demographics of the population of children eligible for Part C services increase the complexity of the dynamics of delivering collaborative services to young children and their families. Part C legislated the notion of early intervention for children who have traditionally not been served under the broader IDEA legislation, that is, children at risk for developmental disability. Although there has been some retrenchment under this provision, states remain committed to serving *all* children who are eligible. Harbin, Gallagher, and Terry (1991) found that of the original 27 states committed to serving children at risk for developmental disabilities when Part H was passed, only 12 states maintained their commitment to serve the at risk population when it came time to approve the policies. In those 12 states the authors noted a range of eligibility criteria: One state included an extensive list of risk criteria, any one of which would qualify a child for services, whereas others cited multiple risk factors and required that more than one factor must be present before a child could be considered eligible for services. The outcome of this study indicated considerable variation among states in determining eligibility for infant and toddler services. Some states now provide early intervention services for both children with disabilities and children with risks, whereas other states still require diagnoses of disability. In spite of our national commitment to delivering services to all children who are eligible, there remains a large group of unserved children and families (Gallagher, 2000).

States have attempted to determine the prevalence of children under age 3 who might qualify for services under each of the three risk categories. Using the criteria for biological, established, and environmental risk, Florida estimated that 28% of infants and toddlers could be considered eligible for Part H services using criteria for one or more risk conditions (Zervigon-Hakes, 1995). When states such as Florida adopt inclusive policies that expand the population eligible for services, they then face more troublesome issues of how services should be delivered; what the overall cost to the state is; how services will be paid for; and, finally, how services will be administered and what agency (or agencies) will be involved.

Identifying the at-risk population and providing it with early intervention services presents the service community a variety of problems. The numbers of children and their families who qualify for services under the biological and established risk categories comprise a small group. However, when children who are considered environmentally at risk are included in the population to be served, the numbers are increased substantially. Beyond the growth in numbers of children and families to be served within the at risk population, the foremost issue is the wide range and interdependency of factors involved in working with a population that includes children and families who live in poverty, teenage mothers, and children who are chronically ill. Social, emotional, and cognitive (multirisk) factors further complicate the outcomes for children and families that comprise this diverse group (Greenspan, 1991; Shonkoff & Meisels, 1991).

Greenspan et al., (1987) followed such a group of multirisk families. These families were identified from several different sources that included medical facilities as well as social service and mental health agencies. On the surface, the presenting risk problems appeared to be social and economic in origin; however, further examination revealed lifelong emotional problems that interacted with social and economic difficulties to produce a much more challenging intervention problem. Early intervention for such a group requires the expertise of many people who represent many professions. This study and others like it (e.g., Sameroff, Seifer, Barocas, Zax, & Greenspan, 1987; Sameroff, Seifer, & Zax, 1982) provide a glimpse of the complex intervention issues that an at-risk population presents to the service community. State and local agencies including the public schools are left with a daunting problem of how to serve families who present multidimensional and complex needs. Who is in charge? What agency or set of agencies is equipped to serve this group? What intervention strategies are appropriate? Who is going to pay?

Components of Effective Programs

Effective systems at the local level are those that can address individual needs in a timely manner and provide families with easy access to all services within the system through a single point of contact. One hallmark of current reform movements in education, health, and human services is the emphasis on local initiatives, such as those discussed elsewhere in this book, to identify needs, locate and develop resources, eliminate redundancy, and allocate personnel and funds to meet the needs of local citizens (Melaville, Blank, & Asayesh, 1993). The goal of these efforts is to provide continuous services that are individually planned and tailored to the needs of the individual and/or family within a community culture. Services are scaled to the diverse needs of the family within a community's culture and its available resources. Across the nation, local volunteer coordinating councils are becoming the stimulus for achieving these community-responsive, locally appropriate services for families and children. Effective collaboration among community groups holds the potential for stimulating a system of seamless services for persons at all ages who experience special needs (Melaville et al., 1993; Schorr, 1988, 1997). Within such a community-based, collaborative delivery system it is essential that the schools become active participants. This reformed social service system requires schools to be integrated into the system and to themselves integrate their programs (Chapter 1; Johnson, Bruininks, & Thurlow, 1987) in order to achieve positive outcomes for children and their families.

One vehicle for this purpose is the Local Interagency Coordinating Council (LICC), a requirement in the implementation of Part C. Its traditional role has been that of a primary advisory and problem-solving panel. In contrast, some states have chosen to channel funds directly to their local councils. In this event, councils maintain separate funding streams to support a variety of programs to benefit children and their families. This active and independent capacity has enabled these councils to blur categories and mesh funds to meet identified needs of children and families at the community level. Obviously the effectiveness of these councils to function as agents for systemic change is dependent on the degree of interagency collaboration and cooperation they are able to establish and sustain over time. Programs for children and their families must be individually crafted to provide services across agencies. The range of options and outcomes for children and families must be extensive.

The mixed role of families in the early intervention system as consumers and interveners is one of many factors in the complex early intervention equation. Families come from different cultures; they are products of value systems and communities that view parenting roles differently. Effective programs and their representative professionals require sensitivity to the diversity of families, their culture, and the communities in which they live. Divergent cultural values about where and how infants and young children should be socialized, the different roles of parents, and how professionals interact with them require that service systems be responsive to families' values, their preferences, and their needs (Kleinhammer-Tramill, Rosenkoetter, & Tramill, 1994; Lynch & Hanson, 1992).

CONCLUSION

In the preceding sections we have described the promise of Part C, the early childhood legislation of IDEA, in terms of its inclusive intent, its focus on families and children, and its promise for development of state and community service capacity-building and coherence. However promising, Part C, with regard to implementation, is falling short of its pledge. The availability of services for all children who qualify for services is unequal within and across states. Many states are not serving infants and toddlers who have risks due to environmental factors. Some states that are serving this population of children have attempted to reduce the ambiguity, short-term costs, and professional discomfort of those who prefer specialized models by developing subcategories of "risk." Although IFSPs are being developed to address the needs of both families and their children, children's needs often remain decontextualized from the family as a system, and families are still relegated to "client" rather than "interventionist" or "participant" roles. As such, the family and service providers are disconnected from one another and from the community.

The operation of state and local Interagency Coordinating Councils (ICCs) and their negotiated interagency agreements have been politicized, and an agency focus predominates. In our own state of Kansas, these councils have not become well integrated with broader service transformations as recommended by Kleinhammer-Tramill et al. (1994). Likewise, Verstegen's (1996) recommendations regarding strategies for blending funding streams to accomplish coordinated services, although a step in the right direction, provide evidence that the complexity of child services and funding arrangements all but defied coordination.

The preschool amendments of IDEA have been in effect for more than 15 years. On the one hand, one might expect the phenomenon of "policy maturation" described by Kleinhammer-Tramill and Gallagher in Chapter 2 to occur within some states. That is, when policies are first developed, prescriptive implementation guidelines may be both useful and necessary. As state and local agencies have more experience with a given policy, they need less guidance and can adapt implementation patterns to best fit local needs. On the other hand, Part C is inextricably tied to IDEA; thus the tendency to replicate its discrete disabilities orientation for defining eligibility, development and implementation of service systems, and acculturation of professionals is a natural outgrowth of more than 25 years of experience in implementing the superordinate policy. As educators we are now very accomplished at categorizing children and services. States that have not attempted to cope with the challenges of serving infants and toddlers who are eligible because of environmental risks provide evidence of application of the reductionistic principles of IDEA. Hehir (1994) notes that a national panel should be organized to develop guidance for states in identifying environmental risks. He suggests that the process of determining what a risk is and what it is not cannot be readily defined by states and communities. Professional acculturation processes must be developed to address broader categories of risk. This appears to be yet another attempt to recreate a disability category in order to determine eligibility and associated services rather than a move to establish a collaborative, broad-based intervention system based on determined needs of children and families.

The evidence suggests that implementation of each of the unique aspects of Part C falls short of either providing a comprehensive base of support for infants and toddlers and their families or transforming the processes for implementation of IDEA for older children with disabilities. To meet its mandates IDEA requires a broader basis for policy and practice that assures that all children have access to a network of supports. Gerry (1996) has noted that the concept of "services" is typically applied only to groups who are not empowered to make choices; for example, poor families receive "child care benefits," "child care services," or "health services." More affluent families select or choose pediatricians, family services they need, and their preschools. We would concur, then, that the idea of "child services" should be replaced by policies that provide for development of a network of supports for all children. We must recapture the original spirit of P.L. 99–457 by acknowledging that the needs of children are not so different regardless of affluence, risks for educational failure, speaking languages other than English, or needing care when they are sick so that both parents can work. Such a support network should acknowledge that child and family needs might be either transient or long term. System transformation means that child supports can no longer be decontextualized from the community or family. Such supports will be community-based and community-specific. Both policies and practices must be transformed to provide incentives for collaborative work to develop a child safety network within economically stressed communities. Such supports must also be family-specific and designed to build on individual family strengths and resources. Families must be fully empowered to determine when and how their child needs to access the support system.

REFERENCES

Bowe, F. G. (1995). Population estimates: Birth-to-five children with disabilities. *Journal of Special Education, 20*, 461–471.

Boyle, C. A., Decouflé, P., & Yeargin-Allsopp, M. (1994). Prevalence and health impact of developmental disabilities in US children. *Pediatrics, 93*, 399–403.

Bredekamp, S. (Ed.). (1987). *Developmentally appropriate practice in early childhood programs serving children from birth through age 8*. Washington, DC: National Association for the Education of Young Children.

Bredekamp, S., & Rosegrant, T. (Eds.). (1992). *Reaching potentials: Appropriate curriculum and assessment for young children (Vol. 1)*. Washington, DC: National Association for the Education of Young Children.

Brody, D. J., Prikle, J. L., Kramer, R. A., Fleagal, K. M., Matte, T. D., Gunter, E. W., & Paschal, D. C. (1994). Blood lead levels in the U.S. population. Phase 1 of the Third National Health and Nutrition Examination Survey (NHAMES III, 1988 to 1991). *Journal of the American Medical Association, 272*, 277–283.

Bronfenbrenner, U. (1979). *The ecology of human development*. Cambridge, MA: Harvard University Press.

Brooks-Gunn, J., McCarton, C. M., & Hawley, T. (1994). Effects of in utero drug exposure on children's development. *Archives of Pediatric Adolescent Medicine, 148*, 33–39.

Children's Defense Fund. (1996). *The state of America's children*. Washington, DC: Author.

Field, T. M. (1979). Interaction patterns of preterm and term infants: Behavior and development. In T. M. Field, A. M. Sostek, S. Goldberg, & H. J. Schuman (Eds.), *Infants born at-risk* (pp. 333–356). New York: Spectrum Publications.

First, L. R., & Palfrey, J. S. (1994). The infant or your child with developmental delay. *New England Journal of Medicine, 330*, 478–483.

Gallagher, J. J. (1984). Policy analysis and program implementation (P.L. 94–142). *Topics in Early Childhood Special Education, 4*, 43–53.

Gallagher, J. J. (1993). *The study of federal policy implementation of infants/toddlers with disabilities and their families: A synthesis of results*. Chapel Hill: Carolina Policy Studies Program, Frank Porter Graham Child Development Center, University of North Carolina at Chapel Hill.

Gallagher, J. J. (2000, April). *Missing infrastructure to support quality services for young children*. Paper presented at the meeting of the Council for Exceptional Children, Vancouver, B.C., Canada.

Gallagher, K. S., & Gallagher, R. J. (1992). Federal initiatives for exceptional children: The ecology of special education. In D. Stegelin (Ed.), *Early childhood education: Policy issues for the 1990's* (pp. 175–193). Norwood, NJ: Ablex.

Garmezy, N., & Masten, A. S. (1994). Chronic adversities. In M. Rutter, E. Taylor, & L. Hersov (Eds.), *Child and adolescent psychiatry* (4th ed., pp. 191–208). Oxford, England: Blackwell Scientific Publications.

Gerry, M. (1996). *Service integration and beyond: Implications for lawyers and their training*. Lawrence: University of Kansas.

Greenspan, S. I. (1991). Comprehensive clinical approaches to infants and their families: Psychodynamic and developmental perspectives. In S. J. Meisels & J. P. Shonkoff (Eds.). *Handbook of early childhood intervention* (pp. 150–172). New York: Cambridge University Press.

Greenspan, S. I., Weider, S., Lieberman, A., Nover, R., Lourie, R., & Robinson, M. (Eds.). (1987). *Clinical infant reports: No. 3. Infants in multirisk families: Case studies in preventive intervention*. New York: International Universities Press.

Guralnick, M. J. (1995). The effectiveness of early intervention for vulnerable children: A developmental perspective. Paper presented at the annual meeting of the American Association of University Affiliated Programs, Washington, DC.

Hack, M., Taylor, H. G., Klein, N., Eiben, R., Schatschneider, C., & Nercuri-Minich, N. (1994). School-age outcomes in children with birth weights under 750g. *New England Journal of Medicine, 331*, 753–759.

Hanson, M. J., & Lynch, E. W. (1995). *Early intervention: Implementing child and family services for infants and toddlers who are at-risk or disabled* (2nd ed.). Austin, TX: Pro-Ed.

Harbin, G. L., Gallagher, J. J., & Terry, D. V. (1991). Defining the eligible population: Policy issues and challenges. *Journal of Early Intervention, 15*, 13–20.

Hehir, T. (1994). *Improving the Individuals With Disabilities Education Act: IDEA reauthorization.* Unpublished manuscript. Washington, DC: United States Department of Education, Office of Special Education Programs.

Huston, A. C., McLoyd, V. C., & Garcia Coll, C. G. (1994). Children and poverty: Issues in contemporary research. *Child Development, 65,* 275–282.

Johnson, D. R., Bruininks, R. H., & Thurlow, M. L. (1987). Meeting the challenge of transition service planning through interagency cooperation. *Exceptional Children, 53*(6), 522–530.

Kelly, J. F., Morisset, C. E., Barnard, K. E., & Patterson, D. L. (1995). Risky beginnings: Low maternal intelligence as a risk factor for children's intellectual development. *Infants and Young Children, 8,* 11–23.

Keltner, B., & Tymchuk, A. (1992). Reaching out to mothers with mental retardation. *American Journal of Maternal Child Nursing, 17*(3), 136–140.

Kleinhammer-Tramill, P. J., Rosenkoetter, S. E., & Tramill, J. L. (1994). Early intervention and secondary/transition services: Harbingers of change in education. *Focus on Exceptional Children, 27,* 1–14.

Lewis, M., & Lee-Painter, S. (1974). An interactional approach to the mother-infant dyad. In M. Lewis & L. Rosenblum (Eds.), *The effect of the infant on its care giver* (pp. 21–48). New York: John Wiley & Sons.

Lynch, E. W., & Hanson, M. J. (1992). *Developing cross-cultural competence: A guide for working with young children and their families.* Baltimore: Paul H. Brookes.

McCormick, M. C., Workman-Daniels, K., & Brooks-Gunn, J. (1996). The behavioral and emotional well-being of school-age children with different birth weights. *Pediatrics, 97,* 18–25.

Meisels, S. F., & Wasik, B. A. (1990). Who should be served? Identifying children in need of early intervention. In S. J. Meisels & J. P. Shonkoff (Eds.), *Handbook of early childhood intervention* (pp. 605–632). New York: Cambridge University Press.

Melaville, A. I., Blank, M. J., & Asayesh, G. (1993). *Together we can: A guide for crafting a profamily system of education and human services.* Washington, DC: U.S. Government Printing Office.

NEC*TAS. (1998). Conflict management in early intervention. *Infants and Young Children, 11*(1), 28–39. Chapel Hill, NC: National Early Childhood Technical Assistance System Publication Office.

NEC*TAS. (1999). Assuring the family's role on the early intervention team. *Infants and Young Children, 12*(2), 17–29. Chapel Hill, NC: National Early Childhood Technical Assistance System Publication Office.

Osofsky, J. D. (1995). The effects of violence exposure on your children. *American Psychologist, 50,* 782–788.

Osofsky, J. D., Hann, D. M., & Peebles, C. (1993). Adolescent parenthood: Risks and opportunities for mothers and infants. In C. H. Zeanah, Jr. (Ed.), *Handbook of infant mental health* (pp. 106–119). New York: Guilford.

Peterson, N. L. (1991). Interagency collaboration under Part H: The key to comprehensive, multidisciplinary, coordinated infant/toddler intervention. *Journal of Early Intervention, 15,* 89–105.

Sailor, W., Kleinhammer-Tramill, J., Skrtic, T., & Oas, B. K. (1996). Family participation in New Community Schools. In G. H. S. Singer, L. E. Powers, & A. L. Olson, *Redefining family support: Innovations in public-private partnerships* (pp. 313–332). Baltimore: Paul H. Brookes.

Sameroff, A. J. (1982). The environmental context of developmental disabilities. In D. Bricker (Ed.), *Intervention with at-risk and handicapped infants: From research to application* (pp. 141–152). Baltimore: University Park Press.

Sameroff, A. J. (1983). Developmental systems: Contexts and evolution. In W. Kessen (Ed.), *Handbook of child psychology: Vol. I. History, theories, and methods* (pp. 238–294). New York: John Wiley & Sons.

Sameroff, A. J., & Chandler, M. (1975). Reproductive risk and the continuum of caretaking causality. In R. D. Horowitz, M. Hetherington, S. Scarr-Salapatek, & G. Siegel (Eds.), *Review of child development research* (Vol. 4, pp. 187–244). Chicago: University of Chicago Press.

Sameroff, A. J., & Fiese, B. H. (1991). Transactional regulation and early intervention. In S. J. Meisels & J. P. Shonkoff (Eds.), *Handbook of early childhood intervention* (pp. 119–149). New York: Cambridge University Press.

Sameroff, A. J., Seifer, R., Barocas, R., Zax, M., & Greenspan, S. I. (1987). IQ scores of 4-year-old children: Social-environmental risk factors. *Pediatrics, 79,* 343–350.

Sameroff, A. J., Seifer, R., & Zax, M. (1982). Early development of children at risk for emotional disorder. *Monographs of the Society for Research in Child Development, 47* (199).

Sander, L. (1962). Issues in early mother–child interaction. *Journal of the American Academy of Child Psychiatry, 1,* 141.

Schorr, L. B. (1988). *Within our reach: Breaking the cycle of disadvantage.* New York: Anchor Press.

Schorr, L. B. (1997). *Common purpose: Strengthening families and neighborhoods to rebuild America.* New York: Doubleday.

Shonkoff, J. P., & Marshall, P. C. (1991). Biological bases of developmental dysfunction. In S. J. Meisels & J. P. Shonkoff (Eds.), *Handbook of early childhood intervention* (pp. 35–77). New York: Cambridge University Press.

Shonkoff, J. P., & Meisels, S. F. (1991). Early childhood intervention: The evolution of a concept. In S. J. Meisels & J. P. Shonkoff (Eds.), *Handbook of early childhood intervention* (pp. 3–31). New York: Cambridge University Press.

Smith, B. J., & McKenna, P. (1994). Early intervention public policy: Past, present, and future. In L. J. Johnson, R. J. Gallagher, M. J. LaMontagne, J. B. Jordan, J. J. Gallagher, P. L. Hutinger, & M. B. Karnes (Eds.), *Meeting early intervention challenges: Issues from birth to three* (2nd ed., pp. 251–264). Baltimore: Paul H. Brookes.

Taylor, L., Zuckerman, B., Harik, V., & Groves, B. M. (1994). Witnessing violence by young children and their mothers. *Journal of Developmental and Behavioral Pediatrics, 15,* 120–123.

Trohanis, P. L. (1989). An introduction to P. L. 99–457 and the national policy agenda for serving young children with special needs and their families. In J. J. Gallagher, P. L. Trohanis, & R. M. Clifford (Eds.), *Policy implementation and P. L. 99–457: Planning for young children with special needs* (pp. 1–18). Baltimore: Paul H. Brookes.

U.S. Department of Health and Human Services. (1995). *Child maltreatment 1993: Reports* for the states to the National Center on Child Abuse and Neglect. Washington, DC: U.S. Government Printing Office.

Verstegen, D. A. (1996). Reforming American education policy for the 21st century. In J. G. Cibulka & W. J. Kritek (Eds.), Coordination among schools, families, and communities (pp. 216-249). Albany: State University of New York Press.

Wolery, M., & Bredekamp, S. (1994). Developmentally appropriate practices and young children with disabilities: Contextual issues in the discussion. Journal of early intervention, 18, 331–341.

Zervigon-Hakes, A. M. (1995). Translating research findings into large-scale public programs and policy. Future of Children, 5, 175–191.

PART II

School Reform and
School/Community Linkages

In Part Two, we move from consideration of the legislative policy realm to that of school reform, and in particular the reform agenda that links educational practices to community supports and services through partnerships formation and innovation in the schools. In Chapter 4, Martin Gerry examines the service integration initiatives of the past three decades and suggests why these fail to go to scale in communities and states. School reform efforts spurred by the publication of *A Nation At Risk* have raised new and important questions about the effectiveness of the hundreds of federal and state grant programs that currently provide categorical services for children and families. Indeed, the impact of unmet child development and wellness needs (e.g., infectious disease, malnutrition, child abuse) on learning is direct and severe. "Service integration" seeks to better coordinate this thoroughly fragmented and inflexible array of categorical grant programs. This chapter examines the background, history, and characteristics of service integration initiatives from the standpoint of their potential contribution to the goals of the contemporary school reform movement. It concludes that service integration approaches—no matter how fully developed, financed, and implemented—cannot meet demands for fundamental systems changes that have been generated by current school reform efforts, and it suggests guidelines for the creation of new, comprehensive, community child development and wellness systems.

In Chapter 5, Jacqui Kearns and her colleagues in Kentucky discuss the implications of KERA-90, Kentucky's school reform legislation, for students with severe disabilities. Kentucky's Education Reform Act has been regarded as the most comprehensive statewide reform effort to date. The basic underpinnings of the reform are presented, as well as full descriptions of each of its eight components and the relationship of each to students with disabilities. Parallels are drawn between Kentucky's Education Reform Act, Goals 2000, and the National Association of State Boards of Education (NASBE) policy standards to illustrate the relationship of education reform efforts and the inclusion of students with disabilities. Reflections from personnel in the Kentucky Department of Education representing both general and special educators reveal both the opportunities and the challenges that the reform act has presented for students with disabilities. Finally, a portrait of an elementary school provides the reader with an image of how the reform is working at its most important level.

In Chapter 6, Nancy Zollers examines the family perspective in the school/ community partnership process. A study of families with significantly disabled children provides insight into what families need from an integrated services model in order to keep their children in their homes, home schools, and home communities—and what they need to bring their excluded children back home. Findings include new information about how families understand empowerment, new insights into the importance of a good school program, and further evidence that mothers especially require new structures of service delivery because they are most often the care givers for their complex children.

Finally, in Chapter 7, Laura Owens Johnson and her colleagues offer a glimpse of another innovative approach to school/community partnerships, one that focuses on the population of students with disabilities entering the transition years. A major purpose of public school programs for students with significant disabilities is to prepare them to live, work, and play in integrated society. The transition years are extremely important to this end. Typically, public school personnel have provided close to 100% of these instructional services until students reach age 21. The Buyout Option may be another way to ensure successful transition from school to adult life. This option maximizes probabilities of learning to live, work, and play in an integrated society by purchasing services from private agencies using public school tax dollars.

CHAPTER 4

Service Integration and Achieving the Goals of School Reform

Martin Gerry

Despite widespread recognition of the need to link a wide range of noneducational grant programs with public education, large numbers of American children (particularly those living in poverty and others with multiple problems) continue to lack the comprehensive and flexible services and supports that they need. As a result, millions of American children experienced preventable illness, injury, abuse, deprivation, and impaired development and learning. Adverse effects on learning have been manifested by disrupted school attendance, impaired classroom concentration, the erosion of self-confidence and self-concept, and the eradication of hope (National Commission on Children, 1991). New community-based systems and expanded infrastructures of supports and services for all children are needed to remedy this problem.

An exploration of the background, history, and characteristics of service integration initiatives from the standpoint of the potential for creating such a system reveals that the time has come to pursue seriously more fundamental system reform. What follows are broad outlines of how such a reform might be structured.

SCHOOL-BASED CHILDREN'S SERVICES

Until the late 19th century, American social policy operated on the assumption that if families were unable to cope with unusual and severe demands on their resources, then neighbors, fellow parishioners, and other concerned community members would be there to help them. Indeed, throughout this period, a network of community institutions, religious organizations, and local associations, autonomous from state control, played the central role in providing support to the family in times of unusual stress or need when demands overwhelmed the capacities of both individuals and families (McKnight, 1995; Olasky, 1992).

From the late 19th century and well into the progressive era of school reform, the healthy development of large numbers of children in immigrant families in the crowded ghettos of many of America's cities was threatened by a range of serious and persistent health, family, and environmental problems. Beginning about 1890, social reformers began to call for school-based health and social services to prevent or remedy the ill health, hunger, and neglect of immigrant children attending the nation's urban schools. The impetus for most of these early school-based programs came chiefly from forces outside the schools who saw the schools as an attractive locus for health and social service reform. Eventually, these services became highly touted panaceas of the progressive era (Tyack, 1992).

Federal Categorical Grant Programs

Prior to the passage of the Social Security Act in 1935, government played a comparatively small role in supporting the healthy development of children. During the mid-1930s the earlier trend of addressing the expanded needs of poor children by investing public money (chiefly local) into the general support for the public schools was replaced during the New Deal by an effort to focus directly on the health and social needs of poor children (Gardner, 1994; Olasky, 1992). However, the original intent of some of these New Deal programs had to be altered to better mesh with the school operations. By 1960, approximately 130 federal categorical grant programs had been created. Virtually all were discretionary, and the amount of money involved was quite small (Tyack, 1992).

From 1960 to 1968, the number of federal categorical grant programs almost tripled. This proliferation appears to have been predicated on a perception by the federal government that it had the resources, technical and administrative capacity, and the will to undertake a major enrichment of domestic life, with states and localities playing the role of service delivery agents (Reischauer, 1986). The objective of most of these new programs was to intervene directly to solve a broad range of problems experienced by various categories of children and families. Over the next 12 years (1969–1980), hundreds of additional federal categorical grants programs were created following this same policy blueprint.

Several factors contributed to this rapid growth of categorical programs during this 20-year period. First, growth was fueled by a desire to circumvent states by establishing new national standards with federal grant money as an enticement. Second, growth was spurred by the reality that the federal administrative base and the new programs' strict eligibility and fund use requirements helped prevent states and localities opposed to new federal civil rights laws from subverting basic program purposes with respect to children in poverty, of color, and with disabilities (Gardner, 1994). Third, several factors combined to make the growth of categorical programs very politically attractive. Growth created significant new fields of employment for a large labor force of service workers drawn primarily from the middle and working classes (McKnight, 1995) and was driven by this lobby through a triangular relationship at federal and state levels among professional organizations, legislators and their staffs, and executive branch specialists in various program areas. The creation of new categorical grant programs also enabled many legislators to take political credit for meeting the needs of various groups of children and families by creating new programs, even if they were actually funded only at token levels (Gardner, 1994).

For a time in the early 1980s, the emergence of new "block grants" threatened to check or even reverse the growth of categorical programs. Early in the Reagan administration the Omnibus Reconciliation Act of 1981 (OBRA) created nine new or revised block grants that consolidated 57 separate federal discretionary grant programs and gave states broad discretion to decide what programs and services to provide. In practice, however, the passage of OBRA did not cause most states to radically alter the structures that were used before consolidation. For example, in programs that incorporated income-based eligibility, states generally tightened eligibility requirements, usually excluding large numbers of children living in near-poor or working-poor families (Hayes, 1995). Over time, the state flexibility intended by OBRA was diminished substantially by increased categorical restrictions created by Congress, new categorical set-asides and expenditure ceilings, and the failure of Congress to increase federal funding of the block grants despite rising service costs. States were left with little choice but to begin restricting eligibility through categorical approaches (Hayes, 1995).

The Personal Responsibility and Work Opportunity Reconciliation Act of 1996 (PRWORA) appeared to herald the beginning of a new era of major block grant legislation. PRWORA makes sweeping changes in a broad range of safety-net programs for the members of large numbers of low-income families. Despite dramatic decline in welfare caseloads across the nation over the last 6 years, many families with children living in poverty have experienced decreases in (a) net family income, (b) access to affordable child care, (c) access to health insurance, and (d) access to child food and nutrition supports (Gerry, 1999). In terms of the evolution of categorical grant programs, it has become increasingly clear that PRWORA did not represent a major shift in direction. In fact, a year after its passage, the Balanced Budget Act of 1997 created two new categorical grant programs, one focused on expanded child health insurance and the other on the welfare-to-work transition, that followed the traditional federal–state administrative model. The FY 1998 Budget approved by Congress and signed by the President included over 500 separate federal grant programs. Of these, over 300 focused on children and families (U.S. Department of Commerce, 1999).

THE EVOLUTION OF SERVICE INTEGRATION EFFORTS

The demand for service integration arose from the proliferation of categorical programs and the failure of large numbers of children and families to gain access to needed children's and family services. As the great expansion of federal entitlement and discretionary grant programs occurred during the late 1960s and early 1970s, several political figures and scholars expressed concern about the proliferation of these programs and the inability of the federal government to manage centrally what were in reality local initiatives (Schultze, 1968). This view was shared by Health, Education and Welfare Secretary Elliot Richardson, who launched a major initiative in 1971 to integrate "allied" services across categorical areas.

By the end of the 1970s and throughout the 1980s, the service integration agenda became subordinated to the OBRA block grant strategy. However, by the mid-1980s, service integration activities at the state and community levels were revived with the original service coordination emphasis. Most of these initiatives have been motivated by a desire for more efficient and effective use of scarce resources. They have also increasingly been seen as effective mechanisms for responding to growing demands for greater accountability. Although numerous state and local service integration initiatives have come and gone over a 20-year period, only a few, such as New Jersey's school-linked service initiative, have been continuously in place over a decade.

What Is Service Integration?

Despite the nearly 30-year history of service integration initiatives at all levels of government, "a clear and agreed-upon definition of service integration has remained elusive" (Kagan & Neville, 1993). Definitions of "service integration" have fluctuated between seeing service integration as a strategy (Gerry, 1999; Lucas, 1975; Rein, 1970) or a process (Agranoff & Pattakos, 1979; Kagan & Neville, 1993), and for over two decades there has been a persistent ambivalence as to its primary goal. Alternative goals have included (a) improving the service system, (b) improving outcomes for families and children, and (c) maximizing the efficient use of limited resources.

Some have argued that at least the first two of these goals are interdependent (Kagan & Neville, 1993), whereas others have maintained that it is possible to have improved outcomes for children without necessarily improving or reforming the underlying systems (Martin et al., 1983). Recent definitions of service integration have also emphasized overall goals and outcomes rather than either strategy or process. These outcome goals include (a) maximizing the independence of families from long-term dependency on government (Bruner, 1989), (b) rebuilding and restoring the capacities of both families and local communities (Gerry, 1999), and (c) expanding social capital, promoting economic development, and increasing parental employment (Annie E. Casey Foundation, 1995). I suggest the following as an inclusive, working definition:

> Services integration is a set of strategies by which a community seeks to
> ensure the immediate and uninterrupted access of all children and families

to those children's services and family supports needed by the family to optimize the cognitive, social, emotional, and physical development of each of its children, and to ensure the healthy functioning, stability, social and economic integration, and economic self-sufficiency both of the family and of the neighborhood of which it is a part.

A Variety of Service Integration Approaches

Service integration initiatives under way throughout the nation can be described in terms of four basic features: (a) target populations and services; (b) the locus of service coordination; (c) the strategies used to link and coordinate services; and (d) the nature of governance and accountability mechanisms.

Target Populations and Services

Significant variation exists among current service integration efforts as to the population of children to be served. Virtually all current statewide service integration efforts are targeted on specific subpopulations of children, most frequently described as economically disadvantaged or as "at-risk." Although both universal and categorical service approaches are being pursued at the community level, most of the initiatives that have adopted a universal approach to child access serve geographic areas with high concentrations of categorically eligible children. Child-focused service integration initiatives are almost always family-centered, whereas most youth-focused service integration initiatives are not (Kagan & Neville, 1993).

The services that are "integrated" by these initiatives vary widely, depending on the age of the children involved, the comprehensiveness of the vision, the locus of activity, and the availability of resources (Levy & Shephardson, 1992). The children's services that form the grist for most include (a) education, (b) health services, (c) food and nutrition services, (d) mental health services, (e) early care and education services, and (f) child welfare services. For youth-focused initiatives, substance abuse prevention and treatment, pregnancy prevention, delinquency prevention, and school-to-work transition are also likely to be part of the mix. The menu of family-centered benefits, services, and other supports provided in most of these initiatives includes prenatal care, family counseling and family preservation services, adult education, and job training and employment support (Gerry, 1999).

Locus of Service Integration Activity

Among current service integration initiatives focused on children, the approaches used to structure the relationship between the school and other children's and family services are community-based, school-linked, or school-based (Chaskin & Richman, 1992; Levy & Shephardson, 1992). Rather than as discrete strategies, these approaches might more accurately be seen as points on a continuum that ranges from no relationship to the school site or to school operations, at one extreme, to school-based and school-operated at the other.

In the school-based approach, the school is the center for a wide range of psychological, health, social, recreational, and treatment services. The vision of a "full service school" is one of a hub for comprehensive services directed not only at educational remediation but also at changing a whole array of negative behavioral outcomes (Dryfoos, 1994). Important components of emerging full-service school models include school-based health centers, family resource and youth service centers, and settlement house-in-the-school programs.

Along the continuum, school-linked services approaches see schools as active collaborators (but not necessarily the drivers or hub) in providing integrated services to children and their families. Other collaborators are usually health care providers and social service agencies. Here, services are provided at a site near the school (e.g., community clinic) with the active cooperation of school staff. The agencies providing health and social services are often encouraged to move some of their staff and/or services to the school to facilitate coordination (Larson et al., 1992).

Community-based service integration initiatives are usually sponsored either by community-based, nonprofit organizations separate from the public service delivery system or by health or human services programs that maintain strong links to a local government agency or program (Chaskin & Richman, 1992). By definition, they are not formally linked to schools.

Although most researchers and practitioners would probably agree that schools should serve as the hub of service coordination if they have become true community institutions (i.e., trusted centers of community activity), several have pointed out that where no trust exists between families and schools, any other community site would be a better locus for such efforts (Chaskin & Richman, 1992).

Governance and Legitimacy

Across current service integration sites, a wide range of strategies are used in an effort to improve the coordination or to integrate the provision of services to children and families. Interagency service coordination involves linking and integrating the work of different agencies and professionals. A combination of managerial, operational, organizational, and physical linkage strategies have been used by service integration initiatives (Kagan & Neville, 1993).

"Governance" refers to the permanent consolidation of leadership and decision making that is needed within local communities to improve the delivery of services to children and families (Center for the Study of Social Policy, 1991) and to promote and facilitate citizen participation in planning and decision making (Chaskin & Garg, 1995).

In practice, the governance structures of multiagency service integration initiatives vary greatly, based on the initiative's goals and objectives and the politics of agency relationships and government entities within the community (Gardner, 1992). The most important and controversial variables associated with these structures have proven to be (a) the legitimacy of "community" representation and participation within the governance structure, (b) the relationship between governance and government within the affected community, and (c) the functions and responsibilities of the governance entity (Center for the Study of Social Policy, 1991).

Numerous issues have arisen in many of these initiatives regarding the participation by families in their governance. The manner of structuring this type of community participation often has proven crucial to their overall success because the perceived legitimacy of this family participation can make a real difference in its credibility—it is seen as truly connected to, and acting on behalf of, the interests of the community (Chaskin & Garg, 1995).

Arriving at the proper linkage of government and governance within a service integration initiative is primarily an issue of organizational structure. Most community-level initiatives have used one of the following structures around which to organize: (a) an institution parallel to local government that offers an alternative mechanism for providing services and supports; (b) a separate but complementary institution to local government; (c) incorporation into local government, usually through the creation of a formal subunit of government (Chaskin & Garg, 1995); or (d) vouchers or similar arrangements that enable families to select among competing institutions (Gerry, 1999).

Financing Service Integration

Today the watchword of almost every service integration initiative at both the state and community levels is *accountability*. The actual success of a particular accountability mechanism is likely to hinge on the degree of agreement on the meaning of *accountability* among families and those agencies and professionals who are to be held accountable.

Flexible financing strategies are an important component of most comprehensive service integration initiatives. They reinforce the initiative's underlying policy and programmatic direction and ultimately influence how useful services are to families (Farrow & Joe, 1992). The two most important flexible strategies that have been used singly or in combination to support service integration initiatives are (a) the decategorization of funding streams, through waivers, pooling arrangements, and blended funding approaches, and (b) the increased leveraging of federal entitlement funds (Center for the Study of Social Policy, 1991).

Beyond Service Integration

Despite over 25 years of development and refinement, service integration efforts predicated on a categorical grant-based funding structure will never meet the overall demands for fundamental systems-change needed to effectively support the current wave of educational reform. Accordingly, it is important that no matter how uninviting the current political landscape appears, we begin to expand the focus of our efforts to include the creation of a new, national network of comprehensive, community-based infrastructures of supports and services for children. I do not suggest that we abandon or even diminish current efforts at service integration. Rather, I am arguing that we go beyond them.

As we begin to consider the design of such an infrastructure, it is essential that we examine the validity and reliability of six major policy assumptions that underlie and dominate current program structures and service integration efforts.

1. Only Some Children Need Services and Supports

The policy assumption that only some children need and deserve access to services and supports external to the family and the public schools to support their optimal development, learning, and well-being rests on two important policy myths. First, the *myth of family self-sufficiency* portrays "healthy" families as those with children who need no outside services or supports for healthy development and views the need for such external services and supports as evidence of a flawed or deficient family (Graham, 1993; McKnight, 1995). In reality, child outcomes are the product of both personal factors and environmental factors, and *all* children need access to supports external to the family. What most differentiates children and families within current structures is not whether or not they have needs but rather the severity and multiplicity of those needs, and the access the child and family enjoy to the resources that must be brought to bear if those needs are to be met successfully (Gerry, 1999; Gerry, Fawcett, & Richter, 1996).

Second, the policy assumption rests on the *myth of undeserving children*, which asserts that regardless of how many children need publicly funded services, only some deserve access to them. The attempt to separate out the mythic "deserving child" from the other equally (or even more) needy children who are not "deserving" is simultaneously a morally bankrupt and a technically impossible undertaking. Ironically, the sorting process that lies at its heart inevitably attaches labels, which are pejorative at best and destructive at worst, to the very children who are found to be "deserving." Indeed, these labels often are used to rationalize the setting of lower institutional and professional expectations for the child. The notion of the mythic "deserving child" also conflicts directly with the central tenet of American educational policy—that all children have access to public education.

2. Child Needs Stem From Internal Deficiencies of the Child or Family

A second major policy assumption is that the primary reason for the existence of unmet child needs are internal deficiencies of the child and/or the child's family. The powerful link between family poverty and child outcomes (e.g., impaired health, undernourishment, abuse, and neglect) belies the wisdom of such an assumption (National Center for Children in Poverty, 1990; National Commission on Children, 1991).

Although the link between poverty and impaired outcomes for children is clear, some have argued that the external social, economic, and political environment is simply a stage upon which more deeply rooted pathologies are played out (Olasky, 1992). This argument ignores the fact that for the last three decades, the number of middle-class children living in single-parent families as a result of divorce has greatly exceeded the number of children in never-married single-parent families (U.S. Department of Commerce, Bureau of the Census, 1999). If the absence of paternal love and discipline is a key to problems having to do with children's well-being, then why have the outcomes for children in working-, middle-, and upper-middle-class families not been similarly affected?

Others have argued that, although the socioeconomic background, education, occupation, and race of the parents of a child have some bearing on whether that child will live in poverty as an adult, the most important predictor is parental intelligence as measured by IQ (Herrnstein & Murray, 1994). Numerous reviewers have pointed out the flaws in this analysis (DeAngelis, 1995; Hunt, 1995; Jacoby & Glauberman, 1995). The National Commission on Children (1991) implicitly rejected such an interpretation, pointing out that children growing up in poverty experience the most health problems but live in the least healthful environments and have the least access to medical care. They are at the highest risk of academic failure but often attend the worst schools. Their families experience the most stress but have the fewest social supports.

3. The Needs of Children Are Best Met by Service Professionals

A third major policy assumption that underlies and dominates current program structures and service integration efforts is that the needs of children and families can be met only by external professional services.

Despite the fact that child development, learning, and well-being are inexorably tied to the community (Gerry, Fawcett, & Richter, 1996), this assumption is premised on the notion that it is the service professional who produces and the child and/or family who consumes. Once agreed to, this premise works to rule out other answers to child and family needs that focus on family and community problem solving. The first step in this process is to translate the needs of children and families into deficiencies, which, in turn, dramatically reduces the likelihood that friends, neighbors, coworkers, and others within the community will perceive themselves as competent to act upon solvable problems (McKnight, 1995). The second step is to label this "deficiency" as internal to the child and family. Indeed, the tools and techniques (i.e., services) that can be paid for are usually limited to those that involve an interaction between the child and/or family and a service professional. Here the tool too often defines the problem, rather than the problem defining the tool. The third step is to attach a label and use technical language to translate the need for assistance into professional and categorical terms. This works powerfully to dissuade families from attempting to solve their own problems (McKnight, 1995).

4. Compartmentalized Services Are an Appropriate Strategy

A fourth policy assumption underlying current structures is that a child can be seen "as a set of manageable parts, each with its own service mechanic," which is improved or "fixed" by a series of competently provided compartmentalized services (McKnight, 1995, pp. 30–31). From this viewpoint, each service is seen as making a discrete and incremental contribution to the child's overall development (Gerry, 1999).

Children are first and foremost organic creatures. No two children are exactly alike, and each child is constantly changing through a variety of interactions with other adults and children and with the social and physical environment. Experience has repeatedly demonstrated that the provision of individual, compartmentalized services to children, particularly those with multiple and complex needs, is not likely to result in any significant improvement in overall child outcomes. For example, no matter how well designed an instructional program may be, educational improvement is unlikely for a child who is chronically ill and exhausted, physically abused by a parent, or in need of drug treatment. Indeed, the failure to address any one of these factors might totally defeat any learning improvement which would otherwise occur. In this sense, the use of a single-strategy approach to children with multiple and complex needs is akin to boat building as opposed to house building—the omission of virtually any plank will completely undermine the overall enterprise (Gerry, 1999).

5. There Is an Adequate Supply of Services

A fifth policy assumption underlying most current service integration initiatives is that an adequate supply of the services and supports needed by children currently exists within most communities and only needs to be properly accessed or interrelated. In reality, major gaps exist in the overall infrastructure of services and supports needed by children and their families. For example, the absence of a community-based primary care infrastructure for child health care and other children's services (e.g., child care) presents serious problems of service access to children and families in both rural and urban areas (Gerry, 1999; Gerry et al., 1996).

6. Collaboration Will Solve the Problem

The sixth and final policy assumption underlying virtually every service integration effort is that the key to solving current "system" problems lies in interagency and cross-disciplinary collaboration. From the beginning, cooperation and collaboration of service providers have been viewed as crucial aspects of service integration (Kagan & Neville, 1993). Current service integration efforts use a wide variety of approaches to structure these relationships, but most have adopted a collaboration-focused strategy within which service professionals, across a broad range of programs and disciplines, decide to work together and pool resources to achieve their respective program goals (Gerry, 1999).

The collaboration assumption is based on the idea that improved cooperation, and certainly collaboration, among service professionals will ensure children effective access to the combination of services and supports that will optimize or substantially improve outcomes. In reality, overall child outcomes are not the central focus of even most traditional collaborative efforts. Rather, the motive for working with other agencies and service professionals is to gain help in better accomplishing one's separate programmatic (and usually disciplinary) objectives for a child. On a day-to-day basis, the success or failure of each of the cooperating or collaborating agencies is not based on any collective accountability for child outcomes (Gerry, 1999).

In practice, most cooperation and collaboration strategies pay scant attention to both the reality that some professionals are simply more effective on certain tasks with certain families and that service professionals from different developmental periods may be able to assist each other. The latter point suggests that professionals who encounter children and families early in the developmental process (e.g., public health nurses, child care professionals) may have both important insights into the child's development, parental attitudes, and the home environment and trust relationships with both the child and parents that could be crucial to the success of other professionals trying to work with the child and family at a later stage (e.g., third-grade teacher). In practice, most collaborative efforts fail to include these "earlier" service professionals because none is currently providing services to either the child or the family (Gerry, 1999).

System Reform

Service integration has been the subject of active experimentation involving a broad range of service integration strategies at hundreds of different sites for nearly 30 years. Remarkably, relatively few methodologically sound evaluations of complex service integration initiatives have been conducted (Gomby & Larson, 1992; Kagan, Goffin, Golub, & Pritchard, 1995). Where they have, the results have been inconclusive or mixed (Dryfoos, Brindis, & Kaplan, 1996; Gomby & Larson, 1992).

I believe that the time has come for communities, not schools, to assume the overall responsibility for a more fundamental systems-change, one that would create both a new system and an expanded comprehensive infrastructure of services and supports for children and their families. Within this new community-based system, decision making and control of noneducational resources for children and families would be transferred to community partnerships, owned, controlled, and shared by all of the residents of the community and by the various social, economic, and service systems (e.g., schools, clubs, businesses) that influence the community environment (Gerry, 1999; Gerry et al., 1996). These partnerships would (a) define child and family needs and problems within the community, (b) design and provide access to an expanded infrastructure of integrated services and supports for individual children and their families, and a process for actively addressing cross-cutting issues and problems, and (c) exercise control over the human, material, and economic resources essential to the successful operation of such a system (Gerry, 1999; McKnight, 1995).

The expanded infrastructure of services and supports would include 12 core capacities (in addition to public education): (a) disease prevention; (b) safety and accident prevention; (c) prevention and reduction of high-risk behavior among adolescents; (d) health and developmental screening at all ages; (e) primary care, including dental care, mental health care, and sick-child care; (f) health maintenance; (g) early care and education; (h) hospital or in-patient care; (i) food and nutrition; (j) emergency shelter; (k) family support; and (l) environmental health and well-being. The decision as to how best to make those capacities readily accessible by, and most valuable to, children and their families will be based on the identification of existing channels of influence within the community (Gerry, 1999; Gerry, et al., 1996).

REFERENCES

Agranoff, R., & Pattakos, A. (1979). Dimensions of human services integrations: Service delivery, program linkages, policy management, organizational structure. *Human Services Monograph Series*. Dekalb: Northern Illinois University.

Annie E. Casey Foundation. (1995, August). *The path of most resistance*. Baltimore: Author.

Bruner, C. (1989). State innovations in children and family services collaboration and financing. In C. L. Romig (Ed.), *Family policy: Recommendations for state action* (pp. 163–172). Washington, DC: National Conference of State Legislators.

Center for the Study of Social Policy. (1991, September). *Building a community agenda: Developing local governance entities*. Washington, DC: Author.

Chaskin, R., & Garg, S. (1995). *The issues of governance in neighborhood-based initiatives*. Chicago: University of Chicago, Chapin Hall.

Chaskin, R., & Richman, H. (1992, Spring). "Concerns about school-linked services: Institution-based versus community-based models. *The Future of Children, 2*(1), 107–117.

DeAngelis, T. (1995, October). Psychologists question findings of bell curve. *APA Monitor*.

Dryfoos, J. (1994). *Full service schools: A revolution in health and social services for children*. San Francisco: Jossey-Bass.

Dryfoos, J., Brindis, C. & Kaplan, D. W. (1996, June). Research and evaluation in school based health care. In *Adolescent Medicine: State of the Art Reviews, 7*(2), 207–220. Philadelphia: Hanley & Belfus.

Farrow, F., & Joe, T. (1992). Financing school-linked, integrated services. *The Future of Children, 2*(1), 56–67.

Gardner, S. (1992, Spring). Key issues in developing school-linked, integrated services. *The Future of Children, 2*(1), 85.

Gardner, S. (1994, December). *Reform options for the intergovernmental funding system: Decategorization policy issues.* Washington, DC: The Finance Project.

Gerry, M. (1999). Service integration and beyond: Implications for lawyers and their training. In J. Heubert (Ed.), *Law and school reform: Six strategies for promoting educational equity* (pp. 244–305). New Haven, CT: Yale University Press.

Gerry, M., Fawcett, S., & Richter, K. (1996, July). *Community health and wellness systems for all of our children.* Princeton, NJ: The Robert Wood Johnson Foundation.

Gomby, D., & Larson, C. (1992). Evaluation of school-linked services. *The Future of Children, 2*(1), 68.

Graham, P. A. (1993, February). What America has expected of its schools over the past century. *American Journal of Education, 101*(2), 83–98.

Hayes, C. (1995, April). *Rethinking block grants: Toward improved intergovernmental financing for education and other children's services.* Washington, DC: The Finance Project.

Herrnstein, R. J., & Murray, C. (1994). *The bell curve: Intelligence and class structure in American life.* New York: Free Press.

Hunt, E. (1995). The role of intelligence in modern society. *American Sicentist.*

Jacoby, R., & Glauberman, N. (1995). *The bell curve debate.* New York: Times Books.

Kagan, S., Goffin, S., Golub, S., & Pritchard, E. (1995). *Toward systematic reform: Service integration for young children and their families.* Falls Church, VA: National Center for Service Integration.

Kagan, S., & Neville, P. (1993). *Integrating services for children and families: Understanding the past to shape the future.* New Haven, CT: Yale University Press.

Larson, C., Gomby, D., Shiono, P., Lewit, W., & Behrman, R. (1992). Analysis. *The Future of Children, 2*(1), 6–18.

Levy, J., & Shephardson, W. (1992, Spring). A look at current school-linked service efforts. *The Future of Children, 2*(1), 44–55.

Lucas, W. (1975, December). *The 1975 census of local services integration.* Santa Monica, CA: The Rand Corporation.

Martin, P. Y., Chackerian, R., Imershein, A., & Frumkin, M. (1983). The concept of "integrated" services reconsidered. *Social Science Quarterly, 64*(4), 747–763.

McKnight, J. (1995). *The careless society: Community and its counterfeits.* New York: Basic Books.

National Center for Children in Poverty. (1990). *Five million children,* p. 51. New York: Author.

National Commission on Children. (1991). *Beyond rhetoric: A new agenda for children and families, final report.* Washington, DC: Government Printing Office.

Olasky, M. (1992). *The tragedy of American compassion.* Washington, DC: Regnery.

Rein, M. (1970). *Social policy: Issues of choices and change.* New York: Random House.

Reischauer, R. (1986). Fiscal federalism in the 1980s: Dismantling or rationalizing the Great

Society. In M. Kaplan & P. Cuciti (Eds.), *The Great Society and its legacy* (p. 181). Durham, NC: Duke University Press.

Schultze, C. (1968). *The politics and economics of public spending.* Washington, DC: The Brookings Institution.

Tyack, D. (1992, Spring). Health and social services in public schools: Historical perspectives. *The Future of Children, 2*(1) 19–31.

U.S. Department of Commerce, Bureau of the Census. (1999). *Statistical abstract of the United States, 1998.* Washington, DC: U.S. Government Printing Office.

CHAPTER 5

Yes, and What About...

The Inclusion of Students with Severe Disabilities in Comprehensive Statewide Educational Reform

Jacquie Farmer Kearns, Harold L. Kleinert, Sarah Kennedy, Rebecca Farmer, and Kenneth Warlick

Dramatic, unforeseen changes, both nationally and in Kentucky's educational system, continue to pose tremendous opportunities and great challenges for children with disabilities. Kentucky's Education Reform Act (KERA) has been regarded as the most comprehensive statewide reform effort to date (Steffy, 1993). Given the magnitude of KERA, it was essential that the needs of students with disabilities be addressed in these efforts. Indeed, the National School Boards Association (NASBE) standards for the inclusion of students with disabilities in reform efforts (Roach, 1995) highlighted important implications for students with disabilities in such areas as school governance, assessment, and accountability. This chapter discusses these commonalties and their essential implications for students with disabilities as addressed in Kentucky's educational reform. In addition, we provide specific descriptions of the KERA 1990 programmatic strands such as preschool and primary programs, family resource centers, and curriculum frameworks.

EDUCATIONAL REFORM

Educational reform has been a topic of discourse in American education since the middle 1960s. The Coleman study (1966) and the subsequent Jencks study (1972) concluded that public schools not only failed to help alleviate inequality in the

United States but in fact *contributed* to it. During the 1980s, with the publication of *A Nation at Risk* (National Commission on Education, 1983), educational reform focused on school inputs and increased regulation from a "top-down" perspective. Regulations for enhanced teacher education standards, increased numbers of credits for high school graduation, and curricular requirements were mandated at the state level (Coots, Bishop, Grenot-Scheyer, & Falvey, 1995). More recently, reform efforts have focused on a broader range of student outcomes, including performance-based measures of student learning, and more fundamental school restructuring with increased decision-making responsibility at the building level (Chapter 2).

Yet despite this widespread attention to educational reform, the needs of children with disabilities were largely ignored in reform efforts (Gartner & Lipsky, 1987; Stainback, Stainback, & Forest, 1989). According to Skrtic (1991), this occurred primarily because special education was viewed as a separate system, designed solely to meet the needs of children with disabilities rather than as an integral part of the general education system. Similarly, in a review of ten articles related to children with disabilities and education reform Johnson and Rusch (1993) found that both regular and special educators expressed concern about low expectations, the lack of successful transition to adult life, and the devaluation of certain groups of students in the educational system. In general, although issues of access to schools and the educational system for students with disabilities appear to be receding, issues of quality and effectiveness of the educational process have clearly emerged (Sage & Burello, 1994).

The Basis of Kentucky's Education Reform Efforts

Not unlike educational reform efforts in other states, Kentucky's education reform originated in litigation. In 1985, a class action equity suit, *The Council for Better Education v. Wilkinson* (1985) was filed in Franklin County Circuit Court by former Governor Bert Combs on behalf of 66 school districts, 7 boards of education, and 22 public school students, collectively called the Council for Better Education. The resulting judgment by Judge Ray Corns stated that the funding system for Kentucky's schools was "discriminatory" and "inefficient." The decision was appealed by the state to the Kentucky Supreme Court, which in turn found the entire educational system unconstitutional (*Rose v. Council for Better Education*, 1989). Steffy (1993) noted that although the Council for Better Education argued that funding was the issue, the Kentucky Supreme Court recognized a more fundamental problem. This action required an "absolute duty" on behalf of the state general assembly to "recreate, reestablish a new system of common schools in the Commonwealth" (*Rose v. Council*, 1989, pp. 215–216). The Kentucky General Assembly set about the task of recreating Kentucky schools in January 1990 (Steffy, 1993). This restructuring of Kentucky's elementary and secondary system constituted a massive overhaul of the existing system that has impacted services for children with disabilities.

Governance at the Building Level

Prior to the supreme court decision, local boards of education in Kentucky exerted considerable autonomy over school governance structures (Steffy, 1993). With the advent of KERA, the locus of power and control for Kentucky's schools was returned to the Kentucky legislature, which, in turn, shifted day-to-day school governance from the district central office to the school level. The power of local school boards was effectively reduced, particularly in selecting principals and determining staff assignments. In addition, KERA mandated a provision for school-based decision making that allowed local schools to make many policy decisions at the school level that were made previously at the district level. Now the majority of decisions impacting instruction could be made by school councils, which included teachers and parents from the school's attendance area. By law, school-based councils (SBDM) assume the responsibility for major instructional decisions and resource allocation at the building level. School councils are responsible for planning curriculum and instruction; assigning staff, students, and space; implementing discipline procedures; and determining extracurricular programs (Weston, 1991). The school forms the central unit of accountability in Kentucky's education system. As such, the council's most significant role is in the development of the school improvement plan. To this end, school councils also have direct control over 65% of all professional development money generated from average daily attendance. Moreover, school councils in Kentucky are optional only if specifically exempted by their accountability scores or if they qualified as a single-school district. In 1996, 93% of Kentucky schools were required to have school councils in place (Lindle, 1996). Of the 400 exempted by their 1994 assessment scores, only 183 chose to abolish their council. During the next accountability cycle, 92 of the 183 schools previously exempted were required to reestablish their council (Lindle, 1996). In short, although KERA is clearly a "top-down" or state-mandated reform, it nevertheless returns to schools considerable resources and broad authority to best meet the needs of their own children (Steffy, 1993).

School-based decision making itself has far-reaching implications for students with disabilities. In fact, the mandated parent participation and parent veto power originally incorporated within the 1975 Education for All Handicapped Children Act (P.L. 94-142) may have itself set the clearest precedent for school-based decision making that includes parents of all children. The IEP team has been characterized as the first school-based decision-making committee for a child with a disability, and, obviously, the decisions of that team directly intersect with school council responsibilities (Lindle, 1992). In a position paper, Kleinert (1995) delineated the intersection of the Individuals With Disabilities Education Act of 1990 (20 U.S.C. Sec. 1400 et seq.) with school council authority in Kentucky. An essential theme of that document is that school councils, in the application of their broad authority, must comply with IDEA and may not make decisions that would disregard an Individualized Education Plan (IEP) or fail to allocate resources in accordance with the requirements of the IEP.

The Kleinert (1995) position paper was included as a basic part of *Synergy*, the Kentucky Department of Education's "operating manual" for school councils. The paper provided a coherent set of instructional and curricular strategies that have been shown to be effective in enhancing outcomes for all students. Collaboration and coteaching (Bauewens, Hourcade, & Friend, 1989) and cooperative learning (Hunt, Staub, Alwell, & Goetz, 1994; Johnson, Johnson, & Holubec, 1990) reflected the type of research-based practices that produce positive outcomes for all children. All of these strategies, when implemented at a schoolwide level, allow for the accommodation of diverse learner needs in the context of an educational reform environment.

Given the authority of SBDM Councils in Kentucky to determine the broad parameters of classroom and school-based instructional practices, it is essential that school council members have basic information about these effective practices. As schools increasingly move to school-based decision making at the national level, it is vital that special educators and advocates provide that information to their respective councils (Kleinert, 1995).

CURRICULUM

The advent of KERA fundamentally changed the state's definition of curriculum (Steffy, 1993). Although the Kentucky Supreme Court outlined its consideration of an "adequate education," the 12–member Council on School Performance Standards, appointed by then Governor Wallace Wilkinson, identified what a high school graduate in the year 2000 should know and be able to do. This work involved gathering public input through a series of hearings, surveys, and focus groups. The Kentucky State Board for Elementary and Secondary Education adopted this set of 75 milestones to be incorporated into the curriculum and assessment system. These 75 milestones were called outcomes or expectations. The expectations focused on academic achievement and were linked (Steffy, 1993) to six broad learning goals for the Commonwealth's schools. Students should:

1. Use basic communication and mathematics skills for purposes and situations they will encounter throughout their lives (p. 2).
2. Apply core concepts and principles from mathematics, the sciences, the arts, the humanities, social studies, and practical living studies to situations they will encounter throughout their lives (p. 3).
3. Become self-sufficient individuals (p. 5).
4. Become responsible members of a family, work group, or community, including community service (p. 5).
5. Think and solve problems in school situations and in a variety of situations they will encounter throughout their lives (p. 5).

6. Connect and integrate experiences with new knowledge from all subject matter fields (p. 6).

Statewide stakeholder task forces convened to define these six learning goals operationally into Valued Outcomes (Steffy, 1993), now called Academic Expectations [Kentucky Department of Education (KDE), 1997)]. A valued outcome or academic expectation was defined as the demonstration of consistent, quality performance on authentic tasks related to a skill area, core concept, personal attribute, or thinking process (Council on School Performance Standards, 1991, p. 5).

These learning goals, rather than the traditional subject area organization, formed the organizational structure of the state curriculum framework, *Transformations* (KDE, 1995), which served as a guide for communicating learner outcomes at grades 4, 8, and 12, and included teaching strategy recommendations for a wide variety of learners. These recommendations included but were not limited to student-centered classrooms, heterogeneous learning environments, teaching teams, performance assessments, community-based instruction, as well as alternative demonstrations of learning (KDE, 1995).

It should be noted that Kentucky's six learning goals and academic expectations apply to all students, including students with disabilities. There were and still are no separate outcomes or expectations for any exceptionality. KERA specifically holds schools accountable for ensuring that students meet the learning goals. In addition, school districts must develop policies to remove physical and mental barriers to learning. The instructional strategies identified in *Transformations* (KDE, 1995) and *The KY Program of Studies* (KDE, 1998) included a variety of strategies designed to address the academic expectations and meet the needs of diverse learners.

Cole, a student with autism, working on language arts academic expectations within the context of a general education fourth grade, illustrated the integration of these strategies. Cole's IEP goals focused on improving spelling, staying on topic, sequencing sentences, and typing a final story, while the other fourth-grade students in his class developed personal narratives for their writing portfolios. The academic expectations for the assignment included writing to convey information to a variety of audiences and appropriate writing conventions. First, Cole dictated four sentences to the teacher about the topic "home." The teacher wrote the sentences on sentence strips, leaving out the spelling words. Then Cole arranged the sentence strips and filled in the spelling words. Finally, he typed his story on the computer. The following is Cole's story about home.

At home I eat cookies and hamburger. My dog Angel is at home. Mommy, Daddy, and Julia are at home. I like home. At home on the VCR, I watch movies and videos. Cole

This sample of Cole's writing will be included in the language arts entry of his alternate portfolio along with other samples of his work.

ASSESSMENT

Prior to KERA, students with mild disabilities were generally excluded from testing, whereas students with moderate and severe disabilities were always excluded from assessment. In a national study of state assessments, Ingels (1993) found similar results: that 40% to 50% of students with disabilities, in particular students with learning disabilities, physical disabilities, and limited English proficiency, were excluded from statewide testing.

Kentucky's assessment system uses a combination of authentic, performance, and norm-referenced assessments. These assessments include norm-referenced multiple choice, open response in content areas, and a writing portfolio. The performance assessments or authentic assessments allow students to demonstrate learning in multiple ways, simulate real-life learning experiences, and focus on students' ability to produce a quality product and/or performance. In authentic assessment, effectiveness in problem solving and craftsmanship become more important than merely "right answers"(Wiggins, 1993).

Students in Kentucky elementary, middle, and high schools produce writing portfolios. Portfolios represent a collection of best student work in writing. Teachers evaluate the portfolios using a holistic scoring guide (i.e., portfolio entries are not scored individually, but rather the portfolio as a whole is scored according to the extent to which it embodies key standards across all entries). The holistic scoring guides illustrate performance indicators at four levels: Novice, Apprentice, Proficient, and Distinguished. Each of these terms reflects student growth in the learning process.

All students with disabilities participate in the assessment system in one of three ways. First, students may participate in writing portfolios, on-demand writing assessment, and norm-referenced assessments as do other students with no specific accommodations. Second, students with identified disabilities may receive testing accommodations, as long as those accommodations are documented on the student's IEP, are used as a regular part of instruction for that student, and do not invalidate the construct that the assessment intends to measure. Finally, students may participate in the Alternate Portfolio Assessment. Less than 1% of Kentucky's students participate in the alternate assessment. Specific eligibility criteria limit Alternate Portfolio participation to those students with significant cognitive disabilities (moderate and severe disabilities) who, even with appropriate support and accommodations, are unable to complete the requirements of the regular course of studies (KDE, 1992a). See Chapter 12 in this text for a detailed description of Kentucky's Alternate Portfolio Assessment. Although all students with disabilities in Kentucky participate in the state assessment process in one of these three ways, students' IEP teams determine how each student will participate. For Kentucky as a whole, only a negligible number of students with documented medical exemptions are excluded from participation in the assessment system on a yearly basis; severity of disability does not count as a basis for exemption.

For children with disabilities, Kentucky's assessment system symbolizes both tremendous opportunities and significant challenges. The fact that all students participate in the assessment system is itself an important advance: Inclusion of all students in assessment measures illustrated a profound commitment to the concept of high expectations for all. Students in the Alternate Portfolio Assessment contribute to a school score in the same proportional, numerical weight as do other students (i.e., a Distinguished score on an Alternate Portfolio produces the same effect on a school's accountability index as a Distinguished score in the regular system). Moreover, state-testing data indicated that students with mild disabilities, with proper supports, are able to score at levels commensurate with those of general education students (Trimble, 1998, personal communication). Inclusion in school accountability formulas gives heightened visibility to the needs of all students and helps to ensure that those needs are met within an era of high-stakes accountability. Finally, student scores for accountability purposes are tracked back to the student's neighborhood school (i.e., the school the student would have attended if he or she did not have a disability) to encourage neighborhood schools to assume ownership for the outcomes of all students who reside within their respective attendance boundaries. The fact that a student is sent out of a school's attendance area does not relieve the school of its ultimate responsibility for the education of the student.

Preschool

Evaluation of the KERA Preschool Program indicates that it may be one of the most successful programmatic changes implemented in the reform (Wraths & Fanning, 1993). Early intervention and prevention paradigm shifts identified by Lipp (1992) are also being realized in Kentucky through its Preschool Program. The Kentucky Preschool Model mandated the availability of preschool services to all 4-year-old children who are at or below 130% of poverty indices. In addition, it serves children with disabilities ages 3 to 5, in conformance with IDEA. KERA preschools incorporated principles well documented in child development literature (KDE, 1992b), including comprehensive family-focused planning, inclusionary service delivery, collaborative work among funding sources, and the development of partnerships with community agencies and services. "Comprehensive" describes the family-focused approach via Family Resource Centers for family services and supports. "Inclusionary" defines implementation of services in a mainstream setting for all children. Finally, "collaborative" implies cooperation among funding sources and agencies to meet mutual goals, the development of partnerships across preschool agencies, and an interagency model for planning transition (Early Childhood Collaboration Forum, 1991).

In its efforts to establish comprehensive local school programs for students with moderate and severe disabilities, the Kentucky Systems Change Project found that preschool programs represent the ideal place to begin inclusive programming,

especially in those situations in which preschool children attend their neighborhood schools. In fact, project data indicate that districts that have achieved neighborhood school programs for school-age students have typically placed their integrated preschool programs into the neighborhood schools as well. At this very early
stage in a learner's life, it is critical that the responsibility for the child and his or
her success belong to the school. In addition, the support of the Family Resource
Centers located in many elementary schools link families to other community agencies and services, with the purpose of removing barriers to learning for each child
in the family.

Primary Program

The Kentucky primary program is a classic example of the transition from a traditional educational model to one with potential to reflect the effective practices from
both general and special education. The intent of the primary program is that no
child will experience failure in his or her earliest exposure to school (KDE, 1992b).
The cornerstone of the primary program is the concept that each child will experience continuous progress with no critical gaps in skills as he or she progresses at
his or her own rate through the various skill and content requirements of the
primary curriculum (Burruss & Fairchild, 1993). Primary students are seen as "cre-
ators of meaning and learning" stimulated by teachers, parents, and the community. The philosophy of the primary program involves students in hands-on investigations and interpretive discussions encouraging student-directed inquiry and
exploration (Burruss & Fairchild, 1993).

Seven critical attributes define effective primary programs. These attributes
include developmentally appropriate practices, positive parent involvement, professional teamwork, continuous progress, authentic assessment, qualitative reporting, and multiage/multiability grouping. Of these attributes, Kentucky teachers have
indicated a high level of importance to all but multiage/multiability grouping.
Although studies have shown that about half of the teachers were meeting the
multiage/multiability-grouping requirement (Bridge, 1995), this requirement remains one of the most controversial (De Mesquita & Drake, 1994; Winograd et al.,
1997; Wraths & Fanning, 1993; Wraths, Katz, & Fanning, 1992).

Because of the emphasis on professional teamwork, heterogeneous grouping,
and hands-on learning in the primary program, it appears that special education
services would be more easily delivered in the regular classroom (see Salisbury et al.,
1993). However, in a comparison study of primary programs in Kentucky and
British Columbia, Bruno and Johnson (1994) found that although the attributes
of the primary program were favorable for including children with disabilities,
successful inclusion was more influenced by administrative support, prior education and experience, personal values, and sociocultural factors. In addition, extensive professional development opportunities, including concrete examples of how
to collaborate successfully, were necessary to meet the needs of children with dis-

abilities. These findings suggest that although the attributes of primary programs may provide an optimal place to start including children with disabilities, they are not sufficient by themselves to establish primary programs that successfully include all children. Nevertheless, studies conducted in Kentucky have shown that primary programs appear to have positive academic, social, and emotional effects for children with disabilities (Schack, 1993).

Family Resource and Youth Services Centers

In their description of the Comprehensive Local School, Sailor et al. (1989) detailed a school community in which the local school provides a range of educational and social support. The provision for Family Resource and Youth Service Centers in Kentucky's education reform illustrated this idea. According to Steffy (1993), "A critical component to the success of any education reform is its ability to connect families, teachers, schools, the human service bureaucracy and the educational bureaucracy" (p. 167). This comprehensive statewide initiative, mandated in statute and supported with state funds, provided the linkages between families and service agencies to meet a variety of family support needs.

The goals for the Family Resource Centers include (a) assisting families to address home and community barriers to learning, (b) assisting families to develop parenting skills, (c) ensuring access to and connection with appropriate community resources, and (d) encouraging social support linkages and networks among families. Similar goals exist for Youth Services Centers designed for middle and high school students; however, at the older age levels, emphasis is also placed on developing independence and self-advocacy skills of the individual student. To qualify for a Family Resource or Youth Services Center (FRYSC), a school must have a student body in which 20% or more of the students receive free or reduced-priced lunch. (Olasov & Patrillo, 1994).

Families with children who have disabilities present unique challenges in community and social support linkages in that they very often require the services of a range of community agencies and are often isolated from more informal supports as well (Covert, 1992). The needs of families with children who have disabilities vary widely and are well documented in family support literature (Singer, Powers, & Olson, 1996). This literature suggests that access both to appropriate formal services and more informal support networks (extended family members, friends, church groups, etc.) present a common barrier for these families. Connecting families with the appropriate supports is a vital function for FRYSCs.

Limited data suggest that FRYSCs have a positive effect on at-risk children, both academically and socially. In a 1996 telephone-interview survey of FRYSC directors, Farmer and Kearns (1996) found that center directors had limited access to appropriate resources for families of children with special needs. Like implementing the primary program, establishing family resource centers offers great potential for providing invaluable services to students and their families; however, resources and materials must be available if the family resource centers are to meet the unique needs of families and children with special needs.

Extended School Services

The final programmatic area included in KERA is the provision for Extended School Services (ESS). Like the other programmatic areas, ESS carries important implications for children with disabilities. ESS provides resources for students who are at risk for failure and who require extra time to learn, a position that special educators have long advocated. ESS may take the form of before- and after-school tutoring programs, summer school, and other enrichment activities that support learning. Schools are given considerable latitude in determining the timing of ESS services, so that children can receive additional assistance with essential skills as close as possible to the time the children are initially learning those skills. Schools receive ESS resources on the basis of the numbers of students who qualify for free and reduced-price lunch, with additional allocations available through innovative grants. Okorly and Drake (1996) found that nearly 20,000 students who were referred to the Extended School Services Program for special help were promoted to the next grade or graduated on time. However, there is some evidence that the ESS fails to engage the most needy students. In the second year of implementation, Justice, Farmer, and Hales (1993) found that students with low-incidence disabilities and behavior disorders appeared to be proportionately under represented in ESS. Legislation, which resulted in specific written regulations, corrected this problem. In fact, innovative incentive grants were awarded to local districts that systematically planned for including children with disabilities in ESS. As a result, students with moderate and severe disabilities have participated in integrated summer school programs in their neighborhood school, integrated summer camp programs, and a variety of after school activities.

Technology Links to the Future

A final but no less significant piece of Kentucky's education reform legislation ushered the "information age" into Kentucky classrooms. The Kentucky legislature recognized the importance of technology if individual students in rural Kentucky were to have access to information similar to that available to students in suburban and urban communities. The legislature described a vision of computer linkages in every classroom to a host of information sources, with the Kentucky Educational Technology System (KETS) working to establish those computer links. The current goal for Kentucky's classrooms is to have one computer in place for every six students. Districts and schools, in turn, must develop technology implementation plans that facilitate implementing this important piece of the reform package. Although the implementation of KETS in all schools still has a way to go before all classrooms are linked, students, teachers, and administrators are beginning to use this technology to access information related to various issues, including those related to disability.

Within the context of this initiative, the implications for students with disabilities range from access to information to access to technology and assistive technology. School and district technology plans must address these accessibility issues related to the needs of students with disabilities. Progress has been made toward improving the access of Kentucky's children with disabilities to the network and also toward creating a clearinghouse for assistive devices. The technology budget of KERA, however, falls short in that it doesn't provide for individualized assistive technology that is *not* directly linked to accessing the KETS system.

CONCLUSION: SUMMARY OF MAJOR INDICATORS

Using the indicators defined jointly by the Consortia of Inclusive Schooling Practice and the National State Boards of Education Association, we have reviewed most of the key components of Kentucky's Education Reform Act to determine their potential implications for students with disabilities. The first of these indicators called for "content based, systemic reform" supporting high standards, coordinated policies, and support for all students. As we have noted throughout, Kentucky's education reform meets the definition of a standards-based reform—a single set of academic expectations that apply to all students, and a single, unified funding stream, although Exceptional Child "add-ons" apply a categorically weighted funding-supplements system. Add-ons are generated categorically, but districts are not required to track expenditures categorically. Students with and without disabilities are represented under a single governance structure and are educated under a single curriculum framework that provides a scaffold for the learning of all students. Students with and without disabilities participate equally and consistently in the assessment and accountability system. Moreover, students with and without disabilities participate in a broad set of assessments aligned with state and local standards for curricular content and student performance. Students with all types of disabilities receive assessment accommodations and alternatives as needed, so that no student is excluded. A comprehensive system of professional development exists to develop the capacity of teachers and administrators to work with an increasingly diverse set of learners. Yet, although Kentucky's education reform meets these state-level indicators, the real impact can be measured only at the student level.

In the final analysis, all educational policy and legislation must be measured in terms of student results (Roach, 1995). Mandated legislation and subsequent policy represent powerful but blunt tools in creating an environment for change. Policy and legislation can only create an environment that supports change, but additional strategies may be necessary to achieve better results for all students. The real answers will come as policy intersects with frontline practice, resulting, one hopes, in positive outcomes for students. In Kentucky, as elsewhere, many questions have yet to be answered in terms of inclusive assessments, high-stakes accountability, school governance, and professional development. Finally, landmark legislation and policy can be impacted profoundly by a changing political climate long before educational reforms have produced the systemic effects for which they were created. As U.S. Secretary of Education Richard Riley specifically noted in a July 1996 speech on the state of our nation's schools, systematic change at the level that Kentucky is attempting takes time. He asked the citizens of Kentucky to sustain their effort over the years required for the reforms to take firm root in the cultures of schools. In short, the stage is set, and even 10 years later, the play has just begun to tell the story of improved results for students.

REFERENCES

Bauwens, J., Hourcade, J., & Friend, M. (1989). Cooperative teaching: A model for general and special education integration. *Remedial and Special Education, 10*(2), 17–22.

Bridge, C. (1995). *The implementation of Kentucky's primary program* (Research Rep.). Frankfort: Institute on Education Reform for the Kentucky Institute for Education Research.

Bruno, R., & Johnson, J. (1994). *Mandated primary program: Responding to changing service for children with special needs.* Paper presented at the conference of the Council for Exceptional Children, Denver, CO.

Burruss, B., & Fairchild, N. (1993). *The primary school: A resource guide for parents.* Lexington, KY: The Prichard Committee for Academic Excellence and The Partnership for School Reform.

Coleman, J. S., Campbell, E. Q., Hobson, C. J., McPartland, J., Mood, A. M., Weinfield, F. D., and York, R. L. (1966). *Equality of Educational Opportunity.* Washington, DC: U.S. Government Printing Office.

Coots, J., Bishop, K., Grenot-Scheyer, M., & Falvey, M. (1995). Practices in general education: Past and present. In M. Falvey (Ed.), *Inclusive and heterogeneous schooling: Assessment, curriculum, and instruction* (pp. 7–22). Baltimore: Paul H. Brookes.

Council for Better Education v. Wilkinson. (1985). No. 85-CI-1759. Franklin County Circuit Court.

Council on School Performance Standards. (1991). *Kentucky's learning goals and valued outcomes: Technical report.* Frankfort: Kentucky Department of Education.

Covert, S. (1992). Supporting families. In J. Nisbet, *Natural supports in school, at work, and in the community for people with severe disabilities* (pp. 121–164). Baltimore: Paul H. Brookes.

De Mesquita, P. B., and Drake, J. C. (1994). Educational reform and the self-efficacy beliefs of teachers implementing non-graded primary programs. *Teaching and Teacher Education, 10*(3), 291–302.

Early Childhood Collaboration Forum. (1991). Shakertown, KY: Author.

Education for All Handicapped Children Act of 1975. P.L. 94-142.

Farmer, R., & Kearns, J.F. (1996). Family resource youth service centers and families with special needs. Unpublished manuscript, University of Kentucky, Interdisciplinary Human Development Institute.

Gartner, A., and Lipsky, D. K. (1987). Beyond special education: Toward a quality education for all students. *Harvard Educational Review, 57*(4), 367–395.

Hunt, P., Staub, D., Alwell, M., & Goetz, L. (1994). Achievement by all students within the context of cooperative learning groups. *Journal of the Association for Persons With Severe Handicaps, 19*(4), 290–301.

Individuals With Disabilities Education Act of 1990. 20 U.S.C. Se. 1400 et seq.

Ingels, S. J. (1993). *Strategies for including all students in national and state assessments: Lessons from a national longitudinal study.* Paper presented at the National Conference on Large-Scale Assessment of the Council Chief State School Officers, Alburquerque, NM.

Jencks, C. (1972). *Inequality: A reassessment of the effects of family and schooling in America.* New York: Harrow Books.

Johnson, D., Johnson, R., and Holubec, E. (1990). *Cooperation in the classroom* (Rev. ed.). Edina, MN: Interaction Books.

Johnson, J. R., & Rusch, F. R. (1993). *Educational reform in special education: Foundations for a national research agenda focused on secondary education.* ERIC Database: ED358608.

Justice, T., Farmer, J., & Hales, R. (1993). Effective inclusionary strategies and practices for extended school service programs. Unpublished manuscript, Kentucky Developmental Disabilities Planning Council, Frankfort.

Kentucky Department of Education. (1992a). *Alternate Portfolio Teacher's Guide.* Frankfort, KY: Author.

Kentucky Department of Education. (1992b). *The Wonder Years.* Frankfort, KY: Author.

Kentucky Department of Education. (1993). *Synergy.* Frankfort, KY: Author.

Kentucky Department of Education. (1994). State regulations and recommended best practices for Kentucky's primary program. Frankfort, KY: Author.

Kentucky Department of Education. (1995). *Transformations.* Frankfort, KY: Author.

Kentucky Department of Education. (1997). Kentucky's Learning Goals and Academic Expectations. *http://www.kde.state.ky.us.* Frankfort, KY: Author.

Kentucky Department of Education. (1998). *The Program of Studies.* Frankfort, KY: Author.

Kleinert, H. (1995). *The role of school-based councils in enhancing the educational outcomes of all students.* Lexington: University of Kentucky, Interdisciplinary Human Development Institute.

Lindle, J. C. (1992). School leadership and educational reform: Parent involvement, the Education for Handicapped Children Act, and the principal. *Occasional Papers: School Leadership and Educational Reform* (OP No. 4). Lexington: University of Kentucky.

Lindle, J. C. (1996). School-based decision making. *1996 review of research on the Kentucky Education Reform Act.* Frankfort: The Kentucky Institute for Education Research.

Lipp, M. (1992). An emerging perspective on special education: A developing agenda for the 1990's. *The Special Education Leadership Review, 1*(1), 10–39.

National Commission on Education. (1983). *A Nation at Risk.* Washington, DC: Author.

Okorley, E., & Drake, J. (1996). Extended School Services. *1996 Review of Research on the Kentucky Education Reform Act.* Frankfort: The Kentucky Institute for Education Research.

Olasov, L., & Partillo, J. (1994). Meeting health needs through Kentucky's new family resource centers and youth service centers. *Journal of School Health, 64,* 59–61.

Riley, R. (1996, July). *Lexington Herald Leader.* Lexington, KY.

Roach, V. (1995). *Standards-based policy evaluation.* Washington, DC: National Association of State Boards of Education.

Rose v. Council for Better Education, Inc., No. 88-SC-804-TG (Kentucky, September 28,
1989).

Sage, D., & Burrello, L. C. (1994). *Leadership in educational reform: An administrator's guide
to changes in special education.* Baltimore: Paul H. Brookes.

Sailor, W., Anderson, J. L., Halvorsen, A. T., Doering, K., Filler, J., Goetz, L. (1989). *The
comprehensive local school: Regular education for all students with disabilities.* Baltimore:
Paul H. Brookes.

Salisbury, C., Palumbaro, M., & Hollowood, T. (1993). On the nature of change of an
Inclusive elementary school. *The Journal of the Association of Persons With Severe
Handicaps (18)*2, 75–84.

Schack, G. (1993). The quality in Kentucky's primary program. *Equality and Excellence in
Education, 26,* 37–41.

Singer, G., Powers, L., & Olson, A. (1996). *Redefining family support.* Baltimore: Paul H.
Brookes.

Skrtic, T. M. (1991). The special education paradox: Equity as the way to excellence. *Harvard
Education Review, 61*(2), 148–205.

Stainback, S., Stainback, W., & Forest, M. (Eds.). (1989). *Educating all students in the mainstream of regular education.* Baltimore: Paul H. Brookes.

Steffy, B. (1993). *The Kentucky Education Reform: Lessons for America.* Lancaster, KY:
Technomic.

Weston, S. P. (1991). *School-based decision making: A guide for school council members and
others.* Lexington, KY: Prichard Committee for Academic Excellence.

Wiggins, G. (1993). Assessment to improve performance, not just monitor it: Assessment
reform in social sciences. *Social Science Record, 30*(2), 5–12.

Winograd, P., Petrosko, J., Compton-Hall, M., & Cantrell, S. (1997). *The effect of KERA
on Kentucky's elementary schools: Year one of a proposed five-year study* (Research Rep.).
Frankfort: University of Kentucky/University of Louisville Joint Center for the Study
of Educational Policy, Kentucky Institute for Educational Research.

Wraths, J., & Fanning, J. (1993). *Primary school reform in Kentucky revisited.* Lexington,
KY: Prichard Committee.

Wraths, J., Katz, L., & Fanning, J. (1992). *The status of primary school reform in Kentucky
and its implication.* Report to the Prichard Committee.

CHAPTER 6

Excluded Children and Integrated Services: What Parents Need to Keep Their Children at Home and Their Families Together

Nancy J. Zollers

Various "integrated services" models have emerged as promising ways for human services professionals to serve families of children with complex learning and living needs (Comer, 1987; Gardner, 1992; Usdan, 1990). The objective of integrated services is to create a seamless web of services with coordinated approaches and comprehensive coverage (Kirst & McLaughlin, 1990). Many observers see these models as having the potential to end the fragmentation and incrementalization of current service delivery approaches (Skrtic, Sailor, & Gee, 1996). Despite the increasing popularity of integrated services, many questions remain about their efficacy. A particularly compelling question is whether an integrated services model can enable children with severe disabilities currently being served in out-of-home placements to return to their families. In order to understand the potential of integrated services to preserve or reunite families, this chapter explores parents' perspectives on their service needs. The three cases presented in this chapter illustrate what parents need to keep their children at home through the perspectives of their mothers. Human service professionals must understand what a family needs in order to design an appropriate and effective service integration strategy.

Before we examine the specific cases, let's first take a look at how the various integrated service models have emerged over time. Prior to 1973, students with significant disabilities, such as mental retardation, severe physical disabilities and/ or medical needs, were nearly always denied access to local public schools. Services were based on institutional models (Wolfensberger, 1972), placing children in large congregate centers designed to care for and shelter them rather than teach or habilitate them. Since the passage of the federal right to education laws in 1973, many schools have created programs to educate these students in their own communities. Others, however, congregate their students with significant disabilities in special centers or send them to residential-care facilities, far away from their homes and neighborhoods.

The special center approach to serving significantly disabled children has often been justified as a necessary program model because of the students' multiple needs, including physical, occupational, and speech therapies, and nursing services such as assistance with feeding, breathing, and toileting. The residential option is often sought because of the burden on the family of providing 24-hour care for children with physical or behavior challenges. These programs have been criticized by some researchers as providing an easy and convenient solution to the problems posed by serving these children (Biklen, 1985; Brown, Long, et al., 1989). Rather than schools' meeting the real-life needs of special children, these services are being provided by therapists and nurses, as well as educators. Increasingly, families are requesting that their children with special needs be served by their neighborhood schools.

HOW INTEGRATED SERVICES BEGAN

Integrated services began as a way to effectively serve families at risk of dissolving because of the difficulties posed by caring for children with multiple needs—physical, behavioral, medical, and so on. Children may leave their families for a number of reasons. Sometimes they are placed in the social service or criminal justice system, sometimes in foster homes, and sometimes in residential special education programs because they have severe or multiple disabilities. This chapter focuses on this latter group, children with disabilities and their families. Although the integrated services literature has paid considerable attention to multicultural issues and issues of social context, little attention has been given to the potential for integrated services to reach families who have children with disabilities.

From the onset, integrated services approaches have been viewed as means by which a variety of professionals and their agencies can coordinate their services to meet the needs of families. Essential ingredients include interprofessional dialogue, family empowerment, and strength-based (as opposed to dysfunctional- or deficit-based) service delivery. The integrated services approach is rooted in the premise that education, health, and social services currently provided to children through individual bureaucracies with separate funding streams result in scattered, uneven, and ineffective service to children and families in need. Although implementation has varied, in most cases it has been designed to coordinate educational, health care, family income support, mental health, legal, and other supportive services. Schools are often the host agency for the newly integrated services.

An integrated services approach requires significant organizational changes in the education and human services professions to broaden and efficiently coordinate the array of available services (Knoster, 1995). The approach emphasizes community and family involvement in defining needs and identifying appropriate supports. In this system professionals accept a supportive rather than representative role (Knoster, 1995). Agencies depend on the expertise of both families and professionals (Lerner, 1995). By collaborating with families, experts can come to understand, often for the first time, what services and supports each family needs. Giving voice to parents can lead to shared understandings, family empowerment, increased accessibility to services, improved coordination of services, and cost savings in communities. Although most human service programs recognize the importance of parental involvement, agencies tend to focus instead on superficial procedures or planning processes of services. For integrated services to succeed, the needs of parents must be fully understood. Therefore, this chapter attempts to understand, from parents' perspectives, how coordinated services appear.

We present the perspectives of three mothers of children with significant disabilities who hope to return their children to their homes, schools, and communities. These portraits shed light on the practices and the values that these mothers would expect to find in any integrated service model. Their stories communicate the goal of this chapter: to demonstrate the importance of serving children, whenever possible, in their home communities. Neighborhood schools and natural supports such as friends and extended family provide a network of support including extra hands, expertise, familiarity, and accessibility. The local connections and circles of friends available to students who stay in their community are well documented (Brown, Schwarz, et al., 1991; Kishi & Meyer, 1994). However, any attempt to return children to their homes and local communities must be understood in the context of their families' needs.

Family Supports

Although some families possess the coping and advocacy skills and financial means to meet the multiple needs of children with significant disabilities (Laski, 1991), most families have some difficulty coping with a child's disability (Turnbull, Patterson, et al., 1993; Turnbull, Turnbull, et al., 1992). Family members often suffer anxiety and depression as they strain to meet a child's needs. In many cases, frustration with the human service system can add to the tensions that destabilize families (Cutler, 1993).

The disability community and human service professionals have a solid history of conceptualizing and mobilizing coordinated services for families. These services are often referred to as "family supports." Early family support initiatives were targeted at families seeking to keep their children in their local communities. These initiatives were based on the idea that families should lead the decision-making process concerning the type and amount of support they need (Yuan, Baker-McCue, & Witkin, 1996). However, a variety of factors conspired to limit the success of these early efforts.

Many families did not receive the support their family required. A major impediment to the implementation of a system of full family supports was the perceived cost to the local community of caring for and educating children with significant disabilities. Many communities viewed these students as "severely expensive." To agencies with tight budgets, the notion of returning students with complex needs to their own communities has often been often viewed as a "budget-busting" initiative. Additionally, in many cases the necessary supports were poorly coordinated, placing families and human service agencies at odds. We are optimistic that an effort to listen to families within the context of an integrated services approach will revitalize the ability of agencies to provide "family supports."

The Voice of Families

From the beginning, the integrated services model has been an attempt to coordinate multiple professionals and their agencies around needy children. However, integrated services has more recently been defined as including other essential ingredients such as interprofessional dialogue, family empowerment, and strength-based (as opposed to dysfunctional or deficit-based) service delivery. The integrated services approach is based on the premise that education, health, and social services, currently provided to children under separate funding streams and through individual bureaucracies, create scattered, uneven, and ineffective results. This practice is particularly costly to the very children and families who are most in need. While the integrated services model is operated differently in various communities, it is designed to coordinate—both physically and conceptually—educational services, health care services, family income support, mental health services, legal services, and other supportive arrangements. Schools are often the host agencies for the newly collected services. However operated, an integrated services approach requires significant organizational change in education and the human services professions in order both to broaden the array of services available to families and to coordinate them efficiently (Knoster, 1995). One significant change from traditional ways of operating is that the integrated services model requires an emphasis on community and family involvement in defining needs and identifying the most appropriate supports from professionals (Comer & Haynes, 1991). This approach is most successful when family- and child-driven outcomes are regarded as basic and power is shared. This requires clarifying the professional role as supportive rather than representative (Knoster, 1995) and acknowledging that children need dual experts—the family and the professional (Lerner, 1995). The financial considerations of a fragmented service system have long been understood and recommendations have been offered to reduce the responsibility risks when human service agencies choose to provide services to families (Zollers, 1983). Families in this study, however, when given the chance to contribute their perspectives, point out that financial concerns are only one fallout of fragmented services. Through dialogue with families, we understand for the first time what families view as weaknesses in the current model of service delivery and what they would construct as a system strong enough to keep their family together. Giving parents voice may also lead to shared understandings, family empowerment, more accessibility to services, increased coordination of services, more success for families, and therefore cost savings in communities. Experts may also learn that when parents articulate what they need in order to stay together, their information may be even more practical than the sophisticated expertise offered us in our professional training (Brabeck et al., in press).

Integrated services began as a model built on prevention. One widely understood aspect of prevention by the human service system is the concept of family preservation. Many families are at risk of dissolving under stressful circumstances. Social workers, as well as other human service professionals, have understood that one intervention that keeps families together is the occasional need for intensive services (Maluccio, Pine, & Warch, 1996). Children of all complexities and from all types of families leave their communities, sometimes because that is the only way for them to obtain professional services. These children and youth include students in the social service or criminal justice system sent to live and be educated in facilities away from their communities; students with severe or multiple disabilities who are educated in out-of-community residential special education programs; and foster children temporarily served in new families away from their home communities. These children and youth become invisible members of their communities, out of sight and out of mind.

All of the programs and services available to parents recognize the importance of involving parents and have some framework to do so. Enforcement of preexisting requirements of the statutes governing education could, in itself, contribute to family supports. However, in reality, agencies often focus on procedures or planning processes that are superficial. Important provisions of IDEA and Title I are reduced to little more than paperwork that has slight resemblance to what the families we interviewed said they needed. For integrated services to succeed, the needs of parents have to be fully understood and implemented with their full participation. Recent proposals to promote a value orientation to integrated services—and by doing so promote a more democratic society—add another attractive framework to consider in pursuing integrated services (Skrtic & Sailor, 1996). Under this values orientation, Skrtic and Sailor argue that voice, collaboration, and inclusion are key to a participatory democracy and are closely aligned in the principles that guide the integrated services movement. If this is the case, it is imperative to give voice to *families* as we continue to define this model. The case studies presented here shed considerable light on the practices and the values three mothers would embed in any integrated service model.

Integrated service provision emphasizes providing support for care givers. The burden of care-giving in families with a child with complex needs often falls heaviest on mothers. Without a web of services, the stress, time commitments, and organizational burdens involved in managing and obtaining services are largely placed on mothers. Family preservation and reunification may depend on the extent to which the mothers can obtain services when they cannot meet their child's needs.

Thus the portraits discussed here are based on interviews with mothers of children with significant disabilities.

ETHNOGRAPHIES OF MOTHERS AND CHILDREN

To illustrate what this really means, let's take a look at an ethnographic study of mothers of children with significant disabilities. Qualitative research has a rich tradition in sociology and anthropology. Qualitative traditions are "constructivist" in that they require that generally accepted notions of what is truth be suspended in order for new truths to emerge from the data. Widely accepted terms and definitions such as *interdisciplinary* and *individual education plans* are taken as problematic rather than as givens. Qualitative methods are particularly appropriate here, given the strong tradition of qualitative research for obtaining a consumer's view of human services.

The method of focus groups was chosen because it differed from the traditional "expert-driven" discourse on integrated services (Skrtic & Sailor, 1996). Focus groups are particularly effective in exploratory research (Morgan, 1988). The disclosures we sought were encouraged by the "informal" focus group setting (Krueger, 1994).

The mothers in this study were selected because they have children with significant disabilities placed in residential facilities or at risk of leaving home for such a facility. The mothers were cooperative speakers, thoughtful and articulate. The open-ended nature of the focus groups allowed them to share and explain their experiences with each other and with the authors (Krueger, 1994). Because little data were available on how integrated services could support families of children with significant disabilities, the research questions were ambiguous and required the input of families. Questions guiding the focus groups of the study included:

1. What do you need for your child to be able to return to your family, community, and school under an integrated service approach?
2. How would you design an integrated services approach that would save your child from leaving his or her school and community?
3. How could an integrated services approach empower your family?

THE PORTRAITS

Betty

Betty (pseudonym) is a 14-year-old girl who has been diagnosed as autistic, multiply handicapped, neurologically impaired, and mentally retarded. For 11 years she lived at home despite challenging behavior and learning issues that took a serious toll on her family's stability. She is now in a private residential school about an hour from her mother. Betty's mother would like Betty to return to her community.

Although Betty's mother cannot be sure what effect Betty's disability had on the family's eventual break up, she often ponders what might have happened if she had received "more help" from Betty's school and local human service agencies. She attributes the ultimate need to send Betty away to insufficient services, especially lack of a good school program. She is presently engaged in conversations and negotiations with the school and local human service agencies to determine what the family needs to bring Betty home and keep her there. Betty's mother always needed more help.

Betty's mother recalled the rationale given to her when she was denied additional personal-care-attendant services she had requested. When they advised her that "You have been denied the additional hours because *you* can do it," Betty's mother was convinced that she was being told that care-taking was her job as mother and care giver. She knew that her need for help was real, but she was denied additional support for the role "she was supposed to do." Later, she requested assistance from the school to help her eliminate some of Betty's severe behaviors. The school's response was a complex behavior-modification program that required Betty's mother's constant participation. With her existing commitments, she simply didn't have the time to complete this task. She said, "I didn't have the time to follow her around the house filling in the data collection card on her behavior plan." The agency was willing to give her more work to do in the name of family support but less willing to give her more help for the countless tasks she already performed.

In addition, Betty's services needed to be reorganized, extended in number, and improved in quality and coordination. When Betty was first diagnosed, her mother obtained as many services as she could, ranging from trained caretakers to behavior consultants. However, the lack of a cohesive service system with case-management functions presented her with a new set of problems. She had to work with four major agencies: the public school, the Department of Mental Retardation, the Department of Public Assistance, and the Department of Public Health. These organizations, however, did not work with each other. Betty's mother observed,

> No one listens to anybody, I found out. They don't want to come to a meeting with other agencies. They are afraid they'll be asked to pay for something.

Although providing services in this isolated manner had advantages for the agencies, it had serious disadvantages for Betty's mother. The services Betty received were insufficient and piecemeal. The fragmented services operated within the constraints of particular professional boundaries. The limited communication and coordination reduced the ability of each individual agency to effectively meet the complex needs of Betty's family. This resulted in the family not receiving services that were clearly necessary.

> We received no family counseling although I do think the social workers care about the family in a holistic way. More than the other agencies do anyway.

In an attempt to get the professionals from the school, the Department of Mental Retardation (DMR), and health care professionals to communicate and coordinate their efforts, Betty's family decided to see a team of professionals at a local clinic. The team's intention was to look at the child and family through an interdisciplinary lens and coordinate a habilitation plan. However, Betty's family's experience, described below, illustrates the difference between integrated services and the goal of "interdisciplinary" work.

> I went there. You see the psychologist, the social worker, the pediatrician, the speech and language person. Then they all go around the table and give their report. They told me she was retarded and always will be. I already knew that when we went.

Children's agencies and special-education-related agencies are often run by an "interdisciplinary model." This model has several weaknesses and should not be confused with integrated services. The interdisciplinary model is usually convened around assessment. The objective of the team is to evaluate the child across a number of different professional perspectives. Team members tend to use a deficit model of assessment, detailing only the student's needs and deficits. Team members may also operate in isolation, providing disconnected information; their only coordinated effort is to meet as a group in order to report their findings to families.

The deficit model derives from the medical profession's focus on sickness, identifying weaknesses rather than strengths. The medical profession has traditionally devalued individuals with disabilities. This medical approach often reasserts itself during the family's interaction with health care providers. Betty's mother sees children with disabilities as marginalized by the community and often regarded as nondeserving of human services.

During the course of the conversations, Betty's mother laid out what the family will need if Betty is to return home, including complex in-home supports and a good school program that would teach her new skills and more appropriate behaviors. In addition, Betty needs home health aides to assist in the daily tasks of dressing, bathing, and feeding; and because her mother could no longer work full time if Betty returned home, the family would need income support. The family, especially Betty's brother, would need counseling and support to cope with the challenges posed by Betty's needs and respite services provided by trained staff so that Betty's mother could take time off. None of these needs are excessive. Yet Betty's mother often had difficulty getting local agencies to meet even her most basic needs.

The concept of "wrap-around services" has emerged as a potential way of designing integrated services that would better serve people like Betty. *Wrap around* began as a term to describe flexible funding that could be used to support families in tailored ways rather than through specific agency programs (Katz-Leavy et al., 1992). A wrap-around model increases the power of families to assert their needs and encourages agencies to meet those needs (Knoster, 1995). By requiring human services to provide whatever resources the mother needs to keep the child home, the model turns traditional service delivery on its head.

One of the earliest agencies to adopt wrap-around meetings as a planning model for families was the Philadelphia Department of Mental Health. In one of the first wrap-around meetings, the Department of Mental Health director allowed the most powerful feature of wrap around—parent empowerment—to prevail. Representatives from a variety of agencies sat with parents and discussed what they would need in order for their child to return from a residential mental health facility. Everything the family asked for was recorded and considered legitimate. On one occasion, a mother asked for a "house." The director asserted that this was well within the context of wrap-around service work. The Office of Housing staff in attendance determined that the high-rise project the family currently lived in was, in many ways, an obstacle to successfully returning the child, and they found a public housing option in the neighborhood.

In cases such as these, family support has attempted to eliminate the traditional "blame and shame" approach used by professionals, replacing it with support and encouragement (Karp, 1996). Similarly, integrated services planning should go beyond fitting children into current service configurations and focus instead on meeting families' immediate and long-term needs.

Ryan

Ryan (pseudonym) is a 12-year-old boy with significant physical needs and mental retardation. Nonoral, he is in a wheelchair, has multiple seizure disorders, and suffers from vision impairments. He was fully included in a team-taught elementary program with his brothers and sisters. The program was of high quality and Ryan was accepted as a part of the school community. However, when he reached sixth grade, the lack of a similar middle school program forced Ryan's parents to send him to a private school program.

Like Betty's mother, Ryan's mother reported that Ryan required a good educational program integrated with services provided by other agencies. A good educational program would be based on a vision of what Ryan needs in order to live and work in the community and provide access to social relationships and friendships with nondisabled peers. Lifelong friends made in school are likely to outlive Ryan's parents and can provide support and even advocacy for Ryan in the human service system in his adult life. A model educational program could also alter his future through social role valorization—improving the status of a person with disabilities by planning typical routines, relationships, and activities for him or her. (Wolfensberger, 1972). The status of devalued members of the community is enhanced by associations with higher status community members. Ryan's career as a student and the friendships he made in school enhanced his status in the community. To be educated alongside similarly disabled students creates an environment more resembling a hospital than a school and multiplies the stigma of disability.

For Ryan's family, obtaining and keeping a good school program is a critical aspect of any plan to keep him at home. Still, by itself an educational program cannot adequately address the extended needs of Ryan and his family. Ryan's family requires access to excellent health care, many hours of personal care, respite care, and case management. An integrated services approach would link these services with his school program. For example, Ryan's family needs an after-school program that will involve and engage him. In sixth grade, an after-school program was not provided. The short school day and limited school year created holes in Ryan's schedule that his family did not have the resources to fill. This forced his family to send him to private school. An integrated services approach would focus on filling these holes.

One way to obtain an appropriate program for a child is to be able to articulate the child's needs to professionals. Ryan's mother was concerned that the prevailing attitude in service delivery prevented her from being served effectively. She believed that her concerns and requests fell on deaf ears because professionals often made unilateral decisions about the level of supports she needed. Whether for reasons of equity or funding, her requests for services were often turned down and she grew extremely frustrated by the second-guessing of professionals. Ryan's mother discussed how this attitude would affect parents who did not have her ability or background.

> I am a well-spoken, educated person who has to struggle for wrap-around services. I am also listened to in this urban center because I am white. When I think about all the minority parents and parents who can't advocate for themselves or who are not listened to like I am, I worry.

When families cannot articulate their needs, integrated services should include mechanisms whereby such families are given a voice. Paying attention to social class and, cultural differences and improving consumer empowerment have been methods used by some agencies adopting the integrated services approach. An integrated approach to service delivery should be grounded in regular communication between professionals and family members.

Ryan's mother is the primary care giver of the family and was responsible for managing the in-home help for Ryan during the day. For Ryan's mother, letting strangers into her personal space at all hours of the day strained her coping skills. In addition, the lack of an integrated services approach forced her to try to coordinate disconnected services. In her view, integrated services for families with disabled children needed several fundamental features, including case management to organize services in a flexible way and advocacy to obtain additional family supports. These services had to be based on the premise that parents were doing the best they could in difficult circumstances.

Bill

Bill (pseudonym) has significant physical and cognitive disabilities. From ages 5 to 14, he was educated away from home. The school district told his family that he could return to the community as soon as a program was ready for him. When his residential school closed down, Bill returned home and his school developed a program that resulted in positive outcomes such as academic skills and a circle of friends. At age 21 Bill will no longer be eligible for public education, and lack of a postschool program will threaten the gains he achieved in school.

Bill's family had little connection to Bill's neighborhood school and local district. This is the case for many families when their children are placed in an out-of-district residential facility. However, once the transition was made, Bill's life changed dramatically. His mother described the difference when Bill returned home and began attending his local school.

> I went to the County Fair on opening day with my three boys as we do every year. This year something very different happened. As we entered the fairground the boys' friends called them to join them. Bill was called, too! For the first time I "did" the Fair alone. Usually the boys join their friends and I push Bill through the exhibits. Having Bill home has made a world of difference.

Bill's transition from private school to his community school was difficult. Bill's circle of friends was an important source of support for Bill and his mother. But as Bill began to approach the age of 21, the dark reality of postschool life in the community for him became apparent to his mother. "Post-21" life for students in special education has been likened to falling off a cliff. Although some students find habilitation day programs or supported employment, the vast majority of graduates end up idle, secluded in their homes, losing skills that took years to learn in school (Zollers, 1983).

Little attention has been paid to how integrated services can facilitate the transition to postschool community living for students with disabilities. Our findings in this study regarding the mismatch between the services families need and those they receive could inform current problems in transition from school to work. The relatively reasonable solutions these mothers discussed—having voice, eliminating professional assumptions, and collaborating to create a good program—can inform an effective integrated services model and promote smooth transitions to postschool life in the community.

CONCLUSION

Most children with disabilities in residential placements return to their local communities at some point in their lives. When the child returns home, a fragmented or unilateral approach used by human services agencies will not facilitate the child's transition into the community. We do not believe that any human service agency can by itself prepare a family for reunification or help a family prevent disintegration.

The potential for interprofessional dialogue under an integrated human services model to contribute to the quality and breadth of human services is great. An integrated services model requires professionals such as social workers, psychologists, educators, and health care professionals to become familiar with the knowledge base and practices of other professionals. Armed with this information, these professionals can operate in synchronization, avoiding duplication, mixed signals, and gaps in services that result from limited knowledge and information. Territorial professionalism creates gaps in the service system. The interprofessional dialogue and problem solving envisioned in integrated services can be instrumental in "breaking the status quo" of service delivery design and connecting these gaps to provide a seamless web of services.

The portraits illustrated in this chapter show how listening to the parents' voices can challenge the faulty assumptions held by professionals operating in isolation. The portraits also provide new directions for human service agencies planning for students with significant disabilities and their families. These mothers inform us that an integrated services model can be much more powerful if its design relies on the tradition in disabilities services of "family supports." By working in a partnership with families, emphasizing the families' needs and listening to their voices, professionals in an integrated services model can develop a coordinated program that meets the needs of the child with disabilities and contributes to family cohesion.

Coordinated, wrap-around services that fully meet the needs of families caring for children with significant disabilities are both logical and humane. This service model has the potential to keep families together and children in their communities. If we could solve the problems of uncoordinated services and funding shortfalls, the complexities of designing the best solutions for families would remain. Betty's mother was receiving services for her daughter and had the advice and support of a number of professionals. Yet examination of her case reveals that her family dissolved because the amount of home health assistance was too limited. The requests for more help were denied because the agency concluded that the caretaking was Betty's mother's responsibility.

Similarly, as his primary care giver, Ryan's mother was unable to provide more than she was already providing. A shortened school day made it impossible to keep Ryan at the neighborhood school. The school day was not understood by people outside the family as "the last straw."

As Bill's case illustrates, the natural supports of friends and neighbors made a profound difference for Bill's mother. Such supports are not traditionally on the list of services provided, but they would be under an integrated services model that included the voice of families.

Many unexamined issues in integrated services delivery can be illuminated by mothers of children with disabilities. This becomes clear from the stories. An effective wrap-around service model must include input from the care givers in the family. Prescriptive services and formula-based services cannot meet families' individual needs. Any program designed by agencies—coordinated or not—that does not include a family voice specific to that family's particular needs, in all aspects of raising a child with significant disabilities, may leave critical gaps that will keep some families from "making it." No one expected the Philadelphia mother to request decent housing when she was asked to identify her human service needs. But it was, in fact, her most urgent need. Similarly, it is somewhat surprising that mothers were unanimous about "a good school program" as a top priority for children who have complicated personal-care needs. And families who have exceeded the formula for the allowable number of personal-care attendants may still need more. As the mother of Betty told us, her need for more personal care was urgent, and yet unrecognizable to the agency.

What families need to keep their children at home is both highly individualized and sometimes surprising. Answers to "What do you need to bring your child home?" can be well articulated by care givers. It is apparent that the mothers in this study had thought about this question before and were able to answer with certainty what an integrated service model would mean to them. The value in asking care givers and understanding and responding to their expressed needs puts the theoretical benefits of integrated services in place for families and communities.

REFERENCES

Biklen, D. (1985). *Achieving the complete school: Strategies for effective mainstreaming.* New York: Teachers College Press.

Brabeck, M., Cawthorne, J., Cochran-Smith, M., Gaspard, N., Green, C. H., Kenny, M., Krawczyk, R., Lowery, C., Lykes, M. B., Minuskin, A. D., Mooney, J., Ross, C. J., Savage, J., Soifer, A., Smyer, M., Sparks, E., Tourse, R., Turillo, R. M., Waddock, S., Walsh, M., & Zollers, N. (in press). Changing the culture of the university to engage in outreach scholarship. In R. M. Lerner & L. A. Simons (Eds.), *Creating the New*

Outreach University for America's youth and families: Building university–community collaborations for the twenty-first century.

Brown, L., Long, E., Udvari-Solner, A., Davis, L., VanDeventer, P., Ahlgren, C., Johnson, F., Gruenewald, L., & Jorgensen, J. (1989). The home school: Why students with severe intellectual disabilities must attend the schools of their brothers, sisters, friends, and neighbors. *Journal of the Association for Persons With Severe Handicaps, 14*(1), 1–7.

Brown, L., Schwarz, P., Udvari-Solner, A., Frattura Kampschroer, E., Johnson, F., Jorgensen, J., & Gruenewald, L. (1991). How much time should students with severe intellectual disabilities spend in regular education classrooms and elsewhere? *Journal of the Association for Persons With Severe Handicaps, 16*(1), 39–47.

Comer, J. (1987). New Haven's school–community connection. *Educational Leadership, 44*(6), 13–16.

Comer, J., Haynes, N. (1991). Parent involvement in schools: An ecological approach. *The Elementary School Journal, 91,* 271–277.

Cutler, B. C. (1993). *You, your child and "special" education: A guide to making the system work.* New York: Macmillan.

Gardner, S. L. (1992). Key issues in developing school-linked, integrated services. *The Future of Children,* 85–94.

Karp, N. (1996). Individualized wrap-around services for children with emotional, behavior, and mental disorders. In G. Singer, L. Powers, & A. Olson (Eds.), R*edefining family support: Innovations in public–private partnerships* (pp. 291–310). Baltimore: Paul H. Brookes.

Katz-Leavy, J. W., Lourie, I. S., Stroul, B. A., & Ziegler-Dendy, C. (1992). *Individualized services in a system of care.* Washington, DC: CASSP Technical Assistance Center, Center for Child Health and Mental Health Policy, Georgetown University Child Development Center.

Kirst, M. W., & McLaughlin, M. (1990). Improving policies for children: Proceedings of the 1989 New York Education Policy Seminar. *New York Education Policy Seminar* (pp. 1–31). Albany, NY: The Nelson A. Rockefeller Institute of Government.

Kishi, G., & Meyer, L. (1994). What children report and remember: A six-year follow-up of the effects of social contact between peers with and without severe disabilities. *Journal of the Association for Persons With Severe Handicaps, 19*(4), 1–10.

Knoster, T. (1995). Understanding the difference between "wrap around" and "run around" interagency collaboration under the Cordero court order. *The Association for Persons With Severe Handicaps Newsletter, 21*(11/12), 5–6.

Krueger, R. A. (1994). *Focus groups: A practical guide for applied research.* Thousand Oaks, CA: Sage.

Laski, F. J. (1991). Achieving integration during the second revolution. In L. Meyer, C. Peck, & L. Brown (Eds.). *Critical issues in the lives of people with severe disabilities* (pp. 409–422). Baltimore: Paul H. Brookes.

Lerner, R. M. (1995). Features and principles of effective youth programs: Promoting positive youth development through the integrative vision of family and consumer sciences. *Journal of Family and Consumer Sciences, 87*(4), 16–21.

Maluccio, A., Pine, B., & Warsh, R. (1996). Incorporating content on family reunification into the social work curriculum. *Journal of Social Work Education, 32,* 363–373.

Morgan, D. L. (1988). *Focus groups as qualitative research.* Newbury Park, CA: Sage.

Skrtic, T., & Sailor, W. (1996). School-linked services integration: Crisis and opportunity in the transition to postmodern society. *Remedial and Special Education, 17*(5), 271–283.

Skrtic, T., Sailor, W., & Gee, G. (1996). Voice, collaboration, and inclusion: Democratic themes in educational and social reform initiatives. *Remedial and Special Education, 17*(3), 142–157.

Turnbull, A. P., Patterson, J. M., Behr, S. K., Murphy, D. L., Marquis, J. G., & Blue-Banning, M. J. (1993). *Cognitive coping: Families and disability.* New York: Macmillan.

Turnbull, H. R., Turnbull, A. P., Bronicki, G. J., Summers, J. A., & Roeder-Gordon, C. (1992). *Disability and the family: A guide to decisions for adulthood.* Baltimore: Paul H. Brookes.

Usdan, M. D. (1990). Restructuring American educational systems and programs to accommodate a new health agenda for youth. *Journal of School Health, 60*(4), 139–141.

Wolfensberger, W. (1972). *The principle of normalization in human services.* Toronto: National Institute on Mental Retardation.

Yuan, S., Baker-McCue, T., & Witkin, K. (1996). Coalitions for family support and the creation of two flexible funding programs. In G. Singer, L. Powers, & A. Olson (Eds.), *Redefining family support: Innovations in public–private partnerships* (pp. 357–385). Baltimore: Paul H. Brookes.

Zollers, N. (Ed.). (1983). *The report of the Commission on the Financing of a Free and Appropriate Public Education.* Philadelphia: Research for Better Schools.

CHAPTER 7

The Buyout Option for Students with Significant Disabilities During the Transition Years

Laura Owens-Johnson, Lou Brown,
Jacqueline B. Temple, Beth McKeown,
Charlotte Ross, and Jack Jorgensen

The 1997 Individuals With Disabilities Education Act (IDEA) as amended requires that a free and appropriate education be provided for all students with disabilities. In almost all states this means access to public school services from birth to age 21. Unfortunately, at age 21 students leave educational systems that were supported by legal entitlements and encounter adult services that are based on discretionary eligibility criteria. That is, if adult service agency personnel have the money and choose to serve an individual with disabilities, they do. However, in most states they can choose not to do so, even if they have the necessary dollars. The anticipation of this reality is the cause of considerable stress for vast numbers of parents and individuals with disabilities.

After 21 years of tax-supported education, what should the lives of the most intellectually and physically disabled, who comprise 1% to 3% of our population, look like? What are reasonable postschool outcomes for which to strive? Where should they be 24 hours a day, 7 days a week? Whom should they be with? What should they be doing? How much and what kinds of extra support will they need? How much will it all cost? Who will pay for it?

At the end of their educational careers, with individually determined types and amounts of extra support, most individuals with significant disabilities should be able to perform real work next to nondisabled coworkers. They should live and participate meaningfully in typical homes and apartments that contain no more than two unrelated persons with disabilities, and they should use the same array of recreation–leisure and other community environments they would use if not disabled. In addition, "government" should be involved in their lives as little as possible; they should make more personal choices, have more privacy, enjoy better social lives, and cost taxpayers less than their predecessors. Conversely, there are many postschool outcomes that should be avoided. Among others, such outcomes include inhibiting the growth, achievement, enjoyment, and pursuit of happiness of siblings and parents; wasting human potential; involving individuals with behavioral challenges in the criminal justice system; preventing individuals from contributing their talents and skills to society to the extent they are able; and allowing individuals to take more financial government assistance than they need.

There are some instances when public school officials engage in cooperative agreements with other government agencies such as state vocational rehabilitation departments to assist in providing appropriate services to individuals with disabilities. In most instances, however, government officials contract with private agencies to provide the training and related services needed. In an attempt to delineate many of the major factors associated with the Buyout Option, this chapter addresses the often adversarial relationships between public school personnel and parents of children with disabilities, and between schools and private agencies. However, relationships between parents, schools, and nonschool agency personnel are not inherently antagonistic. That is, all parties can agree that a private or a public nonschool agency is appropriate to provide services. In these cases, public school officials can then contract with that agency and all involved to function in cooperative, collaborative, and wholesome ways for arrangement of the best possible preparatory experiences for a student with disabilities during transition years. Indeed, we strongly endorse any effort to commingle resources, to share responsibilities, and to engage in any other school–community partnership efforts that result in cost-efficient and high-quality services and integrated outcomes.

State vocational rehabilitation agencies generally wait until three semesters prior to graduation before providing funding and transition-related services for students with disabilities. Often this is too late, because students may not have had the experiences in school necessary for them to successfully transition from school to adult life (e.g., development of self-determination and self-advocacy skills, a variety of work experience based on interest). The Buyout Option refers to the practice in which schools contract directly with private adult service agencies to provide transition-related activities such as functional assessments, job development, and on-the-job support 1 to 2 years, prior to a student's graduation from high school.

THE STUDENTS

The students of primary concern are individuals who function—or who are perceived to be functioning—intellectually within the lowest 2% of a naturally distributed school-age population. Historically, such individuals have been described as having IQ scores of approximately 50 and below, or they have been labeled variously as autistic, multiply handicapped, cognitively disabled, psychotic, dual sensory impaired, and moderately, severely, and profoundly retarded. Chances are great that these students experience communication, cognitive, social, physical, behavioral, sensorimotor, and/or other difficulties to such a degree that reasonable persons would consider these difficulties severely or significantly disabling (Sailor et al., 1988). These and associated characteristics cannot be denied, ignored, or minimized in importance. Neither can they be used to exclude or reject individuals from important experiences in integrated settings. Specifically, the students of concern

1. Are likely to learn fewer skills than 98% of all others of the same chronological age.
2. Need more opportunities to learn than almost all others.
3. Will experience more difficulties than almost everyone else in transferring/generalizing skills learned in one set of conditions to others.
4. Will be among the lowest 2% of all those rated on any measure of adaptive behavior.
5. Can learn much, but primarily skills in the lowest difficulty ranges.
6. Are considered "significantly delayed" in all academic subjects.
7. Are likely to forget more than all others if individually meaningful practice is not arranged. If allowed to forget, they will need more instructional opportunities to relearn what was forgotten than almost all others.
8. Will require individually determined but substantial extra support from taxpayers as long as they live. Extra support refers to the personnel, training information, individualized adaptations, money, and other phenomena persons with disabilities and those who interact with them need in order to function acceptably—support that would not be needed if they were not disabled.

EDUCATIONAL ALTERNATIVES

Many parents of such students—and also professionals and taxpayers—are tired of fighting public school officials. What if public school officials refuse to change, to collaborate, to develop meaningful partnerships, to improve, or to at least try? What about those parents and professionals who want to put their energies into generating something good or better in the system, but to do so seems useless? Some of these individuals have meaningful alternatives; some do not. Perhaps it will be instructive to review several alternatives available to many nondisabled students and to consider these in the light of individuals with significant disabilities. If students without disabilities have alternatives to enhance their educational opportunities, why should students with significant disabilities not have those same or similar options?

Private Nonsectarian Schools

Some parents of nondisabled students are able to send their children to private nonsectarian schools. Unfortunately, such schools serve few students with significant disabilities for several reasons. First, most children with disabilities, particularly those who present significant challenges, are de facto excluded. Indeed, these students are usually rejected if they are considered to have become disabled after they enroll. Second, many of these schools are quite costly and therefore beyond the means of many families, even if tax-supported tuition vouchers are available. Third, on average, there are fewer private nonsectarian schools and more students with significant disabilities.

Sectarian Schools

Many parents choose to send their nondisabled children to schools that are affiliated with particular religions. Unfortunately, most sectarian schools exclude and reject children with disabilities, even though they and their families practice the same religion as the schools, even if they would attend them if not disabled, and even though their siblings attend them. Space, therapy services, equipment, expertise, adult-to-student ratios, reputation, accessibility, "We have nothing to offer," and money are the typical justifications offered. In effect, the separation of church and state requirements of the Constitution of the United States and those of most states restrict students with disabilities more than they do students without disabilities. There are notable and, it is to be hoped, increasing exceptions. In 1993 Rachel Holland, a young girl with mental retardation, was welcomed in a "Jewish" school in California, Raphael Oberti, a young boy with Down syndrome, was thriving in a "Christian" school in New Jersey, and Becky Till, a young girl with severe disabilities, was flourishing in a "Catholic" school in Ontario, Canada.

Charter Schools

Many parents, policymakers, professionals, politicians, and other taxpayers are looking for alternatives to traditional public schools. To many parents and nondisabled students, the charter school concept is particularly attractive, as they are supported by tax dollars and are designed to do what in the eyes of some is not being, or cannot be, done in typical public schools. Theoretically, charter schools can be released from many of what are perceived as the negative restrictions, rules, regulations, incompetencies, rigid hours, and working conditions of the public schools and are potentially powerful vehicles for accelerating positive changes in public education. Clearly, the developing charter school movement offers many exciting possibilities and is endorsed by the authors, unless, like most other "school reform" or "school restructuring" movements, charter schools exclude or reject natural distributions of students with disabilities (Zollers & Laski, 1994).

It should be noted that some parents of children with disabilities choose to send them to private schools attended only by students with disabilities. Tax-supported segregated schools are rejected by the authors because, in our view, it is no longer acceptable to raise children with disabilities in isolation, devoid of relationships with nondisabled peers who live in their neighborhoods. Also, the historic costs and outcomes of such schools are unacceptable. The separation of state and segregation is at least as important as the separation of state and church.

Most parents and professionals now realize that segregation begets segregation, that integration begets integration, and that integration is better. Specifically, the more integrated the experiences of students with disabilities during school years, the higher the probabilities are that individuals with disabilities will be able to function successfully and cost-efficiently in an integrated society during postschool years (Piuma, 1989). If integrated postschool outcomes are to be realized, educators are responsible for providing experiences that have preparatory validity. In our view, this means that from birth through about age 5 children with disabilities should function in the same environments they would if they were not disabled, and they should have constructive, supervised, safe, and healthy developmental experiences that are as similar as possible to those of nondisabled peers (Curry-Sontag, 1997; Curry-Sontag, Sontag, & Bohren, 1994). If they were not disabled and would stay home with their parents, attend neighborhood day care centers, Head Start, and integrated early childhood or preschool programs, then this should be the case regardless of their disabilities. However, although integrated early experiences are necessary for children with disabilities, they are not sufficient; these experiences must be supplemented with individualized types and amounts of extra support. Shared information with parents, assistive technology, social relationship engineering, speech and language therapy, physical and behavior therapies, lower adult-to-student ratios, and curricular modifications are a few examples of the supports that may be needed.

From about ages 6 through 18, students with disabilities should be based in the same elementary, middle, and high schools and should function in many of the same regular education classrooms they would be in if they were not disabled (Brown et al., 1989). When young, they should spend virtually all of their time in regular education settings. As they get older, they should spend individualized, increasing amounts of time in the actual integrated and/or respected nonschool environments in which they function during nonschool days and times (Brown et al., 1983). During high school years, they should spend about half their time on school grounds—eating, moving about the school, developing tutor and other relationships with nondisabled peers, learning meaningful attitudes and skills, participating in constructive extracurricular activities, and so on. The rest of their time should be spent learning to function effectively in the array of integrated and/or respected nonschool settings they will use at the conclusion of their school careers (Halverson & Sailor, 1990).

At age 19, most students without disabilities complete their public school careers. Typically, students with significant disabilities remain in school through their 21st birthdays. The options students with significant disabilities have between the time their nondisabled chronological-age peers graduate from high school and the time they themselves complete their public school careers—the transition years—are outlined below.

First, like their nondisabled peers, they can terminate their public school careers at age 18 or 19. This option is rarely exercised because few individuals with disabilities can thrive without extra support paid for with tax dollars. The financially distressed government agencies responsible for supporting adults with significant disabilities have de facto policies that say, "You have legal entitlement to public school tax dollars until you are 21. We cannot use our limited supply of money on you until you have exhausted that alternative. Even then you may not meet our eligibility criteria for us to spend our money on you." As most parents would rather not have their children at home during the day, school careers are usually maintained until legal entitlements end.

Second, they can continue to take courses at their high schools, try to develop new friendships, and so on. In our view, this option is chronologically age-inappropriate in that nondisabled persons from ages 19 to 21 are not present in high schools; high schools become overloaded with students with disabilities; space, transportation, and other costs are inflated; and in too many instances this option offers merely a "stay of execution." Nevertheless, the overwhelming majority of public schools offer this option and almost all families who have children with significant disabilities choose it.

Third, they can enroll in a post-high-school community or technical college. This option is available to only a few individuals with significant disabilities because of costs and lack of collaborative agreements with these institutions.

Fourth, they can remain the responsibility of public school personnel but receive virtually all of their instruction in integrated and/or respected nonschool settings in which they are being prepared to function when they exit public schools. This 100% nonschool instruction provided by public school personnel has been available to some students in several places and is becoming increasingly popular.

Fifth, public school officials can decide to agree with parents, hearing officers, and others that it is no longer appropriate for a student to be their direct responsibility. However, as they are legally obligated to support her or his education until age 21, they can arrange the services needed for reasonable preparation for integrated postschool life from nonschool professionals with school tax dollars. That is, an Individualized Education Plan (IEP) can be designed in accordance with established rules of professional conduct and then implemented by public or private agency personnel. This is the Buyout Option, and it can take many forms: (a) School personnel can provide a student with a voucher than can be used to purchase the services of choice; (b) the student can hire an agent to secure needed services; (c) school officials can contract directly with an agency; (d) funds can be assigned to a trust and designated as necessary; or (e) public school dollars, family contributions, and the resources of the state vocational rehabilitation departments and other public and private agencies can be commingled and dispensed as needed.

FACTORS TO CONSIDER

Opponents argue that the Buyout Option is inherently negative and should not be utilized under any circumstances. They correctly note that it is not a new alternative in that public schools have been purchasing a wide variety of services for their students with disabilities from nonschool agencies for many years. Some argue that this option should be available to all students with disabilities at any age, any time they want to use it, and for anything they need. Others support it only for selected functions, at certain ages, in some locations, for students with particular characteristics, and so on.

Seven factors that typically come to the fore when the Buyout Option is being considered are presented below. These factors are intended to stimulate thought and dialogue, focus debate, engender opportunities, and enhance educational quality so that we may determine the conditions under which the Buyout Option can be best utilized. When it is feasible, we first discuss points typically offered by individuals who oppose or who are suspicious of the Buyout Option, then follow with typical counterpoints from those who support it. Readers are encouraged to consider the factors and the associated points and counterpoints they judge locally appropriate. Our view is that the Buyout Option is viable in some, but not all, circumstances and that the controversial nature of this presentation is real in some instances, but collaborative-cooperative partnerships are also operative.

Locus of Responsibility

Many believe that taxpayers will and should be outraged if public school personnel abdicate their legal and professional responsibilities to provide individually appropriate education to students with disabilities. In their view, citizens pay school taxes for educators, not brokers. If school officials cannot or do not want to do what is necessary, they should learn how or step aside and be replaced with others who can and will. There is no reason to go outside the system. Some public school systems do it well; others can too.

Those who support the use of the Buyout Option argue that (a) the outcome statistics of public schools provide sufficient justifications for the use of rational alternatives, (b) taxpayers and others have lost confidence in too many public school systems, (c) school officials are constrained and diluted by too many extraneous tasks such as hall, bus, lunch, and homecoming-weekend duties and thus cannot focus upon the provision of important instructional services, and (d) whoever can provide meaningful educational services should be given the opportunity to do so (Blackorby & Wagner, 1996; Hayden & DePaepe, 1994; Herrnstein & Murray, 1994; National Commission on Excellence in Education, 1983; National Education Committee on Time and Learning, 1994; Shapiro et al., 1993).

Expertise

Many argue that our best teachers work in public schools. As public school personnel provide cost-efficient and high-quality services to millions of students who are not disabled, they can do the same for students with significant disabilities, if given the proper training, money, and other resources.

Conversely, some argue that the quality of services provided by a private agency through the use of the Buyout Option may be better than that of services that can be provided by public school personnel for several reasons. First, private agencies can offer expertise that is functionally related to the needs of individual students. If a student requires specific kinds of instruction, the agency can hire someone to provide it or can provide training quickly and efficiently. If hirees cannot do the job, their employment can be terminated. This is rarely feasible in public school systems in which incompetence is too often hidden, tolerated, or simply unchallenged. Second, many school districts overuse relatively low-cost and poorly trained paraprofessionals to interact with students with significant disabilities (Salisbury & Chambers, 1994). Too often this denies students access to the professionals with the expertise, commitment, creativity, and ingenuity they so desperately need to learn to function best in integrated society. Third, instruction can be highly individualized. Providing training for a specific job in an actual workplace on weekends, building important after-work relationships with nondisabled coworkers who live in the neighborhood of the student, and arranging participation in an integrated home-to-work carpool are some examples. Few public school personnel are interested in or capable of providing such instruction. Even if they were, their typical work days, hours, and other conditions do not allow them the flexibility to do so.

Laws, Rules, Regulations

Some argue that local, state, and federal laws, rules, and regulations must follow the student. That is, private agencies must meet the same licensing, certification, degree, insurance, adult-to-student ratio, and other requirements that must be met by public schools. Although many school districts contract privately for medical, legal, physical therapy, and personnel training services, the professionals who provide these services are licensed, certified, or have degrees that qualify them to do so. If private agencies had to meet the same requirements public schools face, they would experience the same problems and inhibitors.

Those who support the Buyout Option offer several important counterpoints. First, many states and school districts have been "monitored" and declared "in compliance" with local, state, and federal laws, rules, and regulations. However, they still offer low-quality, segregated, and cost-inefficient services by untrained or undertrained personnel with unacceptable outcomes for students. Indeed, some estimate that 25% of all special education "teachers" working in public schools in the United States are not "certified" to teach the students with disabilities for whom they are responsible (Shapiro et al., 1993). Second, if many states and school districts are not in compliance with local, state, and federal laws, rules, and regulations, why should private agencies be? Third, public school personnel may be degreed, certified, and licensed, but they may not be able or willing to do what is needed. Private agency personnel may be able and willing to do what is needed but may not be degreed, certified, or licensed. Those who are most likely to get the job done should be given the resources.

Fourth, most school districts function from interpretations of rules, regulations, traditions, schedules, tort liability fears, and superstitions that disallow the provision of the most appropriate and individually meaningful educational experiences to students with significant disabilities. For example, some school districts have arrangements with their insurance companies that preclude the provision of individualized instruction in nonschool environments. Confining the instruction of students with pronounced generalization and transferring of training difficulties to school grounds is educationally absurd. Private agency personnel may be unencumbered by the rules, regulations, group-instruction proclivities, inhibiting management-labor contractual agreements, personnel transfers based on seniority, and inflexible work days and hours that characterize most public school districts. Indeed, if private agencies were to adhere to the same interpretations of laws, rules, and regulations as public schools do, they would be just as cost-inefficient and unable to produce the favorable outcomes so needed by individuals with disabilities.

Fifth, there is the issue of the "spirit" of the laws, rules, and regulations and the quest for competent professionals and effective services for individuals with disabilities. At least from age 18 through 21, students with disabilities and their families should receive rational and responsible relief from the rules, regulations, and the interpretations thereof that suppress, compromise, inhibit, and dilute the effectiveness of too many public school services. In effect, students with disabilities need and deserve one last chance to benefit from an IEP as the concept was originally conceived through the "spirit" of IDEA.

Finally, some argue that most laws, rules, and regulations were established because, in the past, students with disabilities were excluded from school entirely or from certain activities in school, or they were provided a range of services that was too limited. If these laws, rules, and regulations are changed or abandoned, many fear that services to a truly needy segment of our society will disappear; they may be made discretionary rather than mandatory, or they may not be funded at all. Conversely, many argue that most of these laws, rules, and regulations were generated with admirable intentions and it may not be necessary to modify or abandon all of them. However, the impact each has on the educational services provided individual students with disabilities must be scrutinized carefully. If "admirable intentions" are not converted to actual practices that produce meaningful outcomes, changes are in order.

Competition

Some argue that the Buyout Option does not guarantee that a student will get the most appropriate preparation. Private agencies, as they have in other instances, will take the money but will not provide services of reasonable quality or will take only students through whom they can make money. This "creaming," taking on students with less significant disabilities who are more cost-effective, will leave the "truly disabled" students in public schools. In addition, relatively few communities have private agencies that can provide students with significant disabilities with the services necessary to learn to function meaningfully in integrated and/or respected work, play, domestic, and general community settings and activities. Until such agencies are available and learn to serve all well, the local public school system remains the only or the best option (Mank, 1993).

Many who support the Buyout Option suggest that public school systems have no real competition. Like most monopolies, they too often become inert, cost-inefficient, arrogant, and resistant to change. Parents are too often told to "take it or leave it." "Leave it" usually means, "Shut up," "Move to another district," or "Teach your child at home." When advised to move elsewhere, a few do, but most do not want to or otherwise cannot. Even if they could, where can they go? Will another school district provide the necessary supports and services to ensure the quality education to which students with significant disabilities are entitled? Or will parents and students run into the same or similar issues in a new school district? Private agency personnel will be more responsive and accountable to consumers and taxpayers. If they do not do the job, they lose the contract. School districts receive tax subsidies without such accountability contingencies. If public schools have competition for jobs, money, prestige, and community respect, they will be more responsive to students with disabilities and their families. This competition and the associated principle of supply and demand will reduce waste, increase productivity, and otherwise improve performance. Real competition will encourage public schools to accept the inherent challenges and engender the "best practices" and "state-of-the-art" services.

Unions

School-affiliated unions are threatened and offended by the Buyout Option and will resist it. Their obvious fear is that the number of jobs and the amount of money available to public schools will be reduced and job security challenged. Recently, the American Federation of Teachers, a 750,000–member union, called for a moratorium on students with disabilities moving to regular education schools and classes from special education setups. However, the same people want to keep students with disabilities in public schools (Shanker, 1994/1995). Teachers' unions also fear the "slippery slope" that might result if students under the age of 18 with and without disabilities are allowed access to versions of the Buyout Option. If every parent had such an option, too many would exercise it and threaten the very nature of the public schools. Finally, many school administrators would rather have "labor peace" than allow even a public discussion of the Buyout Option.

Conversely, many have concluded that far too often the wages, hours, and working conditions of teachers and other professionals interfere with students' real educational achievement. Many teachers cannot or do not want to teach public bus riding, street crossing, and restroom skills during the times and in the actual places they must be taught. These skills are necessary for students with significant disabilities to succeed in real-work settings and to function effectively in integrated society. If school professionals do not want to or cannot do the job, they should step aside and give someone else a chance.

Cost

Assume that a 19-year-old female student with significant disabilities meets with the important persons in her life to design a qualitatively acceptable IEP, that is, one in accordance with all relevant laws, rules, regulations, and with reasonable professional standards of good practice. This IEP includes, but is not limited to, teaching the student the following:

1. To prepare for work, to rest, dress, and groom appropriately.
2. To function in a subsidized and integrated carpool that will get her from home to work and back.
3. To perform actual work in a real workplace next to nondisabled coworkers from 8 A.M. to 12 P.M. five mornings per week.
4. To take breaks and eat lunch with nondisabled coworkers at her workplace, at a nearby park, and at a restaurant.
5. To function in an apartment with as little extra support as possible, that is, cleaning, cooking, and using appliances.
6. To recreate and spend her leisure time in a wide array of personally desirable environments and activities.

Consider that if the public school personnel were responsible for implementing this IEP, the cost would be $15,000 for 180 work days per year, including transportation.

Private agency personnel will say that they will implement the IEP for 180 work days per year for $15,000. However, they will also say that this figure should be prorated because a full-time job is 260 days per year. Some public school personnel will say that the cost for implementing the IEP is higher for school districts owing to much higher salaries, fringe benefits, insurance rates, and building costs; therefore private agencies should implement the IEP for less. Other school officials will say, "She is only going to get about $5,000 per year, including transportation costs, from taxpayers when her educational entitlement ends at age 21. She should get used to functioning with less, so let's give her that amount now."

In this scenario, some might say that the system with the lowest cost should prevail; others might say that low cost equals low quality; and still others might say that given equal quality, the lower cost should prevail. Some say it is extremely important that a student with disabilities learn to live, work, and play as productively and cost-efficiently as possible in integrated society. If one system can get the job done, but charges more than another that cannot, cost-efficiency requires that the former get the resources. Some might argue that school district personnel should negotiate with private agencies to provide services for less than they will cost the district. The resulting "savings" can then be used for "other worthwhile purposes." Others say that private agencies should negotiate with public school officials for more than it will actually cost to provide the agreed-upon services. The resulting "profit" can then be used to support other deserving individuals with disabilities who do not generate as much money as they actually cost. This back-and-forth argument could continue forever, as people have nearly as many different opinions about this issue as there are students with disabilities. In the meantime students with disabilities continue to be stuck in the middle of the argument and remain underserved in many instances.

Personal Relief

The Buyout Option provides parents and school officials viable choices to consider. It affords parents who are unhappy with school district personnel and/or services a much-needed and welcome alternative during the last few years of their children's school careers. If, in their view, public school professionals do not know how or do not want to serve their children in ways they deem beneficial, they should be allowed to take their tax dollars and secure the services of those who do. Conversely, school officials who feel they have been beaten down, harassed, dominated, or otherwise inhibited by parents have a choice of giving the money to others and thus ridding themselves of the parents and their children as soon as possible. School officials argue that if the unhappy, crazy, and insatiable parents are bought out, valuable time, energy, and other resources can be devoted to those who are just as needy and who truly appreciate public school services and personnel.

CONCLUSION

From birth to about age 18, students with significant disabilities should attend the same schools and function in the same classrooms and other respected and/or integrated environments that they would occupy if not disabled. Thus we do not recommend the Buyout Option until such a student's comparable class of nondisabled peers are completing public school. These students have been a hidden, misunderstood minority, often routinely deprived of the basic life choices that even the most disadvantaged among us take for granted (Shapiro, 1994). What type of services do students with significant disabilities need from the point at which their nondisabled peers exit public schools until they reach their legal educational entitlement limit? They need those services that validly prepare them to be productive, efficient, successful, and to otherwise enjoy the highest possible quality of life in their postschool years.

If a public school system provides reasonable services during these "transition years," it seems feasible that the students should stay and benefit from them. However, what if a school system does not, cannot, or will not provide valid preparatory experiences for integrated postschool functioning? Or what if it is planning or making progress toward developing this capacity but has not yet reached its goal? It seems fair that students with disabilities be allowed access to the potential benefits of the Buyout Option if a responsible private or public nonschool agency is available.

Our purpose is not to categorically reject public schools as reasonable vehicles to a decent quality of life. In fact, we proudly respect, revere, and salute the historic accomplishments of the American educational system. On the other hand, we argue that many public schools, as they currently function, must be reorganized, restructured, reformed, or otherwise changed for the better, especially in terms of their services to students with disabilities. Let us all address reality and join the quest to realize this improvement.

REFERENCES

Blackorby, J., & Wagner, M. (1996). Longitudinal postschool outcomes of youth with disabilities: Findings from the National Longitudinal Transition Study. *Exceptional children, 62*(5), 399–411.

Brown, L., Long, E., Udvar-Solner, A., Davis, L., VanDeventer, P., Ahlgren, C., Johnson, F., Greunewald, L., & Jorgenson, J. (1989). The home school: Why students with severe intellectual disabilities must attend the schools of their brothers, sisters, friends and neighbors. *Journal of the Association for Persons With Severe Handicaps, 14*(1), 8–13.

Brown, L., Nisbet, J., Ford, A., Sweet, M., Shiraga, B., York, J., & Loomis, R. (1983). The critical need for nonschool instruction in educational programs for severely handicapped students. *Journal of the Association for Persons With Severe Handicaps, 8*(3), 71–77.

Curry-Sontag, J. (1997). Contextual factors influencing the sociability of preschool children with disabilities in integrated and segregated classrooms. *Exceptional Children, 63*(3), 389–404.

Curry-Sontag, J., Sontag, E., & Bohren, J. (1994). The schooling of children with disabilities. *Wisconsin School News,* 18–22.

Halverson, A. T., & Sailor, W. (1990). Integration of students with severe disabilities: A review of research. In R. Gaylord-Ross (Ed.), *Issues and research in special education* (pp. 110–172). New York: Teachers College Press.

Hayden, M. F., & DePaepe, P. (1994). Waiting for community services: The impact on persons with mental retardation and other developmental disabilities. In M. F. Hayden & B. H. Abery (Eds.), *Challenges for a service system in transition: Ensuring quality community experiences for persons with developmental disabilities* (pp. 173–206). Baltimore: Paul H. Brookes.

Herrnstein, R., & Murray, C. (1994). *The bell curve.* New York: The Free Press.

Individuals with Disabilities Education Act (IDEA) Amendments of 1995: Reauthorization of the Individual With Disabilities Education Act. Washington, DC: U.S. Department of Education.

Mank, D. (1993). *The underachievement of supported employment: A call for reinvestment.* Eugene: University of Oregon.

National Commission on Excellence in Education. (1983). *A nation at risk: The imperative for educational reform.* Washington, DC: U.S. Government Printing Office.

National Education Commission on Time and Learning. (1994). *Prisoners of time.* Washington, DC: U.S. Government Printing Office.

Piuma, F. (1989). *Benefits and costs of integrating students with severe disabilities into regular public school programs: A study summary of money spent well.* Unpublished manuscript, San Francisco State University.

Sailor, W., Gee, K., Goetz, L., & Graham, N. (1988). Progress in educating students with the most severe disabilities: Is there any? *Journal of the Association for Persons With Severe Handicaps, 13*(2), 87–99.

Salisbury, C., & Chambers, A. (1994). Instructional costs of inclusive schooling. *Journal of the Association of Person With Severe Handicaps, 19*(3), 215–222.

Shanker, A. (1994, December–1995, January). Full inclusion is neither free nor appropriate. *Educational Leadership,* 18–21.

Shapiro, J. P. (1994). *No pity: People with disabilities forging a new civil rights movement.* New York: Times Books.

Shapiro, J. P., Loeb, P., Bowermaster, D., Wright, A., Headden, S., & Toch, T. (1993, December). Separate and unequal. *U.S. News & World Report,* 46–60.

Zollers, N., & Laski, F. (1994). Charter schools and equity concerns: Serving students with severe disabilities. Paper presented at the 1994 International Conference of the Association for Persons with Severe Handicaps, Atlanta, GA.

PART III

Inclusive Teaching: Building on School and Community Partnerships

In Part Three, we further explore the implications of school/community partnerships by moving from the broad school-reform basis of Part Two to a closer examination of classroom practices. Kathy Gee, for example, in Chapter 8, presents a constructivist approach to inclusion that builds on partnerships. The focus is on instructional strategies in inclusive classrooms and schools for both the individual and the group. A framework for the instructional research base for effective inclusive schools is provided, and key practices and issues regarding the provision of high-quality instruction to students are delineated. Readers are offered an opportunity to consider parallel reforms from both general and special education research. They are also challenged to re-think some current special education practices that serve to separate students and to consider expanding the range of instructional methods used with students who have disabilities.

In Chapter 9, Dianne Ferguson and her colleagues present the case for "mixed-ability groups" in configuring instructional designs for inclusive schools. The authors discuss the ways in which the role of "special" educator has to change as schools restructure into single unified systems. The chapter presents research findings on the role of the "inclusion facilitator/specialist" and discusses the time-limited nature of that role as an option for special educators who previously staffed self-contained classrooms. It describes the ways in which "special" educators might become educators working in collaborative groups with other teachers who have varying expertise to support very diverse groups of students, including all students with disabilities. The chapter offers vignettes from schools that are currently making these shifts, and closes with a discussion of the implications of these changes for separate special education practices such as IEP planning and how these practices, too, can be restructured.

In Chapter 10, Jennifer York-Barr and Robi Kronberg carry this theme further in a discussion of collaboration as the basis for within-school partnerships. The social norms, expectations, and reinforcers in most schools today do not support collaboration among staff or between staff and students. The tradition of teaching as an isolated professional is not easily changed. Collaboration is, however, an essential support in the process of creating inclusive schools. The sharing of resources, experiences, strategies, and perspectives by individuals who share responsibility for groups of students is paramount to school restructuring. This chapter presents common realities faced by many practicing educators related to their efforts to create a more collaborative work culture to better promote the development of unique learners in heterogeneous classrooms. Learnings from school restructuring, positive social interdependence, and strategic change are synthesized to propose effective approaches for sustained change.

Lou Brown and his colleagues, in Chapter 11, examine various teaching models to implement inclusive partnerships. Each year more and more students with disabilities leave or avoid special education schools and classrooms and receive increasing kinds and amounts of educational and related services in regular education settings in home schools. Unfortunately, too few schools that serve students with disabilities in regular education classrooms (students who were formerly excluded or rejected therefrom) carefully analyze a reasonable array of service delivery options before implementing them; nor do they continuously evaluate them with a clear commitment to evolving new and better ones. Three non-mutually-exclusive elementary school service delivery options are addressed: coteaching, team teaching, and consulting teaching. Ten of many possible factors, values, dimensions, and so on, relevant to all are delineated, and some of the major pros and cons of each are presented. The purpose of this chapter is not to explore all the parameters of each option but rather to address some of the structural elements of each in relation to students who were formerly served in special education schools and classrooms.

In Chapter 12, Hal Kleinert and his colleagues enable us to revisit the Kentucky school reform initiative for a look at the formation of a partnership approach to education assessment and accountability. A key component of the Goals 2000: Educate America Act is Title II, National Education Reform Leadership, Standards, and Assessments, which calls for the development of state assessment systems that fully include all students. To date, Kentucky is the only state that fully includes all students, even those with severe disabilities, in its mandatory performance-based assessment system. Within Kentucky's system, students with severe disabilities participate in the Alternate Portfolio Assessment; a student in this program carries equal weight with any other student in determining the school's and local district's accountability index. This chapter focuses on both content and performance standards for the Alternate Portfolio, and the relationship of the Alternate Portfolio to the state's regular assessment system. Finally, recommendations for improving the Alternate Portfolio Assessment program and suggestions for other states to consider in developing inclusive assessment systems are presented.

CHAPTER 8

Looking Closely at Instructional Approaches: Honoring and Challenging All Children and Youth in Inclusive Schools

Kathy Gee

The activities that transpire within classrooms, and the relationships that develop among students, faculty, and related support personnel, can either help or impede students' learning. Meaningful discussion of educational reform, therefore, must have a strong focus directly on the classroom and on the teaching and learning that occur within it. As made clear in the earlier chapters of this book, a major pedagogical, social, and political question for current educational and instructional reform is the extent to which *all* children and youth will be included in the transformation of our school systems, and the extent to which the learning of every child is valued. One underlying premise for this chapter is that the very basis for the transformation cannot occur without the inclusion of all children and youth.

Inclusive education provides a catalyst through which general and special educators, parents, and community members can come together to design schools that foster the development of caring and capable citizens who have been challenged intellectually, socially, and ethically to develop excellence in all areas. The concept of inclusion requires us to frame curriculum and instruction under a different mental model. The purpose of this chapter is to focus on curriculum and instruction within an inclusive, community school. We take a closer look at critical approaches to instructional practice that facilitate success in heterogeneous classrooms and how these approaches provide fertile ground for continued, collaborative thinking about teaching and results for all learners.

BELIEFS, PHILOSOPHIES, AND STRUCTURES

Unfortunately, the term inclusion has been used in so many different ways that it has almost lost its meaning. Inclusive schools, as originally conceived, are those designed to meet the educational needs of all their community members within common, yet fluid, environments and activities (Sapon-Shevin, 1992). For professionals who have been involved in this movement over many years, inclusion signifies something quite different from the earlier "mainstreaming" approach in which children with disabilities were "allowed access" at specified times into general education classrooms (see Chapter 1). An inclusive school moves beyond the integration models by setting a presumption of belonging, with services and supports following. Contrary to what many people may think, the inclusive schools movement represents school improvement on many levels for all children and youth. It is not simply the physical placement of individuals with various abilities and disabilities in general classrooms (Downing, 1996; Stainback & Stainback, 1992; Villa & Thousand, 1992).

Table 8.1 depicts three of the key assumptions in inclusive schools and the differences between a school in which there is some mainstreaming, a school that is integrated, and a school that can be labeled inclusive. Each of these models still exist in our nation's schools. Simply changing the word to describe the same model is not what reform is about. It is hoped that the reader will identify that there are fundamental differences in these concepts, which in turn impact decisions that are made at schools regarding structure, staffing, curriculum, and instruction. Understanding what inclusive schooling really means and then making a commitment to it is the first step needed to form the guiding base or mission at a school. Although there are many "models" of how schools organize themselves to provide inclusive education (see Chapter 1), successful inclusive schools have many things in common.

Some opponents of inclusive schooling make the mistake of thinking that all children will be asked to do the same work at the same level, or that children with some needs that are very different from those of their peers will not receive appropriate instruction. In fact, as identified in Table 8.1, a successful inclusive school promotes the individual nature of each child and, from an instructional standpoint, is characterized by opportunities to value the individual gifts of all students by providing supports to students on an individualized basis. Inclusive, collaborative classrooms hold the greatest opportunity for varied abilities and talents, and varied ways of learning and knowing (associated with gender, culture, learning history, and emotional makeup), to be seen as gifts that should be celebrated, as opposed to problems to be dealt with.

INSTRUCTIONAL APPROACHES

Researchers and teachers immersed in the practice of inclusion have noted both the merger and the "mis-match" of professional practices when "general" and "spe-

Table 8.1. Inclusion, Integration, and Mainstreaming

In an Inclusive School . . .	In an Integrated School . . .	In a School With Mainstreaming . . .
• All students are full members of a general education classroom in the same school their brothers or sisters might attend. Part of *any* student's day might be spent in the community or other parts of the school in integrated learning groups or, at times in one-to-one instruction, depending on his or her needs.	• Students with disabilities are members of self-contained classrooms but may spend part of their day in general education classrooms or in the community and other parts of the school, *depending* on what the special education teacher can arrange. The school is often not the same school where their brothers and sisters attend.	• Students with disabilities are "mainstreamed" into general education classrooms based on their ability to do the work with minimal support from a special education teacher. Students with disabilities go to a resource room for parts of their day for help on their mainstream classes.
• Student needs and abilities are evaluated in the context of teaching. Supports for enhancement of the curriculum, adaptations, modifications, and alternative curriculum are designed by various members of educational teams (including general and special educators, paraprofessionals, parents, and related service professionals). The special education teacher and paraprofessional staff are members of teams that work with all the students but still provide intensive supports for students with disabilities when and where they need it. Person-centered plans guide the IEP and the curriculum. Instruction of goals and objectives is embedded within general class, school, and community activities. Students with disabilities do not lose services or support.	• The special education teacher has the responsibility for arranging and designing instruction for the students with disabilities. If the special education teacher can get general educators to agree to have students with disabilities in their classes for certain periods, she or he works with the general education teacher to plan for successful integration within the particular periods of the day when the student is integrated. The special education teacher and/or a paraprofessional often go with the student when he/she is integrated. Instruction also occurs in the self-contained class, the community, and other parts of the school.	• The special education teacher spends most of the day in the resource room, and students go to this room for support. A paraprofessional is assigned to the students who need more support. The general education teacher gives assignments and the special education teacher tries to provide support and adaptations. The special education teacher also works on basic skills and other curriculum (depending on the age of the students) in the self-contained classroom but does not spend much time in the general education classrooms.
• All students belong. Because students spend lots of time together, the opportunities for friendships are immense. Teachers and paraprofessionals support friendships through informal and formal methods, facilitating relationships through a variety of means. Classrooms foster a sense of community through the types of teaching methods that are used.	• Because students "come and go" often, it is more difficult to facilitate friendships, so if the special education teacher sees friendships as a high priority, he or she arranges opportunities for students to spend time together at recess, lunch, and other leisure times. He or she may use a variety of methods to facilitate the integration of the special education staff and students, and a variety of methods to facilitate	• Typically special educators in this model do not see the facilitation of friendships as a high priority. Because the special educator is not involved in the general classes, it is difficult to get to know the other students and their families.

cial" education teachers and related service providers come together on inclusive educational teams (Billingsley & Kelley, 1994; Udvari-Solner, 1994). Chapter 9 of this book provides a thoughtful discussion of the roles that professionals play and some possible directions that are proving successful for the re-thinking of these roles. The mental model for the basis of inclusion is that everyone belongs. If we accept that all children and youth belong in our schools, our classrooms, and our society, it forces us to rethink how we provide instruction and supports. What we do in classrooms is ultimately our choice. Making bold enough changes in how we determine what we do to successfully support all students will create a climate of self-renewal for both students and staff (Joyce, Wolfe, & Calhoun, 1993). Eight critical approaches to inclusive instruction are identified below. This is not to be entertained as an all-encompassing list. These approaches are purposefully discussed from an inclusive base, without the notion of "special" and "general" education strategies but instead as applicable for students with varying abilities and needs. It is important to remember that each approach is like a strand of thread, each from a different spool of research. In an effective inclusive classroom, these strands are woven together in a tapestry that is richly interconnected and supported by collaborative goal structures.

CONTEXTUALLY ALIGNED CURRICULUM

Despite the fact that IDEA 1997 specifically addresses the need to "align" each child's Individualized Education Program (IEP) goals with the general education curriculum, it is not uncommon to see IEPs that have been written completely from a deficit perspective. When IEPs reflect only the skills that individuals are perceived to lack, these documents make it difficult for many people to see how the individual's needs can be met within a general curriculum, a school, or a community, while he or she is participating in the activities of same-age peers. By using a collaborative assessment model in which information from discipline-specific or performance-based assessment is set in the context of ecologically appropriate curriculum and environments, IEPs become documents that clearly align learning for individual students within their chronological age groups across domains (Giangreco, Cloninger, & Iverson, 1994; Rainforth, York, & MacDonald, 1992). The IEP team uses the following types of sources for setting priorities and instructional contexts: parent/family input; age-referencing (i.e., what activities children of the same age are engaged in, at school, at home, or in the community); curriculum frameworks from the school across all subject areas; and prior experiences/history. In addition, the team collaboratively assesses the student's strengths and needs across disciplines using direct and authentic measures (Snell & Brown, 1999).

There are IEP goals that reflect the context or the curriculum as well as the appropriate challenge or expectation for the student. This means that a team has to know and understand what a typical child would be expected to learn (i.e., the outcomes) in each curricular area in order to determine whether the outcomes for the student with an IEP are the same, or different, and in what way.

For example, using a more traditional, deficit model, the following goals may have been written for Joseph, Bob, and Sara (all seventh graders).

JOSEPH
- Increase his ability to use an object symbol communication system.
- Learn to initiate an "I want . . ." message with a microswitch.
- Learn to use a visual choice system with eye gaze.
- Learn to discriminate the tactile and auditory signals in routines.

SARA
- Read at second-grade level.
- Increase spelling to first-grade level.
- Increase math to fourth-grade level.
- Dictate a story that has a beginning, middle, and end.

BOB
- Increase his site-word vocabulary by learning 20 new words a month.
- Have him use a conversation book to have interactions with nondisabled peers.
- Match functional words in the community.
- Work cooperatively on a group project.

In contrast, if the team operates from a curriculum-aligned and age-referenced perspective, setting the priorities for Sara, Joseph, or Bob starts with considering what seventh graders do at school, at home, and in the community. The following curricular areas and contexts would be priority for seventh graders: world civilizations, science, language arts/literature, math, foreign languages, fine arts (art, band, drama, or orchestra), computer use/word processing, P.E., community skills, futures planning, social and communication skills, and self-management skills. Given that framework, Table 8.2 depicts goals with individualized outcomes for Sara, Bob, and Joseph in two different core areas: world history and community skills.

Team members looking at these IEP goals, regardless of their training, can see how students like Joseph, Bob, or Sara will not only participate in the world civilizations class, but how they will be challenged and educated on goals that are critical to their development. Without giving up the specificity we need, we can place Joseph's goals in the context of the seventh-grade curriculum. This requires the teaching team to understand the many and varied skills involved in each activity and curricular area. In the author's experience, working with numerous teams to identify varied outcomes within both elementary and secondary school general education curriculum, teachers have indicated that this process—whether interpreted linearly or from a cognitive mapping perspective—eventually becomes "second nature." It may not, however, have been a part of their original teacher education.

Table 8.2. Sample of Contextually Aligned Goals

Curricular Domain and Standards for Typical Students	Examples of Goals for Sara	Examples of Goals for Bob	Examples of Goals for Joseph
WORLD HISTORY • Regular framework for seventh grade history or district-adopted curriculum. This will list out concepts that are expected of children at this age and other skills such as research skills, etc. Teachers will also have a set of units of material they need to accomplish.	• Sara will become knowledgeable of world geography to the extent that she can find and name the continents, locate countries on a map or globe, understand the hemispheres, poles, and equator. • Sara will gain an appreciation of other cultures and an understanding of the history of world religions demonstrated by her ability to develop a product that shows the major religions and identifies four key elements of each. • Sara will increase her reading skills to second-grade level using a modified social studies textbook.	• Bob will become knowledgeable of world geography to the extent that he understands the following concepts: ocean, mountains, sea, borders, continents, and countries. • Bob will learn to match key geography words on an enlarged map. • Bob will become knowledgeable of world religions to the extent that he can identify which words are religions (e.g., Buddhism: that's a religion) . . . • Bob will increase his site word reading ability by using key words from the social studies text.	• Joseph will be exposed to the visual and tactile geography of maps and globes; will become knowledgeable of the tactile symbol for globe; and will be able to activate a microswitch to pull up geography information in one file on his computer. • Joseph will demonstrate his choices of and preferences for the music and foods of various world cultures. • Joseph will participate in all projects and class activities through embedded instruction of the following goals: augmentative communication, visual choice making, etc.
COMMUNITY SKILLS • The team would list here what their inventory says that seventh graders in this community typically do; the age-level expectations of seventh graders in this area. • If the school has a community component for all kids, these goals would be listed here as well.	• Sara will learn to independently make purchases in the campus food court, fast-food restaurants, and small stores using the "one-up" strategy. • Sara will participate in the social studies community internship program with adaptations as needed.	• Bob will use his conversation book to initiate dialogue with peers during breaks. • Bob will increase his community grocery shopping skills to the extent that he can find a list of 5 items using a picture list in a familiar store; find the checkout line and wait appropriately; and carry the groceries home, when accompanied by an adult or peer partner. • Bob will participate in the social studies community internship program with adaptations as needed.	• Joseph will increase his ability to stay relaxed, requiring less suctioning, when participating in the community. • At various services and stores in the community, Joseph will make selections of videos he wants to rent, music he wants to check out of the library, stamps he wants to buy, and clothes he wants to buy using his visual choice board. • At various services and stores in the community, Joseph will activate his communication initiation tape to indicate that he needs something.

Embedded Instruction in Meaningful Activities

If we take a look at the rest of these seventh graders' IEPs, we see that Sara has specific reading goals that are not only taught directly with some one-to-one attention but also embedded throughout many of her subject areas and in community activities. Bob uses his conversation book across nearly every period of the day, and Joseph works on his object symbol system throughout every activity. Embedded instruction of skills means that teachers arrange for both basic and complex skills to be learned within the context of age-relevant and functionally motivating activities in the classroom, school, and community (Snell & Brown, 2000). Teachers emphasize higher-order thinking and learning, present tasks as problems to be solved, and ask questions that involve more than one correct answer (Englert, Tarrant, & Marriage, 1992). Students are provided with reasons to learn through the use of motivating projects and problems to solve, creating a feeling that they "know what they need to know" (Brown, 1994; Brown & Campione, 1990).

Embedded instruction is grounded in several theories. Contextual-behavioral theory stresses the importance of instruction within context, or related to the natural cues and consequences presented by the naturally occurring stimuli and contingencies in daily life situations that include both school and nonschool activities (Billingsley, Gallucci, Peck, Schwartz, & Staub, 1996; Horner, Dunlap, & Koegel, 1988). Ecological variables are included in assessment and instruction, and functional assessment of the use and generalization of skills is conducted across numerous settings and situations that occur in the student's lifestyle. In a summary of these concepts, the theory of contextual relevance (Sailor, 1990) was proposed as a means of explaining the "motivational boost" that occurs when students gain competence as they learn new skills when those skills are functionally related to a familiar context.

Constructivists consider embedded instruction to be a key aspect of teaching (Grennon-Brooks & Brooks, 1993; Poplin & Stone, 1992). Classrooms using embedded instruction are often theme-based or project-based. Students are provided with interesting problems and projects that require acquisition of certain skills to solve or complete. A second-grade teacher who is approaching sentence structure and punctuation may, for example, start a letter-writing project with a class in another district, or she may design sentence pyramids or bridges that will "hold up" only with all the correct pieces in place. A high school world history teacher may approach World War II by starting with diaries and biographies of soldiers from both sides, enticing students to want to know more about the events and politics that preceded the war, and so on. A middle school math teacher attempting to teach proportion may combine with the social studies teacher to do a unit on the Egyptian pyramids.

Teams responsible for additional supports to children and youth with more significant disabilities use the principle of embedded instruction to determine where and when instruction of even the most basic skills can occur—making sure that these skills are connected to the natural cues and consequences of age-referenced activities. The team does an activity analysis, determining the underlying skills that are necessary to the activity and which skills are priority for instruction (Snell & Brown, 1999). A team supporting a 10th grader with severe disabilities involved in a science class may see the opportunity for the student to practice visual-motor skills and communication skills within the lab experiments planned for the unit on molecules. A team supporting a student with autism in the second grade may see the opportunity to teach communication skills during the language arts work stations in the class. The teaching team determines where and when the critical moments for instruction on particular objectives/skills from an IEP should take place by taking time to look at units of instruction, activities that will occur in the classroom or the community within the unit, and the supports for learning available.

Designing Teaching Activities That Respect Varied Learning Styles and Intelligences

The work of Howard Gardner (1983) on the theory of multiple intelligence has stimulated numerous research projects in classrooms around the country. Armstrong (1994) has provided some of the most comprehensive work on the application of this theory to the development of instructional units that attend to all "ways of knowing" and provide opportunities for the development of all aspects of intelligence. The research on learning styles has been intersected with multiple intelligence theory by Hanson, Silver, and Strong (1990) in an effort to provide teachers with instructional practices that allow for both processes and products that honor the many different learning styles and intelligences students bring to classrooms.

There is relatively little research and literature related to learning styles and multiple intelligences that include children and youth with serious learning challenges due to their developmental or behavioral disabilities. Why they have been left out of the research and demonstrations in this area in the past is no doubt related to the segregated ways in which they have been taught and the lack of collaborative research across disciplines. Other reasons could be related to the tendency to ignore the cognitive and affective characteristics of students who are exceptional, or the fairly narrow means in which we have defined instructional possibilities for many children with disabilities. Despite the lack of participation in this type of research, investigators concerned with providing support to individuals with serious behavior challenges have documented the importance of looking at learning styles when designing curriculum, instructional strategies, antecedents to behavior, and coping mechanisms (Dunlap, Vaugh, & O'Neill, 1998). Increasingly, researchers and educators in the field have begun to address learning style and different ways of knowing related to communication, cognition, and performance (Gee, Houghton, Pogrund, & Rosenberg, 1995).

In a unique approach to making these important concepts practical for teachers, the Thoughtful Education model (Hanson, et al., 1990) provides teachers with a "window" for planning teaching and learning activities. Teachers use the window as a reminder of the four learning styles and intentionally plan that both input and output methods reflect opportunities for students in all four styles. Strain & Gee (1994, 1995) and Gee (1995) successfully taught in-service and preservice teachers in both general and special education to design units of instruction for literature/social studies at the elementary and secondary school levels on the basis of a combination of the Thoughtful Education model and the concepts of multiple intelligence (Gardner, 1983). In addition, these teachers planned for the ways in which students with severe disabilities could successfully be included in these units. By impacting the *original design of the learning environment and activities*, teachers not only provide a richer instructional milieu but also avoid some of the need for changes and adaptations in lessons/units typically needed for the child with special needs.

Establishing a Community of Learners

Another source of convergence within education fields and related service fields, and perhaps the one that has received the most attention, is the notion of creating communities of learners. Many researchers believe that effective instruction takes place in classrooms where a strong sense of community is reflected (Brown & Campione, 1990). Classrooms as learning communities, composed of the teaching team and the children and youth learning, serve to create powerful insights and knowledge for all (Johnson & Johnson, 1989a; Slavin, 1990; Thousand, Villa, & Nevin, 1994).

Student-to-student dialogue is the foundation upon which cooperative learning (Johnson & Johnson, 1989b) is structured. The social power inherent in the joint and collaborative enterprise of learning communities has the potential for providing students with a greater sense of ownership and agency in their own learning (Fagan, 1989). In these demonstrations classrooms are vital, busy, environments containing groups of students engaged in problem solving around a variety of experiments, research, and productions. Studies report that cooperative learning experiences have promoted interpersonal attraction among initially prejudiced peers and such experiences have promoted interethnic interaction in both instructional and free-time activities (Putnam, Rynders, Johnson, & Johnson, 1989).

More recent studies in cooperative learning have demonstrated the effectiveness of this model for children and youth with learning disabilities and severe disabilities (Hunt, Staub, Alwell, & Goetz, 1994). Villa and Thousand (1992) and Putnam (1994) have reviewed numerous strategies and research on student and teacher collaboration specifically for inclusive schooling. The emphasis on community reflects theoretical assumptions that new knowledge is constructed as a joint venture in the class rather than as a result of individual communication from teachers to students (Lampert, 1990).

Fluid heterogeneous and homogeneous groupings

Research done by Slavin (1990) on groupings in various content areas has shown that cooperative, heterogeneous groups were most desirable for base groups and groups related to content area subjects (such as social studies). His work also supports the use of some small, more homogeneous groups for reading and math instruction. This demonstrates the importance of fluidity in classrooms. Students in effective, inclusive classrooms are not continuously grouped with the same peers. The teaching team utilizes a variety of groupings throughout the day, including large and small groups, heterogeneous groups, homogeneous groups, partners, and individual work time in order to maximize learning and develop community. Multiage classrooms and Montessori models demonstrate much the same fluidity.

Person-centered planning and the learning community

There has been considerable work done in the past several years documenting the preference for and the utility of various "person-centered/family-centered" models for curriculum development and action planning for persons with disabilities (Forest & Lusthaus, 1989; Rainforth et al., 1992). The person-centered process extends the notion of community from the communities created at schools for learning to the communities in which the individual with disabilities lives and will be supported over time. This process incorporates the importance of natural supports and emphasizes the individual as a part of a larger social and community system that extends beyond the school building (Giangreco et al., 1994; Turnbull & Turnbull, 1996). These models stress the ecological and social variables that may influence the student's priorities based on family and community input and the importance of nonprofessional supports.

Social relationships and friendships as educational goals

When teams engage in person-centered planning from a quality-of-life perspective, friendships and social relationships typically rate high, if not at the top, of the list of priorities. Friendships are a key to quality of life and, as many authors have pointed out, children and youth with disabilities often need support and assistance in gaining opportunities to make friends (Strully & Strully, 1989). Numerous studies have documented that inclusion in typical classrooms with nondisabled peers, the provision of supports for communication, and active facilitation of social relationships are important to friendship development (Gee, 1993; Hunt, Alwell, & Goetz, 1988; Hunt, Staub, et al., 1994; Staub, Schwartz, Gallucci, & Peck,

1994). Classrooms and schools that operate from a strong sense of "learning communities" facilitate friendships as well as increased cognitive growth.

Promoting Self-determination, Self-regulated Learning, and Reflection on Learning and Thinking

In the last decade the concept of "self-determination" has received increasing attention as one of the most important educational goals for individuals with disabilities. Sands and Wehmeyer (1996) propose that self-determination is best conceptualized as a dispositional characteristic, a set of attitudes and abilities learned across the life span. Instructional approaches that emphasize self-determination stress promoting a classroom dialogue for self-regulated learning. Teachers involve their students in classroom dialogues about cognitive processes and learning strategies. The teacher still evaluates and gives feedback; however, an additional and important part of the teacher's role in this process is to model and think aloud the thoughts and strategies of a more expert member of the classroom community (Vygotsky, 1978). Teachers have a critical role in being responsive to students and the cognitive process by actually apprenticing students in the language, dialogue, and actions of the skilled problem solver and choice-maker.

> Students help each other with this dialogue, while teachers embed instruction in new procedures and strategies at critical points where such instruction is needed. This results in a complex interplay between the students' growing level of mastery and the teachers' sequencing of prompts and directives. Gradually, cognitive processes that were performed together by teachers and students become internalized by students as the collaborative dialogue becomes internalized. (Englert et al., 1992, p. 72)

Students with severe and profound disabilities have not often been included in the literature related to self-regulated learning and problem solving. One could speculate that this is primarily because of their exclusion from classrooms in which these strategies are being evaluated, but I suggest it is also a function of the emphasis on performance of tasks versus cognitive development in the field so far. Work has been done, however, related to self-determination and problem solving as individuals with severe disabilities are increasingly involved in futures planning, transition planning, and social relationships (Miner & Bates, 1997; Wehmeyer & Kelchner, 1995). There has also been substantial work related to choice-making, communicative intent, and the initiation of communication/dialogue at all levels (Beukelman & Mirenda, 1998).

Recent work described as "context instruction" for individuals with low-incidence disabilities has been designed to parallel the self-regulated dialogue but focuses on individuals who are unable to participate in what we think of as traditional "dialogue." These studies have been conducted on teaching the initiation of new mobility skills (Gee, Houghton, et al., 1995); communication and motor skills (Gee, Graham, Sailor, & Goetz, 1995, 1999); cognitive engagement (Gee, Graham,

& Goetz, 1999) and social interaction skills (Gee, 1993; Hunt, Farron-Davis, Beck-stead, Curtis, & Goetz, 1994). Students in these studies demonstrated the ability to initiate actions and behaviors in order to solve problems. These "problems" ranged from "how do I do something which will engage the peer near me to make something happen so I can go outside?" to "what do I need to do to get these friends of mine to continue to talk to me?"

Students *self-directed* their own learning by providing teachers with indications of the most critical moments for instruction versus teachers' controlling the "when and where" of instruction. Studies involving individuals with very severe behavior challenges have demonstrated the effectiveness of positive strategies that increase student choice, student empowerment, and control. Research also supports the importance of dialogue and increased communicative effectiveness regarding choices and control (Anderson, Albin, Mesaros, Dunlap, & Morelli-Robbins, 1993).

Responsive Instruction

Responsive instruction reflects the notion that students' everyday knowledge mediates their acquisition of scientific concepts (Moll, 1990). Constructivist practice suggests that effective teachers must continually tie new information to known in order to introduce new concepts and develop new understandings at the point where students are making errors or demonstrating confusion (Englert et al., 1992). Vygotsky (1978) suggested that an important aspect of responsive instruction is the extent to which teachers are able to bridge the gap between the level of performance attained by students in independent problem-solving activity and the level attained by students in collaborative problem-solving activity with the teacher or more knowledgeable peers (the zone of proximal development). Teachers must know their students and how they think, and this can only be accomplished through the process of instruction. Errors are seen as opportune moments for instruction, and the teacher responds to errors by starting with familiar or known content and then transforming that knowledge into more conceptually correct assumptions.

The notion of utilizing everyday activities and events familiar to the student to teach new concepts is basic to the literature on acquisition and generalization of new skills with students with severe disabilities (Horner, McDonell, & Bellamy, 1986). An extensive database exists documenting the efficacy of instruction of new skills within functional routines in which the activity itself sets the stage for learning a new skill (Snell & Brown, 2000). Horner, O'Neill, and Flannery (1993) discuss the need to allow errors to occur as instructional moments. Teachers can still guide the student to solve problems using decreasing assistance or errorless learning.

Discrepancies or problems to be solved create the need to learn (Van Dijk, 1989). Understanding clearly where the critical moments are can greatly enhance a teacher's responsiveness (Gee, Graham, et al., 1995). Poplin & Stone (1992) state that learners are most likely to succeed when they are passionately involved in a task. Critical learning moments are the opportunities that bank on that "passion" to learn, but they may need to be *created and enhanced* by the way in which we design instruction (for students with and without disabilities). "Incidental instruction" was designed to utilize moments that cannot be specifically planned or may not have been previously identified as instructional opportunities (Halle, 1987; Wolery, Ault, & Doyle, 1992). Teachers either plan these moments or teach their staff to quickly observe and utilize these naturally occurring moments for instruction. Inclusive classrooms, with the ever-changing activities and social contexts of nondisabled peers, provide individuals with disabilities continuous "incidental" opportunities for instruction. Support staff and teachers need to learn to recognize these opportunities and how to use them.

Systematic Instruction, Ongoing Adaptations, and Assessment Within the Context of Teaching

Behavioral and contextual-behavioral researchers have, for many years, documented the necessity of ongoing assessment within the context of teaching (Snell, & Brown, 2000). Systematic, "data-based" instruction is definitely a continued part of what is considered to be "best practice" in the field of special education. Ongoing measurement while teaching allows instructors to quickly change pace, materials, assistance, and so on. Systematic planning of what the teacher will say and do to facilitate learning, and how the teacher will determine whether or not the method is working, are indicators of successful and effective programs. Making desired outcomes clear and consistent to the learner, with discrete and identifiable measures of progress, is a hallmark of effective instruction (Wolery, et al., 1992).

Active, ongoing assessment while teaching is also a key aspect of constructivist classrooms. These classrooms use multiple measures of change through processes that allow teachers to follow student learning as opposed to measuring it at the end, enabling teachers to be responsive and flexible in their instructional methods (Grennon-Brooks & Brooks, 1993). Montessori models provide a systematic protocol for how a teacher introduces a new activity/skill, at what point a child should receive the opportunity, and how to facilitate a child's problem solving throughout the discovery and mastery of a task. Montessori classrooms provide an excellent learning environment for students with disabilities because of the systematic approach to instruction and the strong embedded skill orientation (Thompson et al., 1996).

A successful inclusive school utilizes research-based, innovative strategies to enhance the learning of all students and seeks new and creative strategies for any student for whom the current strategies aren't working. Ongoing data collection (of various types) within the context of teaching assists teachers to determine if the strategies presently being used should continue. Specific strategies for specific issues or disabilities are researched by the teaching teams and implemented as quickly as necessary. Students are not asked to wait to fail, nor are they asked to wait to be assessed for special services, before direct assistance is given. Support for challenging behavior is seen as essential, and special education teachers work with all team members to develop strategies, model interventions, and directly support students for whom the typical strategies aren't working (Anderson, 1989). Because some students need more intensive instruction to attain their objectives, teachers work in concert to find ways for this to occur.

Positive and Invitational Approaches to Instruction and Behavior

The final key element to the strategies above is the joint celebration of diversity, equity, and excellence. Teaching teams and school administrators who operate from this value base and share common goals regarding the nature and purpose of education will be more successful at designing inclusive schools. Many authors have recently addressed the notion of celebrating diversity—of culture, ability, and gender (Sapon-Shevin, 1992). Inclusive classrooms, by nature of the instructional design, value the differences in each student's abilities. Teachers operating from this perspective value the opportunity to think about learners with varied abilities and styles. They promote self-esteem through their approach to students, other staff, and instructional design.

Teachers operating from a framework of positive behavioral supports (Anderson et al., 1993) utilize curricular and instructional approaches that demonstrate their value for a wide range of learner styles and abilities. Through their instructional strategies they avoid and prevent many behavioral challenges. Teachers also recognize and analyze the communicative bases of challenging behavior and the social context in which it exists (Carr et al., 1994). When students have serious behavioral challenges, teams functionally assess the environments and interactions that form the context for the student's behavior, not just the student's behavior itself. A positive behavioral support plan is designed, implemented, and continuously evaluated and revised. The focus of the plan is to improve the individual's quality of life by assisting the individual to develop effective ways to communicate and ways to satisfy needs that do not interfere with learning, daily tasks, and social relationships. This focus differs from the more traditional focus of simply decreasing an unacceptable behavior (Koegel, Koegel, & Dunlap, 1996).

TEAMING AND COLLABORATION

Teaming and *collaboration* have become some of the key buzzwords in both general and special education in recent years. It was stated earlier that the instructional approaches in the tapestry described above are held together by a frame of "collaborative goals structures." Cooperative interactions are promoted by structuring goal interdependence, resource interdependence, and outcome interdependence (Thousand et al., 1994). The majority of our schools and classrooms, on the other hand, have been structured around competitive and individualistic goal structures (Rainforth et al., 1992). Giangreco, Edelman, Luiselli, and MacFarland (1996) discovered that in fact many "teams" do not collaboratively make decisions regarding how services are delivered, and that when decisions are made by a singular professional discipline, many times the goals of inclusive schooling are at risk.

Examples of team problem solving and strategies for collaboration have been delineated in numerous sources (Giangreco et al., 1994), including chapters in this book. One of the crucial elements to the successful inclusion of individuals with a wide range of abilities is that teams work collaboratively through critical discourse about teaching, and critical discourse about the individuals they serve. In addition, not everyone on the team has to have the same knowledge and expertise. In fact, teams operate more effectively when each person brings a unique contribution (Giangreco et al., 1996). Teams also operate more successfully when they recognize the parents' expertise and the "expertise" that is generated by working as a team, allowing all the different ways we "see" a child to be included in the decision making. Determining how services are provided in an integrated format requires sharing expertise, collaborative problem solving, and collaborative decision making.

CONCLUSION

The evolution of effective practices has not stopped—in fact, it is a continuous spiral that is fueled by the interesting mixture of learners and teachers who "look and see" from different perspectives. Effective schools are by nature inclusive, and inclusive schools promote the constant development of new ideas. Given that the technology and the creativity do exist to teach all students, I return to my earlier question. What will be the nature and extent of the transformation of our schools?

Both school districts and universities often "come to the edge" of change, and, as if looking over a cliff, back away from change that will result in true transformation and self-renewing practices. In school districts this often results in surface changes such as hiring "an inclusion specialist" to "include" a certain number of students whose parents have requested it; the use of terms such as *inclusion students*; inclusion in placement only; inclusion only of students whose parents push and push; or one-to-one paraprofessional programs that preclude cooperative teaching and prevent direct time given to students by the special education teacher. These changes provide a retreat from the cliff and allow schools and districts to pretend they are indeed restructuring. These phenomena might be seen as a temporary step but all too often become the end result of the change.

In high schools and universities, rather than doing the hard work of really thinking through the convergence of practices across content areas and developing meaningful ways for faculty teaming, faculty and administration often end up with surface changes that, in the name of curriculum integration, lose the incredible expertise of faculty who have knowledge in particular content areas. An effective teacher or professor must truly love her or his content area and have expertise in it to inspire the students in a class. Teams of highly motivated educators, each with a high level of expertise, can only increase the success of a class. *Team* is the key word, a team of teachers with varied expertise, as opposed to a team of teachers each with only a little knowledge about everything.

New investigations of learning might well begin to reflect the construction of knowledge within diverse communities of learners, the qualitative dimensions of the nature of effective teaching, the outcomes for the full spectrum of learners, and the organizational strategies that support transformed practices. The strategies reviewed above provide only a beginning for what can "become" when critically pragmatic teachers work together in teams to design instruction that is truly responsive to the heterogeneous groups of students we have in every class.

REFERENCES

Anderson, L. M. (1989). Implementing instructional programs to promote meaningful, self-regulated learning. In J. E. Brophy (Ed.), *Advances in research on teaching* (Vol. 1, pp. 311–341). Greenwich.

Anderson, R., Albin, R., Mesaros, R., Dunlap, G., & Morelli-Robbins, M. (1993). Issues in providing training to achieve comprehensive behavioral support. In J. Reichle & D. P. Wacker (Eds.), *Communicative alternatives to challenging behavior: Integrating functional assessment and intervention strategies.* Baltimore: Paul H. Brookes.

Armstrong, T. (1994). *Multiple intelligences in the classroom.* Alexandria, VA: Association for Supervision and Curriculum Development.

Beukelman, D., & Mirenda, P. (1998). *Augmentative and alternative communication: Management of severe communication disorders in children and adolescents.* Baltimore: Paul H. Brookes.

Billingsley, F. F., & Kelley, B. (1994). An examination of the acceptability of instructional practices for students with severe disabilities in general education settings. *Journal of the Association for Persons With Severe Handicaps, 19*(2), 75–83.

Billingsley, F., Gallucci, C., Peck, C., Schwartz, I., & Staub, D. (1996). "But those kids can't even do math": An alternative conceptualization of outcomes for inclusive education. *Special Education Leadership Review,* 43–55.

Brown, A. L. (1994). The advancement of learning. *Educational Researcher, 23*(8), 4–12.

Brown, A., & Campione, J. (1990). Communities of learning and thinking or a context by any other name. *Development perspectives on teaching and learning thinking skills, 21,* 108–126.

Carr, E. G., Levin, L., McConnachie, G., Carlson, J. I., Kemp, D. C., & Smith, C. E. (1994). *Communication-based intervention for problem behavior: A user's guide for producing positive change.* Baltimore: Paul H. Brookes.

Downing, J. (1996). *Including students with severe and multiple disabilities in typical classrooms: Practical strategies for teachers.* Baltimore: Paul H. Brookes.

Dunlap, G., Vaughn, B. J., & O'Neill, R. E. (1998). Comprehensive behavioral support: Application and intervention. In A. M. Wetherby, S. F. Warren, & J. Reichle, (Eds.), *Transitions in prelinguistic communication* (pp. 343–364). Baltimore: Paul H. Brookes.

Englert, C. S., Tarrant, K. L., & Mariage, T. V. (1992). Defining and redefining instructional practice in special education: Perspectives on good teaching. *Teacher Education and Special Education, 15*(2), 62–86.

Fagan, W. T. (1989). Empowered students; empowered teachers. *The Reading Teacher, 42,* 572–579.

Forest, M., & Lusthaus, E. (1989). Promoting educational equality for all students: Circles & maps. In S. Stainback, W. Stainback, & M. Forest (Eds.), *Educating all students in the mainstream of regular education.* Paul H. Brookes.

Gardner, H. (1983). *Frames of mind: The theory of multiple intelligences.* New York: Basic Books.

Gee, K. (1993). *An experimental and qualitative investigation into the motivation and competence of peer interactions involving students with severe, multiple disabilities in middle school classrooms.* Unpublished doctoral dissertation, University of California, Berkeley.

Gee, K. (1995). Facilitating active and informed learning in inclusive settings. In N. Haring & L. Romer (Eds.), *Welcoming students who are deaf-blind into typical classrooms: Facilitating school participation, learning, and friendships.* Baltimore: Paul H. Brookes.

Gee, K., Graham, N., Sailor, W., & Goetz, L. (1995). Use of integrated, general education and community settings as primary contexts for skill instruction of students with severe, multiple disabilities. *Behavior Modification, 19*(1), 33–58.

Gee, K., Houghton, J., Pogrund, R., & Rosenberg, R. (1995). Orientation and mobility: Access, information, and travel. In N. Haring & L. Romer (Eds.), *Welcoming students who are deaf-blind into typical classrooms: Facilitating school participation, learning, and friendships.* Baltimore: Paul H. Brookes.

Giangreco, M., Cloninger, C., & Iverson, V. (1994). *Choosing options and accommodations for children (COACH): A guide to planning inclusive education.* Baltimore: Paul H. Brookes.

Giangreco, M., Edelman, S., Luiselli, T., & MacFarland, S. (1996). Support service decision making for students with multiple service needs: Evaluative data. *Journal of the Association for Persons With Severe Handicaps, 21*(3), 135–144.

Grennon-Brooks, J., & Brooks, M. G. (1993). *The case for constructivist classrooms.* Alexandria, VA: Association for Supervision and Curriculum Development.

Halle, J. (1987). Teaching language in the natural environment: An analysis of spontaneity. *Journal of the Association for Persons With Severe Handicaps, 12,* 28–37.

Hanson, J. R., Silver, H. S., & Strong, R. W. (1990). Thoughtful education: Staff development for the 1990's. *Educational Leadership, 48*(5), 25–29.

Horner, R., Dunlap, G., & Koegel, R. L. (1988). *Generalization & maintenance: Life-style changes in applied settings.* Baltimore: Paul H. Brookes.

Horner, R. H., McDonnell, J. J., & Bellamy, G. T. (1986). Teaching generalized skills: General case instruction in simulation and community settings. In R. H. Horner, L. H. Meyer, & H. D. Fredericks, (Eds.), *Education of learners with severe handicaps: Exemplary service strategies,* (pp. 289–314). Baltimore: Paul H. Brookes.

Horner, R., O'Neill, R., & Flannery, K. B. (1993). Effective behavior support plans. In M. Snell (Ed.), *Instruction of students with severe Disabilities,* (4th ed.) (pp. 184–214). New York: Merrill, MacMillan.

Hunt, P., Alwell, M., & Goetz, L. (1988). Acquisition of conversation skills and the reduction of inappropriate social interaction behaviors. *Journal of the Association for Persons With Severe Handicaps, 13,* 20–27.

Hunt, P., Farron-Davis, F., Beckstead, S., Curtis, D., & Goetz, L. (1994). Evaluating the effects of placements of students with severe disabilities in general education versus special education classes. *Journal of the Association for Persons with Severe Handicaps, 19*, 200–214.

Hunt, P., Staub, D., Alwell, M., & Goetz, L. (1994). Achievement by all students within the context of cooperative learning groups. *Journal of the Association for Persons With Severe Handicaps, 19*, 290–301.

Johnson, D. W., & Johnson, R. T. (1989a). *Cooperation and competition: Theory and research.* Edina, MN: Interaction Book Company.

Johnson, D. W., & Johnson, R. T. (1989b). Cooperative learning and mainstreaming. In R. Gaylord-Ross (Ed.), *Integration strategies for students with handicaps.* Baltimore: Paul H. Brookes.

Joyce, B., Wolfe, J., & Calhoun, E. (1993). *The self-renewing school.* Alexandria, VA: Association for Supervision and Curriuclum Development.

Koegel, R. L., Koegel, L. K., & Dunlap, G. (1996). *Positive behaviorial support: Including people with difficult behavior in the community.* Baltimore: Paul H. Brooks.

Lampert, M. (1990). When the problem is not the question and the solution is not the answer: Mathematical knowing and teaching. *American Educational Research Journal, 27*, 29–64.

Miner, C. A., & Bates, P. E. (1997). The effect of person-centered planning activities on the IEP transition planning process. *Education and Training in Mental Retardation, 32*, 105–112.

Moll, L. C. (1990). Introduction. In L. C. Moll (Ed.), *Vygotsky and education.* Cambridge: Cambridge University Press.

Poplin, M., & Stone, S. (1992). Paradigm shifts in instructional strategies: From reductionism to holist/constructivism. In W. Stainback & S. Stainback (Eds.), *Controversial issues confronting special education: Divergent perspectives* (pp. 153–179). Boston: Allyn and Bacon.

Putnam, J. (1994). *Cooperative learning and strategies for inclusion: Celebrating diversity in the classroom.* Baltimore: Paul H. Brookes.

Putnam, J., Rynders, J. E., Johnson, R., & Johnson, D. (1989). Collaborative skill instruction for promoting positive interactions between mentally handicapped and non-handicapped children. *Exceptional Children, 55* (6), 550–557.

Rainforth, B., York, J., & MacDonald, C. (1992). *Collaborative teams for students with severe disabilities: Integrating therapy and educational services.* Baltimore: Paul H. Brookes.

Sailor, W. (1990). (1) Behavior management: Issues and strategies, (2) Research seminar on contextual relevance, and (3) The comprehensive local school. Invited presentations to the University of Waterloo, Ontario, Canada.

Sands, D., & Wehmeyer, M. (1996). *Self-determination across the life span: Independence and choice for people with disabilities.* Baltimore: Paul H. Brookes.

Sapon-Shevin, M. (1992). Celebrating diversity. In S. Stainback & W. Stainback (Eds.)., *Curriculum considerations in inclusive classrooms: Facilitating learning for all children* (pp. 19–36). Baltimore: Paul H. Brookes.

Slavin, R. (1990). *Cooperative learning theory, research, and practice.* Englewood Cliffs, NJ: Prentice-Hall.

Snell, M., & Brown, F. (2000). *Instruction of students with severe disabilities* (5th ed.). New York: MacMillan.

Stainback, S., & Stainback, W. (1992). *Curriculum considerations in inclusive classrooms: Facilitating learning for all students.* Baltimore: Paul H. Brookes.

Staub, D., Schwartz, Gallucci, C., & Peck, C. (1994). Four portraits of friendship at an inclusive school. *Journal of the Association for Persons With Severe Handicaps, 19*(4), 314–325.

Strain, K., & Gee, K. (1994 & 1995). *Curriculum, instruction and social networks in heterogeneous classrooms: Creating options for including students with significant disabilities.* University of Kansas. A course for both general and special education teachers.

Strully, J., & Strully, C. (1989). Friendships as an educational goal. In W. Stainback, S. Stainback, & M. Forest (Eds.), *Educating all students in the mainstream of regular education.* Baltimore: Paul H. Brookes.

Thompson, B., Wickham, D., Mulligan-Ault, M., Shanks, P., Reinertson, B., Wegner, J., & Guess, D. (1996). Expanding the circle of inclusion: Integrating young children with severe multiple disabilities. *Montessori Life, 1,* 11–14.

Thousand, J., Villa, R., & Nevin, A. (1994). *Creativity and collaborative learning: A practical guide to empowering students and teachers.* Baltimore: Paul H. Brookes.

Turnbull, H.R., & Turnbull, A. (1996). *Families, professionals, and exceptionality: A special partnership* (2nd ed.). Columbus, OH: Charles E. Merrill.

Udvari-Solner, A. (1994). A decision-making model for curricular adaptations in cooperative groups. In J. Thousand, R. Villa, & A. Nevin (Eds.), *Creativity and collaborative learning: A practical guide to empowering students and teachers.* Baltimore: Paul H. Brookes.

Van Dijk, J. (1989). Techniques for working with children who are deaf-blind. Paper presented at symposium on deaf blindness, July 22–26, University of Washington at Seattle.

Villa, R., & Thousand, J. (1992). Student collaboration: An essential for curriculum delivery in the 21st century. In S. Stainback, & W. Stainback, (Eds), *Curriculum considerations in inclusive classrooms: Facilitating learning for all students* (pp. 117–142). Baltimore: Paul H. Brookes.

Vygotsky, L. (1978). *Mind in society.* Cambridge, MA: Harvard University Press.

Wehmeyer, M., & Kelchner, K. (1995). *Whose future is it anyway? A student directed transition planning process.* Arlington, TX: ARC National Headquarters.

Wolery, M., Ault, M. J., & Doyle, P. M. (1992). *Teaching students with moderate to severe disabilities.* New York: Longman.

CHAPTER 9

From "Special" Educators to Educators: The Case for Mixed-Ability Groups of Teachers in Restructured Schools

Dianne L. Ferguson, Ginevra Ralph, and Nadia Katul Sampson

As we begin a new century, our schools, like society in general, struggle to antici-pate the changes that will be demanded of the next millennium. Recommenda-tions abound and teachers in today's schools feel a constant pressure to change that all too often leaves them bewildered and beleaguered (Fullan, 1996). Teachers are being asked to reexamine how and what they teach. Administrators and school boards are experimenting with new management systems in the face of constantly decreasing resources. University educators attempt to refocus their research and theories to better describe and explain effective teaching and learning as students and teachers experience it in these changing schools. Daily reports in the media urge more and more changes in all aspects of schooling, for all types of students and teachers. At the same time, students are more diverse than ever before—in cultural background, learning styles and interests, social and economic class, abil-ity, and disability. Broadly speaking, however, there are three strands of reforms currently challenging teachers in schools. The first two emerge from "general" education, the third from "special" education.

From a broad national and federal policy level, there is much discussion aimed at making schools more effective in terms of how many students complete school and how well they do on achievement measures [U. S. Department of Education (USDE), 1997]. Indeed, one aspect of this "top-down" reform strand is a call for new, higher national achievement standards, for tests to measure students' accom-plishment of these new standards, and for the consistent use of consequences when standards are not met (Center for Policy Research, 1996; Gandal, 1995; McDonnell & McLaughlin, 1997; McLaughlin, 1995b; Waters, Burger, & Burger, 1995). Al-though there are other features to this broad government-initiated reform strand, increased standards and more consistent national testing stand out as major themes and are echoing throughout state reform legislation, district directives, and teacher staffroom conversations.

At the same time, elementary and secondary teachers increasingly experiment with new curricular and teaching approaches that emphasize students' mastery not just of facts and basic academic skills but also of essential thinking skills like problem solving, analysis, collaboration, and experimentation. Encouraged by business and industry (Carnevale, Gainer, & Meltzer, 1990), various state reform legislation, recommendations of a growing number of educational associations, and some strands of educational research, teachers try to expand their agendas to ensure that students not only learn but are able to use their learning in their lives outside of school (Conley, 1993; Darling-Hammond & Falk, 1997; Eisner, 1991; Sarason, 1995; Wasley, 1994). One additional feature to this second major strand of reform is to enable students to acquire an understanding and appreciation for their own learning. With this capacity they might better pursue ongoing learning in the changing situations our society will present them throughout their lives and long after their formal public schooling is over.

Also, within special education the long-familiar "mainstreaming" or "regular education initiatives" discussions about where our "special" teaching (usually remediation-oriented) should occur (e.g., Biklen, Ferguson, & Ford, 1989; Goodlad & Lovitt, 1993; Lieberman, 1996; Lipsky & Gartner, 1997; Rogers, 1993; Skrtic, 1991; Villa & Thousand, 1995) are gradually being replaced by renewed calls for "integration" and "inclusion." The civil rights logic of integration, which focused more on an end to segregation than on any particularly detailed educational alternative, has now been expanded to focus not just on where children with disabilities should not be educated but also on where they should be educated—general education classrooms and activities—and to what end (full learning and social membership) (Baker, Wang, & Walberg, 1994; Berres, Knoblock, Ferguson, & Wood, 1996; Ferguson, 1995; Janney & Snell, 1997; McLaughlin, 1995a; [National Association of State Boards of Education (NASBE), 1995] Sailor, Gee, & Karosoff, 1993).

In response to the pressure of these three reform strands, and despite ongoing debates, three results are becoming evident. First, classroom diversity in general education increasingly includes the diversity of disability along with race, culture, learning style, intelligences, personal preferences, socioeconomic class, and family and community priorities. When asked to identify changes in education over the last 5 years, any group of educators will quickly identify increasing student diversity near the top of the list. Teachers seem quite clear that the "norm," if it ever really existed in the untidy worlds of schools, has nearly disappeared as a useful construct for the design of learning and management of classrooms (McMackin & Bukowieck, 1997; Pugach & Seidl, 1995; Putnam, Speigel, & Bruininks, 1995).

A second result of various educational reforms is that separate special education classrooms and schools are gradually decreasing in number. Although national educational statistics and reports continue to show dramatic variation in this result from state to state (Davis, 1994; USDE, 1997), the shift to more options for students identified as disabled seems well established. Of course, as students with disabilities move into general education classrooms, they bring still another dimension of the student diversity mentioned above. As a consequence of both these shifts, the third result is a shift in the role and daily duties of special educators, from self-contained classroom teachers to a variety of specialist, support, consultative, and generally itinerant roles. These changes are the focus of this chapter because, regardless of the position one takes on inclusion, or any other of the current reforms in American public schooling, the shifting roles are real for an increasing number of both special and general educators.

We have organized our analysis of these changing roles first to explore the logic presented in much of the special education reform literature for these changes. Second, we briefly present the results of our own research (Cameron, 1994; Ferguson, Ralph, Katul, Cameron, in review; Katul, 1995) with special educators exploring these changes in role. Third, we analyze the limits of special educators' changing roles and propose an alternative. Finally, we explore the implications of this alternative for students with disabilities in schools, for our changing educational policies regarding special education, for teacher education, and for teachers' continuing professional development.

THE ROLE SHIFT FROM SPECIAL EDUCATOR TO INCLUSION SPECIALIST

For some advocates of inclusion the emergence of the new role represents movement toward merging the parallel systems of general and special education into a single unified system of public education that incorporates all children and youth as active, fully participating members of the school community; that views diversity as the norm; and that ensures a high-quality education for each student by providing meaningful curriculum, effective teaching, and necessary supports for each student (Ferguson, 1995, p. 286).

For others, this shift in role threatens a loss of tradition, status, influence, and the very core of what makes special education "special." That special core involves being able to bring highly specialized and technical teaching approaches to individual students in order to attenuate, and sometimes repair, highly individual and idiosyncratic differences in cognitive functioning and learning accomplishments (e.g., Gallagher, 1994; Zigmond, 1995). Regardless of the position one takes, however, the shifting roles are a fact for an increasing number of special educators.

Descriptions of the roles and responsibilities of "inclusion specialists" vary as do the titles assigned these new roles. Sometimes called "integration specialists" or "support facilitators," or even "inclusion teachers," the most consistent themes for these professionals are to be coordinators, developers and organizers of supports for students and teachers in inclusive settings (Stainback, Stainback, & Harris, 1989; Tashie et al., 1993; Villa & Thousand, 1995). In an earlier publication we described them as "adapters of curriculum" and "brokers of resources" (Ferguson, Meyer, Jeanchild, Juniper, & Zingo 1993). Others emphasize being a "team member," or a "provider of technical assistance" (e.g., Sailor et al., 1993; Snell, 1998; Van Dyke, Stallings, & Colley, 1995; Villa & Thousand, 1995).

Our more recent research with 19 teachers in this role turned up 16 different titles—some new, some old—being used by educators who defined themselves as exploring this role (Cameron, 1994; Ferguson et al., in review; Katul, 1995). A quick glance at the list in Table 9.1 confirms the major themes found in the descriptions of the inclusion specialist role by proponents. First, the role is supposed to be less about working with students and more about working with grownups. Most examples include the specifically teacher-oriented language of "consultant," "specialist," or "facilitator." Only the "Teacher of Inclusion" example seems unclear about the intended audience for the role's activities. Second, special educators serving in a wide variety of roles seem to be assuming these responsibilities: In some cases, inclusion support is added to the duties of the Chapter 1 teacher, in others the Special Education Director. In the interest of brevity, we will continue to use the term "inclusion specialist" to describe this role because it seems to us to best capture the various recommendations in the literature.

Table 9.1. Job Titles in Use

- Support Specialist
- Supported Education Consultant
- Instruction Facilitator
- Supported Education Specialist
- District Learning SPED Facilitator
- Inclusion Teacher
- Handicapped Learner Teacher
- Teacher of Inclusion
- Teacher Consultant
- District SPED Coordinator
- SPED Chapter 1 Coordinator
- Education Service District Supervisor
- Collaboration Consultant
- Supported Education Consultant/Autism Specialist
- Educational Specialist
- SPED Director

THE NEW ROLE IN THEORY

As inclusion reforms have spread, a literature has emerged describing the features and duties of the inclusion specialist (e.g., Ferguson & Ralph, 1996; Snell, 1998; Stainback & Stainback, 1990; Stainback et al., 1989; Tashie et al., 1993). One recommended prerequisite for the role is that the person be knowledgeable about available supports and resources for students with disabilities assigned to general education classrooms. An important responsibility of the specialist is to get resources and supports to other members of the school community. A second responsibility, and value, is that the inclusion specialist's work should be "consumer-driven." That is, the requests and needs of students, parents, and teachers should direct the allocation and provision of supports and resources. Being flexible enough to be consumer-driven requires the specialist to be familiar with classroom routines and curricula, knowledgeable about students' learning styles and preferences, and aware of family's priorities so that their advice and assistance is maximally useful. Finally, inclusion specialists are advised to be flexible and "fade" their support when it is no longer needed. Proponents' expectations are that as teachers and students become more adept at supporting each other, more natural support networks will emerge, diminishing the need for an official inclusion specialist. Through all this, the specialist is further advised to act as a "team member" rather than as an expert or supervisor in order to encourage and model an atmosphere of unity and cooperation (Givner & Haager, 1995; Pugach, 1995; Snell, 1998; Stainback & Stainback, 1990; Tashie et al., 1993; Villa & Thousand, 1995; Warger & Pugach, 1996).

Inclusion specialists are now encouraged to support all students in the classroom rather than focus on certain labeled students so that, from a student's point of view at least, all grownups are teachers, no longer labeled by their expertise (Ferguson et al., 1993). Yet even recent educational and informational videos seeking to illustrate the best available inclusion practices (e.g., Dover, 1994; Goodwin & Wurzburg, 1993; New York Partnership for Statewide Systems Change Project, 1994; Thompson, 1991) are peppered with phrases like "these special students" or "my inclusion students," suggesting that both general and special educators struggle still with division of students, tasks, and responsibilities.

Apparent contradictions between the inclusion specialist as envisioned by reformers and as experienced by teachers prompted our further investigation. How much has the role of inclusion specialist actually evolved toward serving all students? Does "serving all students" mean that the need for the specialist's resources and supports will in fact not fade as everyone becomes more comfortable working with a new "inclusion student"? Or, is the strategy of "working with all students" just a tactic to disguise the extra resources and attention afforded labeled students so as to reduce stigmatizing them during this period of adjustment? Is the role really needed or just an administrative strategy for using special educators who no longer have classrooms? Can schools really be organized to educate all students without labeling either students or teachers given current federal and state laws and policies?

THE NEW ROLE IN REALITY

Our own research involved interviews with 19 teachers who understood themselves to be taking on the responsibilities of the inclusion specialist role. In addition to hour-long interviews with each, we shadowed eight of the inclusion specialists during a typical day's routine. We carefully logged the minutes these specialists spent on five tasks: (a) driving, (b) pulling students out or aside for instruction, (c) teaching or observing in general education classrooms, (d) talking with teachers and/or parents, and (e) doing paperwork, phone calls, and other desk work. We also interviewed seven general educators who worked with several of the inclusion specialists we had interviewed earlier, although some of these interviews were more brief. Finally, we collected job descriptions, when they existed, for the 19 specialists we interviewed, as well as records of schedules and appointments to expand our understanding of how inclusion specialists spend their time. We illustrate some of the changing roles and tasks through three composite examples derived from our interviews and observations.

Ben: "Teacher With an Empty Classroom"

After receiving his initial special education license and a master's degree in special education, Ben was hired almost immediately as a resource room teacher at McKenzie Middle School. Ben provided supplemental and remedial instruction in math, reading, and language arts to students designated "learning disabled" in his fully equipped classroom. After his first year, however, the school district decided to adopt a more inclusive model for providing special education services and decided to stop using resource rooms for pullout instruction. Suddenly, Ben found he had a new title, a new role, and an empty classroom.

As a new "inclusion specialist," Ben's job description specified that his primary responsibilities were to provide modified and adapted instruction for "included students" in general education classrooms. He was also directed to monitor their progress on IEP goals and objectives and model appropriate teaching methods for the general education teachers—at least with regard to the students with disabilities. Encouraged by the principal and with the cooperation of several teachers, Ben moved his instruction out of the resource classroom to theirs. His soon became more a place for holding adult meetings than for working with children.

Ben and his students found the transition difficult. With little joint planning time, Ben and the general educators decided that the needs of his students would be best met if they were gathered together into small groups when Ben could come to the classroom. As chairperson and primary author of all the students' IEPs, Ben was naturally more familiar with students' needs. So in the end, Ben transferred the materials and skills he had always used in the resource room to create separate instruction for the "included" students in each of their assigned general education classrooms, remaining responsible for much of their education.

In our school the classroom teacher is the case manager. They are the ones who know supposedly what the kid needs and where they are going. I am just a resource. . . . But under the law, someone needs to be there watching what's happening. I am simply the district watchdog. I can't leave it because sometimes if you leave it up to people who don't know the law, who aren't qualified to know, then we have problems. And so if I see problems, or hear about problems, I step in to problem solve. . . . They are still my kids.

I have some groups in which I teach kids reading and math directly and I handle a large bulk of the paperwork. . . . I attend the meetings for the children that I serve and I also provide consultation through the building [when there are] behavioral or academic concerns. I have periods when I can go observe and provide support—give the teacher a break for instance.

After a relatively short time, Ben and several of the general education teachers decided that trying to teach their separate groups at the same time in the same room was not working well. They believe that the students and teachers were distracted by each other. Besides, Ben now had so many different schedules that sometimes he was late or came early and teachers often were not ready for him. The logistics seemed too difficult, so Ben began to pull students out into the hall or another room, and even into his old empty resource room. No one commented, or perhaps even noticed, as Ben began to repopulate the special education classroom.

Joni: "Teacher Without a Classroom"

Before becoming an inclusion specialist, Joni worked as an educational assistant in a resource room for students with learning disabilities. After earning a teaching license to work with students with moderate and severe disabilities, she began teaching in a self-contained classroom that served more significantly disabled students from several surrounding towns. She and her 9–12 students spent their days in a classroom tucked away at the end of a hall in Alder Elementary. Two full-time educational assistants provided most of the actual instruction that Joni had designed, leaving her able to supervise their teaching, organize and manage everyone's schedules, and manage paperwork.

Worried that she was still not adequately addressing her students' learning and social needs, she convinced the principal to integrate her students into general education classrooms for parts of their day. With little fanfare, students began attending P.E., art, and music classes with their nondisabled peers. Soon Joni started worrying that things still were not working the way she had hoped. Even though one of her assistants accompanied students to their general education classes, the students did not seem to be making friends or meeting the expectations of the general education teachers. Instead, the teachers pretty much left the students alone, expecting the assistants to teach them as best they could.

Given her experiences, Joni was excited when her district decided to reassign her students to schools in their home communities. As the district emptied Joni's classroom, it created a new "inclusion teacher" position that seemed perfect for Joni. She had some experience integrating students into general education classrooms, she wanted to achieve better inclusion, and she had a background in IEP writing and curriculum modification that the district believed would be needed in the inclusion specialist role.

As the "inclusion teacher," Joni now has more students and more assistants (now titled "inclusion tutors") to schedule, coordinate, and manage not only across all the classrooms at Alder Elementary but also across several other schools. She also continues to design instruction for the assistants to deliver in the general education classrooms where unfamiliar and uncertain teachers are eager to have help and support.

Her carefully orchestrated schedule is a masterpiece but frequently unravels as little things happen—a student's mood, an assistant's health, or a classroom teacher's decision to change the lesson.

> Actually, the coverage is so tough. . . . I find myself going to a school for fifteen minutes just to give the inclusion tutor a break. . . . Coverage is a problem. It seems like I am always looking for somebody to cover for something.

Joni is everywhere at once and feels as if she is accomplishing less than ever. Our morning with 6-year-old John is illustrative. His squeals could be heard as we approached the resource room. A couple of doors along the hallway closed softly in response to the noise. Joni walked in and went directly to John, passing the two adults in the room. At first I could only see the top of his head over the standing dividers that surrounded him in the corner of the room. His squeals grew a little louder and consistent as Joni spoke to him in a warm, familiar voice.

After spending 10 minutes getting John focused on playing with some puzzles, Joni found that her questions, "How is Johnny doing today? Anything I need to know about?" were met with an uncomfortable silence and exchanged glances between the educational assistant and the resource room teacher. It turned out that they thought the picture communication board Joni designed was too difficult to use, partly because John was in the kindergarten classroom for some of the day where there was no board. Joni stressed the board's importance and began modeling how to use it with John. After a bit Joni took John outside to play, though the other kindergartners would not have recess for at least an hour. According to Joni, John "rarely" played with the other kids during recess anyway. In fact, John's inclusion was dictated by the various adults responsible for coordinating schedules between the resource room and kindergarten classroom. The teachers did not always know when Joni would arrive, requiring them to switch gears unexpectedly. As a consequence John often had stretches of "down time" when whatever was going on did not seem to "fit." No one was available to figure out what else to do.

When we arrived back in the resource room, the tutor assigned to John was not there and the resource room teacher made no move to assume responsibility for him. Joni decided to have him join the kindergarten classroom, but we arrived to find an empty room. Joni remembered that it was music time and his classmates must be in the music room.

Reflecting on her role to us, Joni puzzles over the tensions in her job:

> [I am] not a direct service person, but I am in the classroom almost every day. I see almost every child every day. . . . If the tutor is having a specific problem around something, I may work with the child myself to get a sense of what the issue is or I will do some modeling for the teachers. . . . I am the chairperson of the child's IEP, so it gives me some nice hands-on time to work with the child.

She still teaches children but not all the time. Students are assigned to her but taught by a variety of others. She must plan the IEP, but the goals and objectives are taught by others during lessons that Joni did not design.

Sonia: "Teacher of Teachers"

Once she received her master's degree and special educator teaching license, Sonia worked for 3 years as a roaming special educator. She wrote IEPs and provided individual and small-group instruction for a wide variety of students across several schools, each of whom was included some of the time in general education classrooms and schedules. She assessed students, designed curriculum, and monitored their progress. She also tried to help them develop friends and support networks as often as she could. Like Joni, she felt uneasy that she could not be available enough for any one student to really provide everything she or he needed. She also worried about what was happening for her students when she was not around, but she had few good ways to find out.

After roaming for 2 years, Sonia took a new job as an inclusion specialist for an intermediate district that provided specialized services for districts in the area. Her new job still kept her moving but doing different tasks. Joni was responsible for 17 schools in two districts. Together with two other specialists in her office, she developed and taught in-services for the general and special educators in their assigned schools. She also coordinated the special education team at each school, guiding team members through the process of creating IEPs, lesson plans, and behavior plans for all the students with disabilities.

She was often called upon to manage the ever-present crises and was lauded as very clever at putting out the fires. When we arrived for an interview, we found her talking on the phone. She cupped her hand over the mouthpiece and whispered, "The biggest issue is behavior. It's not anything else. It is the very biggest issue with teachers that I deal with."

Sonia liked the change in role. She was more and more convinced that her knowledge and skills were best used to help other teachers acquire them for their own use instead of her trying to teach every student. As we arrived at a middle school for a meeting about a child who was presenting some behavior issues, the case manager greeted us with her desperation: "I'm so glad you're here. We're going nuts and I don't think we could hold on one more week the way things are going. We're in trouble."

During the meeting with two educational assistants, the case manager and the resource teacher, Sonia emphasized the importance of safe-space, charting, and meeting regularly. "I hate to say 'I told you so,' but you guys have a crisis that just didn't have to happen. You needed to have regular team meetings about Sadie and it sounds like you haven't met since I was here more than a month ago." As we left for a quick lunch, Sonia vented,

> I just can't believe this team! They don't need me to do this stuff. I shouldn't have to come out here when things fall apart. They wouldn't have fallen apart if they had just kept meeting and talking to each other. I swear, I feel sometimes like I'm case-managing adults!

Sonia worried that "putting out fires" consumed too much of her time and was really a symptom of deeper issues. Besides, she was not always confident that her solutions were really going to last because she often did not have enough time to investigate what caused the crisis in the first place: "The problem is that in most instances, I don't know the students or the situation and often my ideas are a quick fix. Yes, I do fix it quickly, but then it falls apart in two weeks."

On the other hand, although there would always be some kind of crisis to manage, there might come a time—perhaps even before she was ready to retire—when the teachers in her two districts would pretty much know what she knows and would not need her in-services and advice. Still, she consoled herself,

> Teachers are alone, so it is nice to have an educational specialist come in and talk to them. So I will sit and talk with them, and I will listen real well. You have to be a good listener and be able to draw that out of people and then help guide them.

These three role examples capture some of the various experiences inclusion specialists have as they try to meet their new responsibilities. We found the roles to be remarkably consistent across the people we formally interviewed as well as among other inclusion specialists we have encountered in other situations. Our shadowing data also captured this range and balance of task patterns. One teacher spent a little over 40% of the time we shadowed him pulling students out to teach as compared with 8% of his time teaching or observing in general education classrooms and 13% talking with teachers or parents. In contrast, another specialist spent no time pulling students out and nearly 40% of her time in classrooms and talking with teachers. Perhaps the biggest range of difference involved paperwork, with one specialist spending 64% of her time at desk work and another spending only 9%. The patterns reflect the three roles rather well. "Teachers with empty classrooms" are most likely to spend larger proportions of time pulling students out or aside and relatively less time doing paperwork or teaching and observing in general education classrooms. In contrast "teachers of teachers" are most likely to spend the bulk of their time talking with teachers and relatively less time teaching at all.

The Predictable Failure of the Inclusion Specialist Role

All of the inclusion specialists who participated in our research, whom we have met at conferences, who attend our university classes, and whom we work with in schools, are able professionals. Indeed, many are praised within their schools and districts as among the best, most energetic, and most forward-thinking teachers. Nevertheless, almost all experience some of the same worries and dissatisfactions that the teachers Ben, Joni, and Sonia shared with us. Yet it seems to us that these teachers' frustrations are all too predictable, though we admit to the advantage of not only hindsight but also data. There are three main issues special educators are facing in their efforts to adapt to this new form of practice. We offer them as a summary of the reality teachers face.

LOGISTICAL DILEMMAS

As teachers leave their special education classrooms to work in other teachers' classrooms, the logistical problems of decentralized practice become real and challenging. Some must travel between several schools, but even those who travel only within a single building face the management challenge of scheduling time with each of "their students" within the constraints of other teachers' constantly changing and rarely predictable schedules (Wood, 1998). At best, these traveling teachers are able to deliver effective teaching some of the time. At worst, their students may learn less while suffering inadvertent, but increased, visibility as being different by virtue of the special attention and the unresolved question of teacher ownership. It is this very kind of visibility that can risk the fragile social connections the students might otherwise make with peers and that generated the challenge to work with all students instead of just the labeled students.

Furthermore, although "not enough time" is the ubiquitous slogan of all teachers, for these peripatetic teachers it takes on the reality of simple fact: not being able to directly teach dispersed students to their professional satisfaction. Neither can they effectively serve as "curriculum collaborators" and "team teachers" when their students' teachers may be members of many different teams, each demanding a share of the available time. When asked, both general and special educators consistently identify *time* as a critical barrier to accomplishing inclusion, as well as many other school reforms (e.g., O'Shea & O'Shea, 1998; Werts, Wolery, Snyder, & Caldwell, 1996).

PERSONAL LOSS

Special educators, like most educators, enter their professions to teach children and youth. They enjoy being around children. They are challenged by the search for ways to help children learn. They are rewarded by the resulting growth, however small or great, each student achieves. However, many inclusion specialists find themselves asked to shift focus from teaching children to teaching teachers and assistants. All the job descriptions and much of the descriptive literature for this role emphasize this teaching-of-adults function, sometimes in quite informal ways (modeling, collaborating), sometimes quite formal (consulting, offering inservices).

To be sure, there are some unique and important compensations in teaching grown-ups, but many inclusion specialists struggle to find the same satisfactions in these more indirect efforts to influence and enable other educators to teach their previous students. Some worry about the logic of using personnel who were prepared to teach children to supervise teacher assistants who possess no such preparation. Others feel devalued and discouraged by having "team" teaching devolve to being the general educator's teacher assistant (Davis & Ferguson, 1992; Wood, 1998). One such pair of teachers (Keller & Cravedi-Cheng, 1995) describe this process well:

> We both assumed from the beginning that I [Nancy] would be responsible for delivering the content and Lia would assist me in this endeavor. This rather conventional assumption—teacher and teacher assistant—provided the basis for dividing our labor. . . . In other words, I identified the content to be covered, set objectives, and did the majority of lesson planning, teaching and evaluating. Lia verbally and physically prompted students to focus on the instruction, checked their understanding, and limited off-task behavior. (p. 83)

Whether or not the special educator finds a new challenge in working with adults as a teacher or an assistant, the loss of teaching children can be a most personal one.

IRONIES OF EXPERTISE

Special educators become itinerant specialists or support teachers partly on the basis of the assumption that they have a special expertise to share with "general" educators who now have been charged with teaching "their" students. This assumption is grounded in a long history of preparing teachers to work not so much with children or youth but with specific kinds of children. As Seymour Sarason (1990) sees it,

> School personnel are graduates of our colleges and universities. It is there that they learn there are at least two types of human beings, and if you choose to work with one of them you render yourself legally and conceptually incompetent to work with others. (p. 258)

We would add to this observation that our content- and category-driven licensing tradition has led to even greater fractionalizing than "two types of human beings." Many special educators fail to realize that the "attitudinal problems" they decry in their general education colleagues constitute a natural, appropriate, and, indeed, professional response to being asked to teach a child one has not been officially licensed to teach.

Our parallel systems of general and special education are a direct product of the beliefs shared among all educational personnel, families of school children, and school children themselves, after awhile, that:

- Students are responsible for their own learning.
- When students don't learn, there is something wrong with them.
- It is the responsibility of schools to determine what is wrong with as much precision as possible so that students can be directed to the teachers, classrooms, curricula, and teaching practices that match their learning profiles. (Ferguson, 1995)

As special education gradually funneled more and more students away from the general education classroom, general educators became literally less able to accommodate student differences. At the same time, separated from the culture and activity of general education classrooms, special educators became less and less familiar with general education curriculum, developments in instructional strategies, learning theories, and innovative assessment practices. After several generations of creating a system of public education where information as well as people are carefully separated, we now ask inclusion specialists to teach in settings they don't understand, relying on practices that may not be appropriate.

To be sure, special educators sometimes possess quite specific expertise in special instructional technologies, certain forms of assessment, educational law, physical modifications and adaptations, and information about how to manage a variety of other relatively rare events and issues. Unfortunately, when such specialized information is decontextualized, interpolating it for general education content, assessment, and curriculum development is nearly impossible.

THE CASE FOR MIXED-ABILITY GROUPS OF TEACHERS

The "solution" of changing special educators into inclusion specialists emerged from assumptions about student learning and teacher capacity. The limits of this strategy will be overcome only by enlarging the discussion to examine assumptions about learning and teacher capacity that undergird our schooling practices so that we can shift our focus from those that perpetuate the labeling and separation of students, teachers, and curriculum to those that might enable all teachers to creatively blend their various abilities to the benefit of all students' learning (Astuto, Clark, Read, McGree, & deKoven, 1994; Rainforth & England, 1997; Skrtic, 1995). Although this is by no means a small task, we believe it to be both possible and necessary. Other chapters in this book have offered analyses that lead to this same conclusion in one way or another. Our contribution is to argue for redirecting our collective efforts in three areas that we think will contribute to achieving not only "mixed-ability groups of teachers" but reinvented schools as well. In this last section we make our case for shifting attention (a) from a reliance on individual practice to a reliance on group practice, (b) from a focus on teaching to a focus on learning, and (c) from special educators' efforts to "reform" general education to more fundamental collective efforts to restructure education.

From Individual to Group Practice

Having said that, let us hasten to add that we are not arguing for all educators to become "generalists" or "Super Teachers" who are presumed to possess all the skills and information needed to serve the learning of all students. We think it very unlikely that anyone could possibly achieve such mastery and competence. Rather, we propose that instead of assigning only one teacher to a classroom of 20 or more learners, or to a content area with instructional responsibility for 150–250 students, groups of teachers be assigned collective responsibility for groups of diverse learners. Only through group practice will educators be able to combine their talents and information and work together to meet the demands of student diversity in ways that retain the benefits of past practice but overcome its limitations.

Replace Restrictive Assignments With Shared Assignments

Current teacher licensure practices tend to be restrictive, limiting the students an educator can teach to specific categories. Of course, some of these categories are broader than others, ranging from specific disabilities (LD or MR certifications for learning disabilities and mental retardation, respectively) to "levels" of students (mild, severe) to disability types and particular ages (secondary severe, or elementary LD). One key feature of mixed-ability group teaching practice, particularly as we await changes in certification requirements to reflect the restructuring of schools, is that teachers share working with all children and youth as part of a team, regardless of their formal preparation or the labels on their certification. We think this step critical because it is one of the most efficient ways for teachers more narrowly educated to "cross-pollinate," quickly increasing the size of their common ground. More important, shared assignments create the contexts in which genuine collaboration can occur.

We have encountered a number of schools pursuing group practice through shared assignments. A common first step among special educators is to assign various special education support staff within a building—resource room teacher, speech/language specialist, Title I teacher, previous self-contained classroom teacher—to a smaller number of classrooms where they can be responsible for students with all the labels they had each separately served across a much larger number of classrooms. Although the previous resource room teacher may feel unprepared to assist the student with significant multiple disabilities, learning how to gather that information from colleagues with different specialties is a "step on the way" to more complete group practice with general educators.

Other schools we know are beginning to create work groups that include some number of general educators as well as one or more special educators and other certified or classified support staff. During the 1996–1997 school year, South Valley Elementary School, with which we have a long-standing collaborative relationship, reorganized into three smaller "vertical" communities. Each included classroom teachers from kindergarten to grade 5 as well as a special educator and a number of classroom assistants previously assigned to either special education or Title I. These new groups began to construct the kinds of working relationships that supported their various efforts to change their teaching practices, improve literacy, experiment with multiple intelligences theory, and develop better student assessment systems for what they actually teach. New roles developed almost immediately for the special educators as members of the work groups.

Personnel preparation programs are reflecting a transition to group practice as well. More gradually, but increasingly, initial preparation programs are merging foundational general and special education content and licensure outcomes. Some states are simultaneously shifting from restrictive, "stand alone" licensure categories to a greater emphasis on "add on" endorsements to initial, usually broader, licenses. Innovative continuing professional development opportunities also encourage shared general and special educators to study collaboratively with preservice students as they pursue continuing professional development and specialization (e.g., Baumgart & Ferguson, 1991; Ferguson, 1994; Ferguson & Ralph, 1999; Goodlad, 1990). In this way, the directions of ongoing professional development can be determined by the needs of a particular group or school to "round out" or increase some area of capacity, say, in designing behavioral and emotional supports or extending their use of technology.

FROM A FOCUS ON TEACHING TO A FOCUS ON LEARNING

Historically we have cared most about what students *know*. Teachers must "cover" content, making sure that as many students as possible remember it all. We've assured ourselves that our schools are doing well through the scores students achieve on tests that measure their acquisition of this content—at least until the test is over. Much teacher work has involved introducing new material, giving students various opportunities to practice remembering that content, and assuring all of us of their success by frequently testing their memory and mastery in preparation for the official achievement assessments.

The confluence of demands upon schools as we begin exploring the largely unknown demands of a new century is gradually shifting educators' focus away from what gets taught to what gets learned and used. Elementary and secondary teachers everywhere are beginning to experiment with new curricular and teaching approaches that emphasize students' mastery not just of facts and content but also of essential thinking skills like problem solving, analysis, collaboration, and experimentation. Rather than merely measuring what students have remembered about what we've taught, educators are just as interested in how students can demonstrate that they understand and can use whatever they've learned in school and in their various pursuits outside of school. Many promising curricular and instructional approaches are emerging in general education. Some teachers, for example, design learning unique to each student through the logic of multiple intelligences and learning styles. Learning is increasingly active, requiring students not just to listen but also to learn by doing. Teachers are turning to projects, exhibitions, portfolios, along with other kinds of curriculum-based information and measurement strategies, to understand what students have learned and can do with their learning (e.g., Darling-Hammond, Ancess, & Falk, 1995; Fogarty, 1996; Goodwin, 1997; Harmin, 1994; Neill, 1997; Valencia, Hiebert, & Afflerbach, 1994).

STANDARDS? OR STANDARDIZATION?

There is great confusion among teachers about the role of *higher national standards* for learning and the incorporation of diverse learning agendas and accomplishments (Gagnon, 1995; McLaughlin, 1995b; Oregon Department of Education, 1996, Reigeluth, 1997). Does "standard" mean standardization in the sense that every student accomplishes exactly the same thing to the same picture of mastery, performance, or other measurement? If so, how can any standard accommodate diverse students—especially students with disabilities? If the call for higher national standards means that children really excel—push themselves to do, know, understand just a little more than they thought they could—then how can we compare the achievement of high standards from one student to the next, let alone from one school, one district, or one state to the next?

Our work with schools suggests that the entire standards discussion is confusing the requirements of program evaluation—*that is, how well are our schools helping the students collectively to achieve our articulated standards of learning accomplishment?*—with teacher, student, and parent needs for individual student evaluation—*how is Sarah accomplishing our articulated standards of learning accomplishment? And how does that make sense for her?* Within any group of students, learning accomplishment for some proportion of the group will not necessarily look or be exactly the same as that for others in the group. In fact, it would be very surprising if there weren't several different patterns of accomplishment in any group of students.

Finding a way to legitimize that some students in any group can accomplish a "standard" in different ways is at the heart of the standards dilemma. If "accomplishment" can mean different things for different students—certainly a logical outcome of the individually tailored curriculum and teaching practices being encouraged—then the various student accomplishments are difficult to "add up" in any straightforward way. Yet adding up accomplishments against a single defined standard is the essential requirement of program assessment. If everyone is achieving the standards in different ways, how can we know how well our schools are doing collectively?

We think this dilemma is possible to resolve if the requirements of program assessment are separated from the requirements of student assessment. Each student and his or her parents should receive individual feedback about how well the student is learning, how much growth she or he has accomplished during some period of time, and how his or her accomplishments compare with the national or community standard established for our students as a group. However, discretion must be possible in letting any individual student know how he or she is compared with others.

FROM "FIXING" TO JOINING GENERAL EDUCATION

The very notion of an inclusion specialist is predicated upon the idea that general educators simply do not know how to teach students with disabilities and that we special educators must teach them our special knowledge. We have argued here that this idea is fundamentally flawed—many general educators do know a lot about teaching students who are different, even disabled, when given the chance. We've also suggested that the expectation that special educators will pass on their knowledge, thereby risking their future as educators, is equally flawed. Our proposal to think instead of "mixed-ability groups of teachers," each with different specialties to contribute to the teaching of very diverse groups of students, is one way to integrate the uniqueness of the previous separate "general" and "special" educators into a single, multitalented teaching corps. We need schools that benefit from the experience of both general and special educators in the design and accomplishment of student learning. We hope to contribute to an effort to shift from our tendencies to frame issues and understanding as "either/or" to a new tendency to seek "both/and."

REFERENCES

Astuto, T. A., Clark, D. L., Read, A., McGree, K., & deKoven Pelton Fernancez, L. (1994). *Roots of reform: Challenging the assumptions that control change in education.* Bloomington, IN: Phi Delta Kappa Educational Foundation.

Baker, E. T., Wang, M., & Walberg, H. J. (1994). The effects of inclusion on learning. *Educational Leadership, 52*(4), 33–35.

Baumgart, D., & Ferguson, D. L. (1991). Personnel preparation: Directions for the future. In L. Meyer, C. Peck, and L. Brown (Eds.), *Critical issues in the lives of people with severe disabilities* (pp. 313–352), Baltimore: Paul H. Brookes.

Berres, M., Knoblock, D. L., Ferguson, D., & Wood, C. (1996). *Creating tomorrow's schools today: Stories of inclusion, change and renewal.* New York: Teachers College Press.

Biklen, D., Ferguson, D. L., & Ford, A. (Eds.). (1989). *Schooling and disability. Eighty-eighth yearbook of the National Society for the Study of Education, Part II.* Chicago, IL: University of Chicago Press and The National Society for the Study of Education.

Cameron, S. (1994). *What is an inclusion specialist? A preliminary investigation.* Unpublished master's project, University of Oregon, Eugene.

Carnevale, A. D., Gainer, L. J., & Meltzer, A. S. (1990). *Workplace basics: The skills employers want.* San Francisco: Jossey-Bass.

Center for Policy Research on the Impact of General and Special Education Reform. (1996). *Standards-based school reform and students with disabilities.* Alexandria, VA: U.S. Department of Education.

Conley, D. T. (1993). *Roadmap to restructuring: Policies, practices and the emerging visions of schooling.* Eugene: ERIC Clearing House on Educational Management, University of Oregon.

Darling-Hammond, L., Ancess, J., & Falk, B. (1995). *Authentic assessment in action: Studies of schools and students at work.* New York: Teachers College Press.

Darling-Hammond, L., & Falk, B. (1997). Using standards and assessments to support student learning, *Phi Delta Kappan, 79*(3), 190–99.

Davis, C., & Ferguson, D. L. (1992). Trying something completely different: Report of a collaborative research venture. In P. Ferguson, D. Ferguson, & S. Taylor (Eds.), *Interpreting disability: A qualitative reader.* New York: Teachers College Press.

Davis, S. (1994). *1994 Update on inclusion in education of children with mental retardation.* Arlington, TX: The Arc of the United States.

Dover, W. (1994). *The inclusion facilitator video.* Manhattan, KS: The MASTER Teacher.

Eisner, E. (1991). What really counts in schools. *Educational Leadership, 48*(5), 10–17.

Ferguson, D. L. (1994). Is it inclusion yet? Bursting the bubbles. In M. Berres, D. Knoblock, D. L. Ferguson, & C. Woods (Eds.), *Creating tomorrow's schools today: Stories of inclusion, change, and renewal* (pp. 16–37). New York: Teachers College Press.

160 Inclusive Teaching

Ferguson, D. L. (1995). The real challenge of inclusion: Confessions of a "rabid inclu-
sionist." *Phi Delta Kappan, 77*(4), 281–287.
Ferguson, D. L., Meyer, G., Jeanchild, L., Juniper, L., & Zingo, J. (1993). Figuring out what
    to do with grownups: How teachers make inclusion "work" for students with dis-
    abilities. *Journal of the Association for Persons With Severe Handicaps, 17*(4), 218–226.
Ferguson, D. L., & Ralph, G. (1996). The changing role of special educators: A develop-
    ment waiting for a trend. *Contemporary Education, 68*(1), 49–51.
Ferguson, D. L., & Ralph, G. (1999). *Building capacity for sustainable change: Final report.*
    Eugene: Schools Projects, Specialized Training Program, University of Oregon.
Ferguson, D., Ralph, G., Katul, N., & Cameron, S. (in review). What's becoming of the
    special educator? *Journal of the Association for Persons With Severe Handicaps.*
Fogarty, T. (1996). Getting reform right: What works and what doesn't. *Phi Delta Kappan,*
    74, 745–752.
Fullan, M. G. (1996). Turning systemic thinking on its head. *Phi Delta Kappan, 77*(6), 420–
    423.
Gagnon, P. (1995). What should children learn? *The Atlantic Monthly, 276*(6), 65–79.
Gallagher, J. (1994). The pull of societal forces on special education. *Journal of Special*
    Education, 27, 521–530.
Gandal, M. (1995). Not all standards are created equal. *Educational Leadership, 52*(6), 16–
    21.
Givner, C. C., & Haager, D. (1995). Strategies for effective collaboration. In M. A. Falvey
    (Ed.), *Inclusive and heterogeneous schooling: Assessment, curriculum, and instruction*
    (pp. 41–57). Baltimore: Paul H. Brookes.
Goodlad, J. (1990). *Teachers for our nation's schools.* San Francisco: Jossey-Bass.
Goodlad, J., & Lovitt, T. (Eds.). (1993). *Integrating general and special education.* New York:
    Merrill.
Goodwin, A. L. (Ed.) (1997). *Assessment for equity and inclusion: Embracing all our chil-*
    dren. New York: Routledge.
Goodwin, T. C., & Wurzburg, G. (1993). *Educating Peter.* New York: Ambrose Video.
Harmin, M. (1994). *Inspiring active learning: A handbook for teachers.* Alexandria, VA:
    Association for Supervision and Curriculum Development.
Janney, R. E., & Snell, M. E. (1997). How teachers include students with moderate and
    severe disabilities in elementary classes: The means and the meaning of inclusion.
    Journal of the Association for Persons With Severe Handicaps, 22(3), 159–169.
Katul, N. (1995). *Inclusion specialists: Are they really fostering inclusion?* Unpublished
    master's project, University of Oregon, Eugene.
Keller, N., & Cravedi-Cheng, L. (1995). Voice of inclusion: Developing a shared voice—
    yours, mine, and ours. In R. Villa & J. S. Thousand (Eds.), *Creating an inclusive*
    school (pp. 80–86). Alexandria, VA: Association for Supervision and Curriculum
    Development.
Lieberman, L. M. (1996). Preserving special education . . . For those who need it. In
    W. Stainback & S. Stainback (Eds.), *Controversial issues confronting special education:*
    Divergent perspectives (2nd edition, pp. 16–27). Needham Heights, MA: Allyn & Bacon.
Lipsky, D. K., & Gartner, A. (1997). *Inclusion and school reform: Transforming America's*
    classrooms. Baltimore: Paul H. Brookes.
McDonnell, L. M., & McLaughlin, M. J. (Eds.). (1997). *Educating one and all: Students with*
    disabilities and standards-based reform. Washington, DC: National Academy Press.

McLaughlin, M. J. (1995a). Defining special education: A response to Zigmond and Baker. *Journal of Special Education, 29*(2), 200–208.

McLaughlin, M. J. (1995b). *Improving education through standards-based reform.* A report by the National Academy of Education Panel on Standards-Based Education Reform. Stanford, CA: The National Academy of Education.

McMackin, M. C., & Bukowieck, E. M. (1997). A change in focus: Teaching diverse learners within an inclusive elementary school classroom. *Equity & Excellence in Education, 30*(1), 32–39.

National Association of State Boards of Education. (1995). *Winning ways: Creating inclusive schools, classrooms and communities.* Alexandria, VA: Author.

Neil, D. M. (1997). Transforming student assessment. *Phi Delta Kappan, 79*(1), 34–40, 58.

New York Partnership for Statewide Systems Change Project. (1994). *Inclusion in New York: An inside view.* Syracuse: New York State Education Department.

Oregon Department of Education, Office of Assessment and Evaluation. (1996). *Performance Standards.* Salem: Author.

O'Shea, D. J., & O'Shea, L. J. (1998). Learning to include: Lessons learned from a high school without special education services. *Teaching Exceptional Children, 31*(1), 40–48.

Pugach, M. C. (1995). On the failure of imagination in inclusive schooling. *Journal of Special Education, 29*(2), 212–223.

Pugach, M. C., & Seidl, B. (1995). From exclusion to inclusion in urban schools: A new case for teacher education reform. *Teacher Education, 27*(4), 379–95.

Putnam, J., Spiegel, A., & Bruininks, R. (1995). Future directions in education and inclusion of students with disabilities: A Delphi investigation. *Council for Exceptional Children, 61*(1), 553–576.

Rainforth, B., & England, J. (1997). Collaborations for inclusion. *Education and Treatment of Children, 20*(1), 85–104.

Reigeluth, C. M. (1997). Educational standards: To standardize or to customize learning? *Phi Delta Kappan, 79*(3), 202–206.

Rogers, J. (1993). The inclusion revolution. *Phi Delta Kappa: Research Bulletin, 5*(11), 1–6.

Sailor, W., Gee, K., & Karasoff, P. (1993). Full inclusion and school restructuring. In M. E. Snell (Ed.), *Instruction of students with severe disabilities* (4th ed.) (pp. 1–37). New York: Merrill.

Sarason, S. (1990). *The predictable failure of educational reform.* San Francisco: Jossey-Bass.

Sarason, S. B. (1995). *School change: The personal development of a point of view.* New York: Teachers College Press.

Skrtic, T. M. (1991). *Behind special education: A critical analysis of professional culture and school organization.* Denver, CO: Love.

Skrtic, T. M. (1995). *Disability and democracy: Reconstructing (special) education for postmodernity.* New York: Teachers College Press.

Snell, M. E. (1998). Characteristics of elementary school classrooms where children with moderate and severe disabilities are included: A compilation of findings. In S. J. Vitello & D. E. Mithaug (Eds.), *Inclusive schooling: National and international perspectives* (pp. 76–97). Mahwah, NJ: Lawrence Erlbaum.

Stainback, W., & Stainback, S. (1990). The support facilitator at work. In W. Stainback & S. Stainback (Eds.), *Support networks for inclusive schools: Interdependent integrated education.* Baltimore: Paul H. Brookes.

Stainback, S., Stainback, W., & Harris, K. (1989). Support facilitation: An emerging role for special educators. *Teacher Education and Special Education, 12*(4), 148–153.

Tashie, C., Shapiro-Barnard, S., Dillon, A., Schuh, M., Jorgensen, D., & Nisbet, J. (1993). *Changes in latitudes, changes in attitudes: The role of the inclusion facilitator.* Concord: Institute on Disability/University Affiliated Program, University of New Hampshire.

Thompson, B. (Executive Producer), Ciersdorff, M. (Producer/Director), Bradley, P., and Ault, M. M. (Associate Producer). (1991). *A circle of inclusion* [Videotape]. Lawrence: University of Kansas.

U. S. Department of Education. (1997). *To assure the free appropriate public education of all children with disabilities: 19th annual report to Congress on the implementation of the Individuals With Disabilities Education Act.* Washington, DC: Author.

Valencia, S. W., Hiebert, E. H., & Afflerbach, P. P. (Eds.). (1994). *Authentic reading assessment: Practices and possibilities.* Newark, NJ: International Reading Association.

Van Dyke, R., Stallings, M. A., & Colley, K. (1995). How to build an inclusive school community: A success story. *Phi Delta Kappan, Inc., 76*(6), 475–479.

Villa, R. A., & Thousand, J. S. (Eds.). (1995). *Creating an inclusive school.* Alexandria, VA: Association for Supervision and Curriculum Development.

Warger, C. L., & Pugach, M. C. (1996). Forming partnerships around curriculum. *Association for Supervision and Curriculum Development, 53*(5), 62–65.

Wasley, P. A. (1994). *Stirring the chalk dust: Tales of teachers changing classroom practice.* New York: Teachers College Press.

Waters, T., Burger, D., & Burger, S. (1995). Moving up before moving on. *Educational Leadership, 52*(6), 35–40.

Werts, M. G., Wolery, M., Snyder, E. D., & Caldwell, N. K. (1996). Teachers' perceptions of the supports critical to the success of inclusion programs. *Journal of the Association for Persons With Severe Handicaps, 21*(1), 9–21.

Wood, M. (1998). Whose job is it anyway? Educational roles in inclusion. *Exceptional Children, 64*(2), 181–195.

Zigmond, N. (1995). An exploration of the meaning and practice of special education in the context of full inclusion of students with learning disabilities. *Journal of Special Education, 29*(2), 109–115.

CHAPTER 10

From Isolation to Collaboration: Learning from Effective Partnerships Between General and Special Educators

Jennifer York-Barr and Robi Kronberg

In many school communities nationwide, teachers are working together more closely, teaching and learning in their shared work of facilitating the development of today's young people. Increasingly, the traditional school culture of isolation is giving way to a culture of collaboration. Why are collaborative relationships becoming more prevalent and why now? Perhaps the most compelling reason is that today's student population is increasingly diverse and their lives more complex. Diversity and complexity require more varied perspectives on and approaches to creating relevant and successful educational experiences (Gomez, 1994). Establishing effective collaborative relationships among educators provides the communication channels through which varied perspectives and knowledge can be shared. Relationships in organizations are an essential pathway for learning (Wheatley, 1999). Schools must become learning communities—for adults and children—in which collaboration is the dominant cultural norm.

The chapters in this book have shown how over the past 25 years, since passage of Public Law 94-142 (reauthorized as the Individuals With Disabilities Education Act, or IDEA), relationships between general and special educators have progressed from a parallel and relatively separate existence to shared instructional responsibility for students in heterogeneous general education classrooms. Johnson and Pugach (1996) offer the perspective that a new wave of collaboration is emerging in schools. They state,

> In this third wave [of collaboration], special educators must expand efforts to include reforming the broader educational system so that it is increasingly responsive to diversity . . . a collaborative orientation in which all members of the school work together and are collectively accountable for the program of all students. (p. 201)

This perspective asserts a valuable and expanded role for special educators in general education school improvement. It implies an expanded role for general educators as well. It requires shared vision and responsibility by all educators to create learning environments in which all students learn well. In Chapter 1 of this book, Sailor describes the current phase of inclusive education as involving local decision making about resource allocation to improve the quality of education for all students. There is no more important resource than the teachers themselves. How this vital resource is allocated and supported does, indeed, make a profound difference in practice. Strengthening instructional partnerships among educators with varied backgrounds and experiences has the potential to unleash the energy and expertise required to create extraordinarily effective educational experiences.

There is an abundance of literature that provides a compelling rationale for collaboration, presents step-by-step strategies for engaging in collaborative practices, and describes skills that promote collaboration (Dettmer, Thurston, & Dyck, 1996; Evans, 1991; Friend & Cook, 1992; Johnson & Johnson, 1994; Morsink, Thomas, & Correa, 1991; Pugach & Johnson, 1995). Why, then, has collaboration remained so elusive? Certainly the stronghold of isolated school cultures is not easily undone. Insufficient resources for staff learning are a factor. A more subtle and less talked about reason involves the personal realities of undergoing substantial shifts in professional practice.

Only recently has increased attention been paid to the highly personal process of changing from isolated to collaborative practice (Arnold, Gombos, Truex, & York-Barr, 1998; Salend et al., 1997). Making the transition to new ways of doing, thinking, and being is difficult. Facing changes in practice can evoke feelings of uncertainty, and even fear, resulting in holding on to what is familiar and comfortable (Tertel, Klein, & Jewett, 1998), even when prospects for improvement are great. For most educators, the emotional stakes around relationships with students and issues of teaching and learning are high. The process of transition is personal and involves loss as well as opportunity. Transitioning to something new starts with an ending—leaving old realities, old identities, old familiarity behind (Bridges, 1991). In a study of teachers who made a transition from teaching in a self-contained wing to supporting students in inclusive classrooms, one special educator stated:

> We cried. We still need to occasionally get together to connect. We all shared this common goal and then we went out and it was important for us to become part of the new school. . . . We were leaving something we were used to and very comfortable with to something better for kids. Yet, for us personally, we needed to maintain those relationships with people who had been friends. (York-Barr, Schultz, Doyle, Kronberg, & Crossett, 1996, p. 98)

Special educators have commented about feeling loss of control of schedules, curricular content, and instructional strategies. Some special and general educators mourn the loss or change in their relationships with students. One general educator shared,

> I would never go back to serving kids that old way, but one thing I will always miss is the level of intimacy I had with my students when it was just me and my 30 students in my classroom.

By recognizing loss as an inherent part of the transition process, educators may feel some assurance that their feelings and experiences are a normal part of moving to new ways of thinking, being, and doing. Understanding may also result in a conscious effort to be aware of and embrace the emerging possibilities and positive realities for themselves and for their students. Understanding also has implications for how teachers are supported in their process of reflecting on current practices, considering changes in their practice, and moving forward to implement changes in practice.

In this chapter, we share a true story about general and special educators moving from isolated to collaborative instructional practices in inclusive classrooms. We offer our perspectives on why the instructional partnerships were initiated and why they have been maintained. We emphasize the personal transitions in the process of change and the central importance of building effective professional relationships. Later in the chapter, we highlight some of the shifts in purpose, roles, and structures experienced by special educators.

The general and special educators in the story created their own ways of joining together to form instructional partnerships in order to more effectively promote student learning in the context of general education classrooms. Significant in the story are the centrality of the professional relationships that developed among the teaching partners and their focus on students and student learning. The story features a middle school (grades 5–8) in which general-educator/special-educator instructional partnerships were initially formed to support students with severe disabilities who were included in general education classrooms. The partnerships, using a cross-categorical approach to service provision, expanded to support all students with IEPs. In this school, the instructional partnerships challenged the dominant culture norms of isolated work. Responsibility for students became shared. Instructional repertoires were expanded. Teaching styles emerged as complementary. Collaborative practice became commonplace and was viewed as a source of instructional improvement and professional growth.

STORY OF A MIDDLE SCHOOL

Several years ago, the principal and special education team at Norquist Middle School were informed that students with severe disabilities who had been included in general education classrooms in an elementary school (grades K–4) in the district would soon be making the transition to the middle school. Norquist Middle School was a grades 5–8 school and enrolled about 800 students. It was located in a medium-sized town in central Minnesota. The year before the transition of the elementary students was to occur, the middle school staff was presented with an opportunity to participate in a university-sponsored project to develop inclusive models of special education service provision. The principal and other key personnel decided to join in a formal partnership with the university-based team.

Planning, Preparation, and Transition

An inclusion team (referred to as the I-Team), comprised of general and special educators and facilitated by project staff from the university, was established to plan for the transition of the targeted fourth graders with disabilities from the elementary to the middle school. Because educating students with moderate to severe disabilities in general education classes was a new experience for the middle school staff, a multifaceted transition plan was created that focused on supporting both students and staff. The I-Team met four times in the spring of the school year before the students would arrive at Norquist Middle School.

A number of supports for the transition were put in place. In the spring, fifth- and sixth-grade middle school teachers visited the elementary school to meet the students and staff and to observe the students in their classroom settings. Representatives of the sending elementary teams and the receiving middle school teams also met to exchange information about students and about classroom and school expectations. Individual student profiles were completed on each identified student and on most of the other transitioning fourth graders as well. Profiles included information about interests, strengths, abilities, and challenges. Middle school staff was available to respond to fourth graders' questions about fifth grade and about attending the middle school.

Transition supports also occurred just before school started in the fall and during the first few weeks of school. The week before school was to begin, all staff involved with fifth and sixth graders convened for a day to review why the students with disabilities would be included in general education and how the staff might work together to support the students and each other. The principal had an instrumental role during this session. He took this opportunity to share with his staff his view that the move toward greater inclusion of students with disabilities was complementary to the school-wide vision and values. He shared the following values and assumptions intended to guide his school's practices for students with disabilities:

- *School community*—The starting place for each student with disabilities will be the regular classroom. No matter where students are eventually educated throughout the day, all students are full members of the school community.

- *Process to help students learn and thrive*—Special education service delivery will be developed by determining what makes sense one student at a time. A fluid problem-solving process will be used as we create plans where each student can learn and thrive within the school community.
- *Special education is a service, not a place*—Students don't "go to" special education. The level of support for each student is based upon his or her needs determined in context of the school community.
- *Knowledge of students' goals*—Teachers have to know what the students with special needs are accomplishing in their classrooms.
- *Efficient, creative program*—We seek creative service delivery for students with disabilities that is also efficient. The 1 : 1 assignment of instructional assistants to students will no longer take place as instructional assistants are assigned to the building. Their daily tasks will be based upon the needs of students and assigned by the special education teachers and principal.

The principal was integrally involved throughout the planning and implementation of inclusive educational services at the middle school. He maintained a constant presence at planning meetings, student study team meetings, and I-Team meetings. He provided a clear and consistent voice of support for inclusive practices, "With restructuring we're thinking about the whole child. With inclusion, kids learn in context of their whole lives. Philosophically, it makes sense."

During the first 2 weeks of school, each classroom that included a student with severe disabilities had an additional adult available to assist and to informally assess the initial inclusion experiences. Additional adult coverage in each classroom was possible because related services personnel, in addition to paraprofessionals and special educators, were utilized. Classroom team meetings were held 2 weeks into the school year to share information about how the students were doing in the classroom, to identify specific and individually appropriate learning objectives and instructional strategies, and to talk about how and when team members should communicate with one another.

Implementation Year 1

During the first year of inclusion at the middle school, the students with moderate to severe disabilities were physically present in general education classes for almost all of the school day. Identification of relevant learning outcomes and the implementation of appropriate instructional support varied from student to student. As the year went along, general educators, special educators, and parents indicated they were generally pleased (some were surprised) with the progress made by most of the students with IEPs. Only a few general educators questioned the effectiveness of inclusive placements, usually citing concerns about cost, appropriateness given ability levels, and potentially negative effects on students without disabilities.

Special educator caseloads remained categorical. This meant that each special educator had students in just about every grade level and in many classrooms throughout the school. They spent most of their time moving throughout the building to check in with identified students, paraprofessionals, and general education classroom teachers. They felt fragmented and overwhelmed trying to support students, getting to know teachers, and learning about many classroom contexts throughout the school. General educators were confused about which special educator was attached to which students. The presence of a paraprofessional in the general education classroom was felt to be awkward, with questions emerging about responsibility for training and supervision.

At the end of the year, students were viewed as doing well and making progress in the inclusive model. The adults were frustrated and struggling with how to best meet the individual needs of students with disabilities in the context of the general education classroom. The combination of student progress but adult frustration resulted in a commitment to continue the pursuit of inclusive services but to consider alternative ways of working together.

After conversing about a number of alternative support and scheduling options, the teachers decided to shift from a categorical to a cross-categorical approach to providing special education services. It was felt that this would allow the special education staff to be more responsive in providing support to students, paraprofessionals, and teachers in the general education classrooms, to be more effective in designing adaptations in content of the classroom, and to engage in more consistent communication among service providers. With this approach, one special educator would be assigned to each grade level and would assume responsibility for implementation of IEPs to all students with IEPs at the respective grade level.

There were a number of variables that substantially influenced and supported the ultimate move toward a cross-categorical model of support: (a) frustration with the current delivery system; (b) willingness on the part of general educators to try a new delivery system; (c) release time in the spring of the first year for the special educators to design a service delivery system that met their specific needs; (d) the ongoing use of the I-Team to provide feedback relative to the redesigned service delivery system; and (e) two days of planning time in the summer to formalize the day-to-day implementation strategies. Each of these influences and supports is described more fully below.

Frustration With the Existing Service Delivery System

As mentioned previously, both general and special educators were dissatisfied with the way in which special education services were scheduled and delivered. It was extremely challenging for special educators to serve students effectively across multiple grade levels and classrooms. They had difficulty becoming familiar with the general education curriculum and communicating with the large number of adults who worked with the students on each of their caseloads. Special educators felt as if they were reacting to the most urgent needs of staff and students rather than proactively supporting the success of students in general education environments. End-of-the-year interviews held in May of the first year captured staff members' frustrations. The following comments convey some of the feelings of the special educators:

> It has been a tough year . . . having so many adults to work with. I'd like to be more of a team.

> Looking back at the year—that's why we changed, we knew there were difficulties.

> Finding time to meet with all the teachers and instructional assistants is frustrating.

General educators felt the categorical service delivery system was confusing and inadequate. Some had to communicate with up to four different special educators. Special educators were rarely available because they were spread throughout the entire building. General educators shared the following:

> About inclusion, I think it's a great idea but it was a struggle for me as a first year teacher. I was trying to get to know the curriculum. I had no idea what anyone else was going to do to help me. It was said that the special education teacher was going to help with plans and materials. I didn't see that much at all.

> There were so many different special education people assigned to the kids, sometimes you didn't know who to go to for help.

> We haven't had much communication with special education teachers.

> About working together for stuff like modifications—we have ideas but that's not our background. It took us a long time to get to the point of doing things that are different. We were really unsure. We needed their help.

At the conclusion of year 1, the shortcomings of a categorical approach to support inclusive student placements were readily apparent to all who had struggled through the first year of service delivery. The students, however, were perceived to be doing well in their general education environments. A sense of urgency existed to design a service delivery system in which special educators could support students and teachers more effectively in the inclusive general education environments.

Willingness of General Educators to Try a New Delivery System

Partly because of the frustration of receiving inadequate support from special education, the majority of general educators were willing to try a different way of meeting the needs of students with disabilities in their classrooms. In the year-end interviews, general educators expressed optimism and ideas for a better system of serving students:

> The special education teacher should be a part of the hub [a two or three member teaching team at a single grade level] or the grade level team and really work with us so that we know we can count on that person—making that person be part of our grade level. Then they can really know the curriculum.

> Maybe if a special educator was assigned to a hub, you could get rapport and know who to go to.

The interest on the part of general educators for including special educators as members of grade-level teams provided encouragement to the special education staff to consider service delivery options. Although both general and special educators were uncertain as to how expertise might be shared in general education classrooms and how the logistics of such an arrangement might work, they were hopeful and willing to try something different.

Release Time for the Special Educators

Committed to continuing the inclusive placements for students, but frustrated with the initial approach to service provision, the special educators met and identified the following outcomes of a redesigned service delivery system: (a) a more effective and efficient system for meeting the needs of students with disabilities; (b) better communication with general education staff; (c) greater flexibility with scheduling; and (d) less time spent in designing classroom adaptations.

The special educators came up with six possible approaches to providing services, then chose a cross-categorical model that allocated one full-time special educator each to fifth and sixth grades, one part-time special educator to the eighth grade classes housed off campus in a community site, and a part-time special educator to the seventh grade and the remainder of the eighth-grade classes housed at the middle school campus. The process by which special educators were assigned to specific grades included consideration of the needs of students with disabilities at each grade level and the categorical licensure area of each special educator. With the projected move to a cross-categorical system of service delivery, all special educators agreed to provide instructional support to any student on an IEP at their assigned grade level(s).

The Ongoing Use of the I-Team

Following the redesign session, the special educators met with members of the I-Team to share the projected cross-categorical service delivery plan. Because the I-Team had been an integral part of the inclusion efforts, it was natural that the I-Team be the vehicle for feedback relative to the redesign of the service delivery system. At its inception, 2 years earlier, the I-Team was designed to be a representative group of staff members who were interested in providing input about the implementation of inclusive practices at the middle school. The I-Team responses were captured as follows,

> This will be a positive step towards assisting a variety of students who need help.

> This feels like we are moving toward our goal. I like the idea of working with one person.

> With this model, adults will be better able to collaborate more effectively to support the efforts already underway.

Two Days of Planning Time in the Summer

Although the special educators were enthused about the potential of the cross-categorical service delivery system, they were apprehensive about certain aspects of the model, namely, whether they would be perceived by their general education colleagues as contributive members of a grade-level team, how they would schedule their time each day, and what their roles would be in the context of the general education classrooms. Special educators were also apprehensive about how proficient they would feel working with students whose educational needs were less familiar than those of students matching their area of categorical licensure.

Given the overall framework of the new service delivery system, two planning days in the summer provided an opportunity for the special educators to more finely tune their anticipated roles, responsibilities, and schedules. The special educators also clarified their philosophy relative to the cross-categorical model of service delivery. The philosophy was articulated as follows:

> We are part of a grade level team, with our primary focus being the enhancement of learning for special education students who are in the team. Our role will positively benefit all individuals involved. We will be using our special education expertise to facilitate the inclusion as well as social and academic success in the inclusive classroom environment.

Implementation Year 2 (Cross-Categorical)

With the shift to a cross-categorical approach to service provision, the special educators provided instructional support to any student on an IEP at the special educators' assigned grade levels. Realizing that it would take time and intentional effort to develop expertise supporting students with disabilities different from each teacher's licensure area, the special educators chose to retain formal "case manager" responsibilities for those students categorically matching the teachers' respective certification areas, regardless of students' grade placements. The grade-level special educator, however, was responsible for understanding the demands and opportunities for students in the general education context. They also developed the closest working relationships with the students and the teachers. Responsibility for communication with families and facilitation of IEP meetings was shared between the grade-level special educator and the "categorical" case manager. This joint responsibility for students necessitated that special educators maintain effective and consistent communication with one another. The shared responsibility also presented an urgent need for special educators to share their expertise, because their special education colleagues were working with some students whose teaching and learning needs were less familiar. A new sense of positive interdependency was created as special educators relied on each other for information, knowledge, and support to problem-solve a myriad of student-specific issues and challenges.

In addition to developing new strategies to better meet the educational and social needs of students on IEPs, the second year of inclusive efforts involved developing and maintaining collaborative adult-to-adult relationships. As each special educator formed new working relationships with members of the grade-level team, efforts were increasingly made to clarify roles and responsibilities within a framework of shared instructional responsibility for all students. Given the reduced number of classrooms with which to interact, working relationships were forged between general and special educators. In addition, the two full-time special educators (in grades 5 and 6) were able to block-schedule their time in general education classrooms (see Figure 10.1 for a sample schedule). This scheduling format allowed the special educators to be immersed in the classroom contexts for longer blocks of time. This facilitated learning about the general education curriculum and instruction and understanding both the opportunities for and demands on students with disabilities in general education classes. As contextual understanding increased and collaborative partnerships evolved, special educators were able to more effectively design and implement meaningful instructional supports for students and staff. They also began to engage in coteaching, provide short-term support to any student in need of intensive study skills, share expertise about specific learning strategies, and offer direction and instructional support as needed.

The initial year of implementing a cross-categorical approach to special education service provision was perceived positively by most of those involved; certainly it was regarded as more successful than the previous year. The year was not

Figure 10.1. Weekly Schedule for Special Educator Assigned to Fifth Grade (Eight Classrooms, Four Teams)

Monday	Tuesday	Wednesday	Thursday	Friday
Grade 5, Team B (2 classrooms)	Grade 5, Team A (2 classrooms)	Grade 5, Team C (2 classrooms)	Grade 5, Team D (2 classrooms)	Morning
				• Child study meeting
		10:00–10:45 Grade-level meeting		• Meet with all special educators to teach and learn from each other (cross-categorical support)
	1:10–1:40* Small group pullout in media center for math	Team C (continued)		Afternoon (flex time)
				• Back in classrooms
1:45–2:15** Study skills lab	1:45–2:15** Study skills lab	1:45–2:15** Study skills lab	1:45–2:15** Study skills lab	• Conference with individual students
				• Develop adaptations
Team B (continued)	Team A (continued)	Team C (continued)	Team D (continued)	• Refine instructional programs

*After providing integrated special education services in the general education classroom, the fifth-grade team decided to conduct a small pullout group for fifth-grade students experiencing significant challenges in math. This group was held once (sometimes twice) each week and led by the special educator assigned to the fifth-grade team.

**The Study Skills Lab was a 4-week session for small groups of fifth graders who needed extra assistance with study skills. This group was held 4 days a week and was led by the special educator assigned to the fifth-grade team.

without its challenges, however. Special educators, in particular, seemed to continually grapple with roles, responsibilities, and expectations. They articulated several challenges that remained at the end of the first year of implementing a cross-categorical approach to service provision: (a) maintaining proactive time for special educators to teach and learn from each other related to meeting the needs of students; (b) feeling less effective when working with unfamiliar types of student needs; (c) losing continuity with students across grade levels; (d) having less involvement with students who were on the special educator's case management list but not at that educator's assigned grade level; and (e) finding a collaborative role in certain classroom contexts. Each of these challenges is explored below.

Time to Teach and Learn From Each Other

The special educators proactively addressed the need for time to share their categorical expertise with one another by scheduling a consistent weekly time to meet (see Friday schedule in Figure 10.1). A 45-minute block of time was allocated every Friday after the special education team meeting and the Student Study Team (SST) meeting. The team meetings and the collaborative teaching and learning time were part of a larger afternoon block of time designed to create time for the special educators to complete paperwork, conduct assessments, participate in IEP meetings, communicate with families and relevant agencies, connect with itinerant service providers, or provide instructional support to students.

Despite the provision of weekly time to meet the anticipated need of teaching and learning from one another, it was consistently difficult for special educators to use this time in the manner in which it was intended. Although special educators needed to connect with one another to share challenges, seek input, and jointly brainstorm solutions, the allotted time for discussion was consistently usurped for other needs. Sometimes one or both team meetings ran late; other times a crisis in a classroom necessitated that a special educator give priority to the crisis rather than to the meeting time. Mostly, special educators said that the shared teaching and learning time never seemed as urgent as many of the daily demands present in the general education classrooms.

Working With Unfamiliar Types of Student Needs

Although the cross-categorical service delivery model reduced the number of general education classrooms and grade levels for each special educator, it increased the breadth of student needs on each special educator's caseload. Although attempts were made when assigning special educators to grade levels to align special education expertise, each special educator had students at her or his assigned grade level who had needs with which the special educator was less familiar. Feelings of diminished effectiveness were attributable to several sources: (a) Special educators did not have a multiyear history with some of the students and therefore did not know what kinds of instructional support were the most helpful; (b) special educators were less familiar with students whose disabilities were different from those the special educator had both training and experience to work with; and (c) special educators lacked a relationship with the families of some of the students.

Despite the difficulties in maintaining the weekly proactive time to teach and learn from each other, the special educators were able to provide informal support to one another via sharing materials, brainstorming solutions to challenging instructional issues, conducting tandem meetings and phone calls to parents, and providing moral support when times got rough. Toward mid-year, the special educators reported feeling more comfortable with meeting many of the students' needs.

Losing Continuity With Students Across Grade Levels

After implementing cross-categorical services for the first half of the school year, the special education staff began to discuss plans for the following year. Paramount in the discussion was whether all or some of the special educators would move to the next grade level along with the students on their caseload or remain at their current grade-level assignment and receive a new caseload. The special educators examined the advantages and disadvantages of each option.

Advantages of transitioning along with the students concerned the ability of special educators to maintain continuity with students. Special educators realized that it had taken them awhile to establish positive and informed teacher–learner relationships with the students, and they were reluctant to repeat the process with a new group of students. They also felt much more familiar with the instructional needs of individual students and worried that their successes would be lost as the students transitioned to yet another unfamiliar special educator. Special educators also verbalized their discomfort in losing the relationship with parents and family members that had been built throughout the year. In some instances, they felt that trust was just beginning to emerge between home and school.

Conversely, clear disadvantages to switching grade levels were articulated by the special educators. Relationships between special educators and their respective general education colleagues had taken time and effort to build. In several teams, roles were still emerging and trust was still tentative. Many general education teachers felt that they had worked out some of the early glitches of the team arrangements, had arranged their schedules to accommodate the special educator, and were gaining familiarity with what their special education team member had to contribute. For these and other reasons, general educators expressed a preference for maintaining continuity with the same special educator. Relative to their experience with similar adult teaming issues, special educators shared concerns about the energy that had been spent in becoming part of a team and said that when all of the factors were considered, it made more sense for special educators to remain at their assigned grade levels.

Special Educator as Case Manager

Despite the clear rationale as to why each special educator maintained case-management responsibilities for students matching his or her categorical licensure area in addition to being responsible for a grade-level caseload, all of the special educators found this dual role difficult. Primarily, the difficulty concerned the lack of time that a special educator spent with students whom they case-managed and who happened to be at a grade level different from the one assigned to the special educator. Given that the primary instructional responsibility fell to the special educator assigned to each student's grade level, the case manager was in a position to attend an IEP meeting in which he or she lacked direct involvement with the student and therefore felt less informed as to the needs of the student. This lack of direct involvement with some students also complicated communication between the case manager and students' families.

Finding a Collaborative Role

Given their history of playing autonomous roles, special and general educators initially found it difficult to create mutually satisfying collaborative roles. Over time, it became clear that some instructional styles had greater potential for enhancing shared roles in which both general and special educators felt contributive. In such classrooms, the teaching method incorporated a blend of large-group, small-group, and individual instruction as well as experiential activity-based instruction. In these classrooms, it became easier for the special educator to find a collaborative role for such teaching responsibilities as facilitating a small-group discussion, providing assistance to individual students, demonstrating an additional learning strategy to a heterogeneous group, or coteaching a lesson to the entire class.

The instructional style that favored a more didactic approach to learning resulted in classrooms in which the special educator found it difficult to create a role that was contributive to the learning of students, both with and without disabilities. In these classrooms, the special educators reported that they felt more like instructional assistants than they did equal teaching partners, and they also articulated feeling, at times, like guests in the classroom.

STORY CLOSING

Subsequent to the first year of implementing a cross-categorical approach to special education service provision, general and special educators and paraprofessionals have continually worked to refine and improve their collaborative practices. One grade-level team has been particularly innovative in designing a restructured approach that greatly maximizes the differing strengths and talents of staff and students. The planning and implementation done by this team is consistently guided by the question, *"What's best for the kids?"* Evident in this team are the commitment to meeting the needs of all students, the enthusiasm derived from working collaboratively, and the constant sense of personal renewal and professional growth. As so aptly described by one of the educators on the team, "It's better for the kids and it's fun for us. We can figure it out together."

LEARNING FROM NORQUIST MIDDLE SCHOOL

When we reflect on the process and changes that occurred at Norquist Middle School, several important lessons about supporting implementation of new practices become apparent. Specific insights about changing from isolated to collaborative practices between general and special educators emerge as well. Following are the authors' perspectives about why and how the individuals in this collaborative partnership initially became involved in the change efforts and why their involvement sustained itself over time.

What Initiated the Changes Toward More Collaborative Practice?

In this school, *increasing student diversity* was the primary factor that initiated consideration of changes in current practice. Teachers at the middle school had increasing numbers of students who were experiencing academic challenges. A second contributing factor can be thought of as *internal capacity*. First, each building had an administrator who was interested in exploring more collaborative approaches to service provision between general and special educators. Second, the faculty included teachers who were willing to consider alternative approaches to meeting the needs of a more diverse student population. A third contributing factor for initiation was the synchronous (and voluntary) opportunity to take advantage of *external support* from a nearby university. Support from the university project team included a part-time lead facilitator for each building, money for release of staff, and knowledge that had been gained through experience in providing inclusive special education services in other schools.

We argue that the three contributing factors identified here—*student diversity, internal capacity, and external support*—had a cumulative effect in moving staff at the school toward considering changes in service provision. Absence of any one factor may have yielded significantly different results. For example, it is unlikely that the school teams would have accepted external support unless the specific support offered aligned with their particular internal needs.

How Were Changes Maintained?

When we consider why the changes in practice were maintained and continued to evolve, at least four factors emerge as significant. First, the teachers believed that students benefited from the changes in practice. Teachers also viewed themselves as contributing to student success. Second, relationships among teachers became mutually supportive and enjoyable. The instructional partnerships became a source of continuous professional development. Third, the teachers had ownership and power in the process. External partners intentionally adopted a facilitative rather than a directive role. Even when options for service design were introduced by the external partners, the teachers were the central decision makers when deciding on and tailoring the specific approach they would implement. They also assumed a lead role in making adjustments when needs arose during implementation. Finally, building and central office administrators were supportive, if not enthusiastic, about the movement toward greater instructional collaboration between general and special educators.

Reflections on Shifting Purpose, Roles, and Structures

The shift from isolated to collaborative and inclusive practices involves substantial changes in how educators view their purposes and their professional roles and contributions. In effect, the meaning of work shifts, sometimes substantially. Also affected are the structures in which they are accustomed to operating on a daily basis, including how and where time is scheduled, how instruction is provided, and what skills and competencies are required. Both general and special educators experience these shifts. Special educators, however, seem especially impacted in the move from isolated to collaborative practice.

As special educators move toward more inclusive and collaborative service provision models, they undergo many changes that can be experienced as loss. They work in another person's turf—physical, curricular, and instructional. They frequently interact less with special education colleagues because their days are spent in the mainstream, moving among classrooms. Their relationships with special education students can become less direct. Certainly they lose a significant amount of instructional control as they work to integrate individualized instructional approaches into the general education context. These changes can lead them to question their purpose, role, significance, and competence, until they begin to establish new relationships and come to understand their contributions to the new work setting. A new set of opportunities can then be recognized: opportunities to know how students function in a richer context surrounded by a wide range of peers; opportunities to make a direct impact on the instructional environment in which students spend most of their school days; opportunities to develop relationships with and learn from general educators; opportunities to be involved with and affect many students, not just those with disabilities; and opportunities to learn about the larger context of mainstreamed-education life and to assume a greater presence and influence therein. The Chinese symbol for change has two parts, one of which represents crisis and one of which represents opportunity. The change from isolated to collaborative practice creates both crisis and opportunity. Table 10.1 reflects some of the changes or shifts

Table 10.1. Changes Experienced by Special Educators Moving From Isolated to Collaborative and Inclusive Practices

	Isolated Practice	*Collaborative Practice*
MEANING AND PURPOSE *(Why?)*	Teach some students	Support some students
	Prepare students for regular class, school, community life	Maximize meaningful student participation in regular class; prepare for life in an integrated world
	Focus on academic skills	Focus on academic skills, learning strategies, social competence, self-esteem
ROLES AND CONTRIBUTIONS *(What?)*	Provide services to students with IEPs	Provide services and support to all students
	Provide categorical special education services	Provide cross-categorical special education services
	Remediate deficits	Compensate for deficits; build from strengths to enhance participation and success in integrated context
	Teach alone	Teach together, modeling teamwork
	Make autonomous curricular and instructional decisions	Collaborate in making curricular and instructional decisions
STRUCTURE, SCHEDULE, SKILLS *(How?)*	Work in a separate space, isolated from general educators	Work in a shared classroom on a teaching team
	Schedule time with special education students	Schedule time with classrooms of students
	Provide individual or small-group instruction to homogeneous group of students	Provide whole class, small-group, individual instruction to many students with varied needs
	Follow a prescribed separate curriculum	Know and flexibly adapt from the regular curriculum
		Develop competence as a collaborator

in meaning, purpose, roles and contributions, and structures experienced by special educators.

CONCLUSION

A growing number of educators are realizing the potential of collaborative partnerships, especially when working with diverse student populations in schools where the value of inclusivity is embraced. Partnerships between general educators and special educators are just one of the many types of collaborative relationships emerging in today's schools. Pugach (1995) asserts that the benefits of such partnerships can and should extend far beyond individual students with IEPs. She promotes a *generative* approach, as opposed to an *additive* approach, to inclusive schooling. She explains that in most schools, inclusion has been *additive*, meaning that students with disabilities have been *added to* general education classrooms, and then a personalized set of curricular, instructional, and social adaptations have been put in place around individually "included" students. With an *additive approach*, there is little or no impact on the curricular, instructional, or social realities for other students in the class. In contrast, a *generative* approach to inclusive schooling results in substantial change in the general education environment. Existing assumptions about teaching and learning are challenged. New approaches to curriculum and instruction are created to maximize learning for students with a wide range of interests, experiences, and potential. New knowledge about effective instruction emerges from within the complex realities of today's classrooms and schools. Collaborative partnerships can provide an invaluable energy source for effective teaching and learning. The collaborative partnerships and instructional practices evidenced in the story in this chapter provide examples of movement toward a more generative approach to inclusive schooling.

ACKNOWLEDGMENTS

We extend our gratitude to the educators and students in the Cambridge-Isanti school district in Minnesota who provided us with the opportunity to learn about creating effective collaborative partnerships. Your openness to our participation and documentation is deeply appreciated. Thank you.

Development of this chapter was supported in part by Grant #H086R40012, Creating Capacities Within Inclusive Schools, awarded to the Institute on Community Integration at the University of Minnesota by the United States Department of Education, Office of Special Education and Rehabilitative Services. This chapter does not necessarily reflect the position of the United States Department of Education and no official endorsement should be inferred.

REFERENCES

Arnold, K., Gombos, S., Truex, S., & York-Barr, J. (1998). Case study: Collaboration in two multiage classrooms. In R. Kronberg & J. York-Barr (Eds.), *Differentiated teaching and learning in heterogeneous classrooms* (pp. 59–80). Minneapolis: University of Minnesota, Institute on Community Integration.

Bridges, W. (1991). *Managing transitions: Making the most of changes.* New York: Addison-Wesley.

Dettmer, P., Thurston, L. P., & Dyck, N. (1996). *Consultation, collaboration, teamwork for students with special needs.* Boston: Allyn and Bacon.

Evans, S. (1991). A realistic look at the research base for collaboration in special education. *Preventing School Failure, 35*(4), 10–13.

Friend, M., & Cook, L. (1992). *Interactions: Collaboration for school professionals.* New York: Longman.

Gomez, M. (1994). Teacher education reform and prospective teachers' perspectives on teaching "other people's" children. *Teaching and Teacher Education, 10*(3), 319–334.

Johnson, D. W., & Johnson, R. T. (1994). *Leading the cooperative school.* Edina, MN: Interaction Book Company.

Johnson, L., & Pugach, M. (1996). The emerging third wave of collaboration: Beyond problem-solving. In W. Stainback & S. Stainback (Eds.), *Controversial issues confronting special education: Divergent perspectives* (pp. 197–204). Boston: Allyn and Bacon.

Morsink, C. V., Thomas, C. C., & Correa, V. I. (1991). *Interactive teaming: Consultation and collaboration in special programs.* New York: Merrill.

Pugach, M. C. (1995). On the failure of imagination in inclusive schooling. *Journal of Special Education, 29*(2), 221–223.

Pugach, M. C., & Johnson, L. J. (1995). *Collaborative practitioners. Collaborative schools.* Denver: Love.

Salend, S. J., Johansen, K., Mumper, J., Chase, A. S., Pike, K. M., & Dorney, J. A. (1997). Cooperative teaching: The voices of two teachers. *Remedial and Special Education, 18*(1), 3–11.

Tertel, E. A., Klein, S. M., & Jewett, J. L. (1998). *When teachers reflect: Journeys toward effective inclusive practice.* Washington, DC: National Association for the Education of Young Children.

Wheatley, M. (1999). *Leadership and the new science: Discovering order in a chaotic world.* San Francisco: Berrett-Koehler.

York-Barr, J., Schultz, T., Doyle, M. E., Kronberg, R., & Crossett, S. (1996). Inclusive schooling in St. Cloud: Perspectives on the process and people. *Remedial and Special Education, 17*(2).

CHAPTER 11

Serving Formerly Excluded or Rejected Students with Disabilities in Regular Education Classrooms in Home Elementary Schools: Three Options

Lou Brown, Paula Kluth, Joanne Suomi, and Jack Jorgensen

Most of the students of primary concern in this chapter can be described in two ways. First, they are individuals whom teams of professionals have historically evaluated and judged as too disabled, handicapped, disordered, or the like, to be allowed opportunities to function in the schools they would attend if not disabled and/or in regular education classrooms. These students were previously diverted directly to special education schools and/or classrooms. Second, they are individuals who were initially given opportunities to function in regular education settings. However, after trial periods they were evaluated and judged by teams of professionals to be too disabled, handicapped, disordered, or the like, and then remanded to special education schools and/or classrooms.

Increasing numbers of legislators, parents, judges, due process hearing officers, professional educators, and others are reaching three important conclusions regarding these students. First, students with disabilities should be given access to the same schools and classrooms in which they would function if they were not disabled (Brown et al., 1989; Hunger, Twiss, Singer, & Lee, 1993; *Sacramento v. Holland*, 1994; Smith, 1997; Will, 1986). Second, once placement therein is arranged, they should be provided the "supplementary aids and services" that are so critical for success (Etscheidt & Bartlett, 1999; IDEA, 1997; *Oberti v. Clementon*, 1992). Third, if they cannot thrive therein, or if they interfere substantially with the achievement of others, placement elsewhere can then be considered (Brown et al., 1983; Halverson & Sailor, 1990; Owens-Johnson et al., (Chapter 7). "Elsewhere," in this context, refers to respected school and nonschool environments such as streets, libraries, cafeterias, parks, workplaces, and homes. Special education schools and classrooms, resource rooms, and other segregated or devalued settings are not considered acceptable.

Now that students with a wide array of disabilities who were formerly served in special education settings are being allowed access to regular education environments, many are asking how they should be distributed across classes and teachers. How can we benefit from the experiences of others? What are the new responsibilities of regular and special educators, therapists, and paraprofessionals? What are the concepts, values, and principles that should drive services? What should we consider before we establish a service delivery option? If we start with one option, when should we change to another? Is there a hierarchy through which we should progress? What kinds of preservice and inservice training are needed? How can we change attitudes?

This chapter addresses three elementary school service delivery options: co-teaching, team teaching, and consulting teaching. The position taken here is that if school personnel are planning to serve the students of concern in regular education classrooms in home schools, it is extremely important that they consider versions of at least these three options, combinations thereof, and their pros and cons *before* deciding upon a local service plan. Further, if school personnel are operating versions of these or other options or combinations thereof, it is extremely important that they be evaluated and improved over time.

Before we can proceed, several points must be made: Many refer to the three options with different labels or use the same labels to refer to different phenomena; some schools offer more than one option; there are options and combinations thereof that are not presented here that may be the most efficacious for individual schools; the options are addressed only in relation to elementary schools; and it is extremely doubtful that the options of today will be acceptable in the near future. Finally, it should be noted and emphasized that only some of the structural elements of three of many possible service delivery options will be addressed. The reader interested in the many complex and interactive instructional, grouping, and other elements that must be honored within each are referred elsewhere (Cook & Friend, 1995; Jakupcak, 1993; Udvari-Solner & Thousand, 1995a, 1995b).

FACTORS

In this chapter we first delineate five factors that should be addressed in the process of selecting, evaluating and/or evolving to the best possible integrated elementary school service delivery models for the students of concern, and then we discuss each. Our major purposes are to engender dialogue and discussion, to clarify values, and to force stands on difficult issues.

1. Regular Education Classes in Home Schools

The Individuals With Disabilities Education Act (IDEA) as amended in 1997 requires that students with disabilities be educated in schools close to their homes and with students who are not disabled to the "maximum extent appropriate" (IDEA, 1997). However, the act does not specify how close to home, with how many other students, and with which nondisabled students. The position taken in the act is that students with disabilities should have opportunities to attend the same schools and be based in the same regular education classrooms they would be in if they were not disabled. Although this interpretation may not apply in all situations, any departure from it should be scrutinized carefully. Exceptions should be made only when absolutely necessary.

In this context *home* rather than *neighborhood* is used to refer to the schools of concern. Many students who are not disabled prefer not to attend schools in their neighborhoods for several reasons. First, contact with those who are potentially negative influences, for example, gang members, can be reduced. Second, some school districts operate "magnet" schools and students choose to travel long distances and experience the associated inconveniences to attend them. Third, some school districts transport large numbers of students across traditional attendance boundaries for purposes of racial balance. Fourth, some schools set aside percentages of their capacities and offer "choice" or "random selection" to a limited number of students who do not live in the immediate neighborhoods. Fifth, some school districts serve only certain grade levels while neighboring districts serve others.

Should students with disabilities have the same opportunities as peers who are not disabled? Yes, and at least one more. Specifically, they should be allowed opportunities to attend the schools that serve the preponderance of peers without disabilities who live in their neighborhoods. There are many reasons for such a position: Health, best uses of time and energy, family access to schools and vice versa, and cost are a few. However, the primary reason stems from the reality that most students who are not disabled have social, physical, athletic, and other attributes that allow them to attend schools outside their neighborhoods and still develop the social networks critical for a stimulating life after school, on weekends and holidays, and during summers within their neighborhoods. Students with disabilities do not have this flexibility. If they do not attend schools that serve the preponderance of peers without disabilities in their neighborhoods, it is virtually impossible for them to build relationships at school and then express them during nonschool days and times. Far too often the tragic results are social isolation, harsh pressures on family members, low self-esteem, and underachievement.

2. Supplementary Aids and Services

IDEA requires that students with disabilities receive "supplementary aids and services" in regular education environments *before* they are placed elsewhere. Consider the following:

> Any modifications to the regular education program, i.e., supplementary aids and services that the IEP team determines that the student needs to facilitate the student's placement in the regular educational environment must be described in the student's IEP and must be provided to the student. While determinations of what supplementary aids and services are appropriate for a particular student must be made on an individual basis, some supplementary aids and services that educators have used successfully include modifications to the regular class curriculum, assistance of an itinerant teacher with special education training, special education training for the regular teacher, use of computer assisted devices, provision of note takers, and use of a resource room, to mention a few. (Heuman & Hehir, 1994)

In almost all instances, if appropriate supplementary aids and services are arranged, a student with disabilities can realize individually meaningful success in regular education settings at reasonable cost without interfering with the achievement of peers who are not disabled (Sharpe, York, & Knight, 1994). Further, it is the responsibility of the professionals involved to learn about, create, and utilize the best available supplementary aids and services. Ignorance of that which is constructive professional practice elsewhere is not acceptable (Etscheidt & Bartlett, 1999).

Certainly, the possibility exists that all reasonable supplementary aids and services will not result in a student's thriving in a regular education classroom or will not prevent her or him from interfering substantially with the achievement of classmates who are not disabled. In such improbable instances it is considered acceptable for the student with disabilities to function in other integrated environments. Special education classrooms and resource rooms, in our view, do not qualify.

3. The Natural Distribution

Students with disabilities should be distributed in schools and in regular education classes as they would be if they were not disabled. Violations of natural distributions should be avoided if at all possible because, when students with disabilities are grouped, clustered, piled, tracked, or channeled, they overwhelm the environment, important opportunities are denied, and negative outcomes almost always result. Conversely, when they are distributed in schools as they are in families and communities, realistic opportunities for positive outcomes ensue. Stated another way, a child with a disability should be based in a regular education classroom only if he or she would be based therein if not disabled. It is also important that students with many kinds and degrees of disabilities be distributed naturally. For example, if three children with physical disabilities or four with autism or five with Down syndrome attend the same regular education classroom they would attend if they were not disabled, so be it. However, in almost all instances extraordinary administrative actions are necessary to generate such phenomena.

4. Local Management and Commingled Resources

A reasonable array of resources should be assigned to a school, and those responsible should have the flexibility to utilize a substantial proportion of these resources as they judge appropriate. For example, there are instances in which the ratio of students to professionals is so high that meaningful education is de facto disallowed. There are instances in which students with disabilities put extraordinary pressures on those who function nearby. These pressures often require meaningful reductions in ratios between students and professionals. If resources are assigned to schools and those who are responsible for managing them have the flexibility to make allocation decisions, generating ratios that are individually appropriate is often feasible. This is in contrast to functioning in response to externally determined ratios—for example, 15 students with mild disabilities to 1 teacher, 9 students with severe disabilities to 1 teacher—that do not allow for individual modifications or that require assigning or binding resources to an individual.

There are instances in which the resources available to a regular education teacher are not sufficient to allow the provision of a reasonable educational program. There are instances in which a special education teacher has more than enough money, equipment, space, assistants, and therapists to operate an effective educational program but cannot do so because she and her students are segregated from both peers without disabilities and regular education teachers. If regular and special education resources are commingled, in concert with the spirit of local, state, and federal laws and regulations, better returns can be realized than if they are not (McGregor & Vogelsberg, 1998; Roach, 1995).

5. Collaboration

As more and more students with and without disabilities learn to function together effectively in regular education settings, so must the professionals who serve them. As discussed in Chapter 8, the term typically used to refer to the need to cooperate, to arrive at the most effective divisions of labor, to problem-solve jointly, to compromise, to push the limits without offending, to synergize expertise, and to filter in the quest for excellence is *collaboration* (Idol, Nevin, & Paolucci-Whitcomb, 1994; Udvari-Solner & Frentz, 1996). Indeed, without collaborative teamwork, reasonable achievement in integrated schools and classrooms is jeopardized. Thus it is extremely important that those involved make clear commitments to working together; that the needs, values, and interests of all are stated and respected; that the time and other resources necessary for meaningful collaboration are made available; and that training pertaining to how to work effectively in teams is provided.

In sum, these are several of many feasible factors that are related to the design, implementation, and evaluation of three elementary school service delivery options for selected students with disabilities. One possibility for us would have been to reference each factor to each option sequentially and cumulatively. We chose not to do so because we think the better strategy is for concerned individuals to delineate and analyze that which they think is most important. Also we appreciate the non-mutually-exclusive nature of both the service options and the factors. At any rate, a relatively large amount of information about the parameters of each option is readily available in the professional literature, and we hope that readers will supplement the information offered as they judge necessary to create a blend that is most meaningful locally.

THE COTEACHING OPTION

Coteaching options are those in which a regular and a special education teacher function in one classroom. They are usually responsible for approximately 20 students without disabilities and 12 who have been ascribed special education labels and IEPs. In addition, at least one full-time special education paraprofessional and the necessary array of related service personnel are available for individually determined amounts of time. Readers interested in other important elements of coteaching are referred to the excellent papers of Cook and Friend (1995) and Dieker and Barnett (1996).

In Support of the Coteaching Option

Coteaching is probably the most utilized of the three options. Indeed, it seems to be the substitute of choice for special education classrooms and resource rooms. Those who endorse it typically offer the following reasons for doing so:

- It is the easiest to establish administratively.
- The special education teacher and the paraprofessional are with their students with disabilities throughout the school day.
- The special education teacher has to establish and maintain a working relationship with only one regular education teacher.
- The regular and the special education teacher have enough daily interactions to learn each other's methods, share curriculum strategies, adapt, modify, plan, evaluate, develop materials or otherwise "collaborate" effectively.
- The relatively large number of adults in the room allows more individualized attention for all.
- When regular and special educators share resources efficiently, students with and without disabilities can benefit more than when these resources are expended separately.
- If the regular and the special education teacher work well together, they can experience a "year in heaven."

Challenges to the Coteaching Option

Some who have tried versions of the coteaching option are pleased with both the process and the outcomes and are not interested in changing or evolving to another version. Others who have tried versions of it have decided that the attendant difficulties are too powerful and that alternatives must be pursued. Some of the major difficulties associated with coteaching options are presented below:

- Coteaching options require unnatural proportions of students with disabilities. These overloads inhibit the development of a wide array of social relationships with classmates who are not disabled, place too many curricular modification pressures on too few teachers, and do not allow sufficient numbers or ranges of appropriate models. Indeed, some question whether it can be referred to as an "integrated" option because the natural distribution is violated so blatantly.
- Quite often there are too many adults in the classroom at one time.
- Regular education teachers at the school who are not directly involved in the coteaching option do not develop the attitudes, skills, and values necessary to serve students with disabilities in their classrooms. In fact, it encourages the perpetuation of the ineffective traditions of "referring problems to special education"; perceiving special education as a place rather than an array of portable services; and believing that there are special education children who are substantively different from regular education children.
- Too often the coteaching option classroom becomes a repository for students with disabilities, particularly those with learning, physical, or behavioral difficulties.
- In many instances, students who have been referred to special education, but have not yet been evaluated or who are "at risk" of same, are assigned to these already overloaded classrooms.
- There is a strong penchant to "ability group." As a result, students with disabilities often function only or primarily with special educators.
- If the regular and the special education teacher do not work well together, they can experience a "year in hell."

THE TEAM TEACHING OPTION

Typically, team teaching option calls for three regular education teachers, one special education teacher, at least one paraprofessional, related service personnel as determined by IEP teams, and about 75 students without disabilities and 12 students with a natural array of disabilities. In many instances, one large room or open area is used. In others, a group of professionals functions as a team but in adjacent classrooms. Readers interested in other elements of team teaching options are referred to the abundance of professional literature (Bauwens, Hourcade, & Friend, 1989; Morsink, Thomas, & Correa, 1991; Udvari-Solner & Thousand, 1995b).

In Support of Team Teaching Options

Those who endorse versions of the team teaching option typically offer the following reasons for doing so:

- The team is, or is close to, serving a natural distribution of students with and without disabilities. This allows opportunities to develop a wide array of social relationships with peers who are not disabled and the use of many heterogeneous instructional groupings.
- Three regular education teachers develop the skills, attitudes, and values necessary to serve a wide array of students with disabilities in regular education settings.
- Instructional and management responsibilities for students with disabilities are diffused across four teachers. This reduces the pressures on one or two.
- Physical proximity and frequent, common, and intense experiences allow for efficient collaboration.
- Many special and regular education resources can be commingled effectively.
- Enough adults are available so that talents, inclinations, and expertise can be counterbalanced through divisions of labor and responsibility rotations.

Challenges to Team Teaching Options

The major difficulties associated with team teaching include:

- In some instances, students with disabilities are homogeneously grouped, tracked, or channeled.
- Although good morale and effective operation of the team require that everyone make contributions in fair and decent ways, the responsibility for planning, teaching, and adapting curricula for students with disabilities is sometimes made the exclusive responsibility of special educators. That is, shared responsibility across regular and special educators is sometimes minimal.
- In many instances, particularly if a team operates in one large room or in a confined area, too many adults are present and the intimacy of a classroom is compromised.
- Many school buildings are not architecturally arranged to allow for meaningful teaming.
- If one teacher does not "carry his load," the overall effectiveness of a team is compromised.
- Some teachers function quite well in a room in which they are the "person in authority." When required to function "out in the open" or as an equal member of a team, they are not as effective or comfortable. Indeed, individual weaknesses are exposed for many to see. This is extremely upsetting to some.
- If more than one classroom is used, the special education professionals may not be in the physical presence of students with disabilities at all times. Although this situation is revered by some, it is unsettling to others.

THE CONSULTING TEACHING OPTION

Consulting teaching options usually consist of one special education teacher who provides some direct instruction and a substantial amount of technical assistance, modified or alternative materials, grouping and teaching strategies, and so on, to five regular education teachers. In addition, one full-time special education paraprofessional and the related service personnel determined by IEP teams are available. The ratio of students with to those without disabilities in many versions is about 125 to 12. Readers interested in other elements of consulting teaching options are referred to the professional literature (Idol, 1989; West & Idol, 1993).

In Support of Consulting Teaching Options

Those who support consulting teaching options typically offer the following reasons for doing so:

• Students with and without disabilities are naturally distributed across five regular education classrooms.
• There is systemic shared responsibility across special and regular educators.
• Regular education teachers can call for help, but only in extreme instances can they refer a student with disabilities to other places. They must assume direct instructional, advocacy, monitoring, protective, and other supportive responsibilities. Thus many regular educators learn to teach students with a wide array of disabilities and special education becomes a cluster of portable services rather than a place.
• Students with and without disabilities experience teachers with a wide array of competency levels and other characteristics and learn to function in heterogeneous groupings.
• If the regular education teachers and the consulting teacher are competent, flexible, creative, fun to work with, and assume responsibility for educating students with and without disabilities, "school is as good as it gets."

Challenges to Consulting Teaching Options

Some who have tried consulting teaching options are pleased and not interested in changing or evolving to something else. Others have experienced advantages as well as disadvantages. Some of the major difficulties associated with consulting teaching options are presented below:

• Too often special educators are "spread too thin." That is, they provide a little assistance in too many places. In some instances, it may be better to provide more assistance to the same number of students in fewer places.

- Developing positive working relationships with five regular education teachers is an extremely complex social challenge. Not many have the qualities necessary to cultivate and maintain such a wide array of relationships.
- Functioning in five classrooms in one day is extremely difficult physically. Many teachers cannot meet such strenuous demands on a sustained basis.
- The depth and breadth of knowledge needed to contribute meaningfully to five regular education curricula and the alternatives and modifications needed for a wide array of students with and without disabilities are in the repertoires of relatively few.
- The time available to plan, collaborate, and generate curricular modifications and alternatives is limited under any circumstances. However, when a special education teacher must work with five regular education teachers in as many classrooms, the time necessary to engender quality may not be available.
- Because the special education teacher spends relatively little time in many places, she or he is often dependent upon paraprofessionals, tutors, and therapists to provide much direct instruction. Sometimes instructional quality suffers (Brown, Farrington, Knight, Ross, & Ziegler, 1999; Giangreco, Edelman, Luiselli, & MacFarland, 1997.)
- If the professionals at a school are relatively stable across time, the consulting teaching option often works well because experience, expertise, and collaboration strategies can be accumulated gradually. However, if personnel turnover is high, too much valuable time is spent building new relationships rather than nurturing existing ones.

DISCUSSION

Which option is best? Who knows? The ideal option, the one that is best for all parents, teachers, administrators, students with and without disabilities, and taxpayers, has yet to be validated. Thus we are obligated to realize that the one we select will probably be less than ideal. Sometimes the option teachers like will not be the best one for students with disabilities, and sometimes the preferred option of parents who have children with disabilities will interfere substantially with the growth of classmates who are not disabled. Sometimes the personality of the teacher precludes or determines the use of an option.

Is there a hierarchy? We are not sure. In our view, the coteaching option is the easiest to generate but the most problematic in the long run. Given low personnel turnover, the consulting teaching option has many more advantages than disadvantages. The coteaching option in a third-grade classroom is not feasible if only two students with disabilities in that age range are enrolled in the school. The team teaching option is best for some but certainly not for all. Indeed, all models are to a large degree personality-driven.

We are encouraged when we interact with professionals who established one option, explored parameters thoughtfully, tinkered with relevant dimensions, and made improvements or evolved to something better. We are disheartened when we interact with professionals who established one option and learned of its short-comings but did little to evolve. The quest for continuous improvement is an essential professional responsibility for inclusive education to be successful.

The options are presented in relation to elementary schools. When middle/junior high and high schools are considered, other factors prevail. For example, in high schools much instruction should be provided in nonschool settings. Thus generating integration in high schools is often easier than in elementary schools because there are fewer students with disabilities on school grounds at one time and because there are significantly more regular education teachers, courses, classes and activities from which to choose.

Finally, it seems reasonable to assume that the number of students with disabilities who function in regular education settings will continue to increase (Udvari-Solner, 1996b). This will necessitate the expenditure of large amounts of resources on inservice training because interacting with students with disabilities will be new to so many. Three hypotheses seem reasonable. First, the professionals of the future will be different from those of the past because they will have grown up with students with disabilities. Second, each spring thousands complete teacher training programs in regular education, get jobs, and experience students with disabilities for the first time. Then they and their administrators realize that they are in need of inservice training. Each spring thousands complete teacher training programs in special education, get jobs, and are required to serve students with disabilities in regular education settings for the first time. Then they and their administrators realize that they are in need of inservice training. Obviously, there is a clear need for all prospective teachers to receive special and regular education training at the preservice level (Chapter 14). Then they can assume both roles and responsibilities that are awaiting them at the point of licensure at substantially less cost. Third, all three models do away with the practice of using categories and levels as the basis for placing grouping students with disabilities. Thus teacher training programs based on categories and levels are becoming increasingly difficult to justify.

REFERENCES

Bauwens, J., Hourcade, J. J., & Friend, M. (1989). Cooperative teaching: A model for general and special education integration. *Remedial and Special Education, 10*(2), 17–22.

Brown, L., Farrington, K., Knight, T., Ross, C., & Ziegler, M. (1999). Fewer paraprofessionals and more teachers and therapists in eductional programs for students with significant disabilities. *Journal of the Association for Persons with Severe Handicaps, 24*(4), 250–253.

Brown, L., Long, E., Udvari-Solner, A., Davis, L., VanDeventer, P., Ahlgren, C., Johnson, F., Greunewald L., & Jorgensen, J. (1989). The home school: Why students with severe intellectual disabilities must attend the schools of their brothers, sisters, friends and neighbors. *Journal of the Association for Persons With Severe Handicaps, 14*(1), 8–13.

Brown, L., Nisbet, J., Ford, A., Sweet, M., Shiraga, B., York, J., & Loomis, R. (1983). The critical need for non-school instruction in educational programs for severely handicapped students. *Journal of the Association for Persons With Severe Handicapps, 8*(3), 71–77.

Cook, L., & Friend, M. (1995). Co-teaching: Guidelines for creating effective practices. *Focus on Exceptional Children, 28*(3), 1–16.

Dieker, L., & Barnett, C. (1996). Effective co-teaching. *Teaching Exceptional Children, 29*(1), 5–7.

Etscheidt, S., & Bartlett, L. (1999). The IDEA amendments: A four-step approach for determining Supplementary Aids and Services. *Exceptional Children, 65*(2), 163–174.

Giangreco, M., Edelman, S., Luiselli, T., & McFarland, S. (1997). Helping or hovering? Effects of instructional proximity on students with disabilities. *Exceptional Children, 64*, 7–18.

Halverson, A. T., & Sailor, W. (1990). Integration of students with severe disabilities: A review of research. In R. G. Ross (Ed.), *Issues and research in special education* (Vol. 1, pp. 110–172). New York: Teachers College Press.

Heumann, J., & Hehir, T. (1994). *Questions and answers on the least restrictive environment requirements of the Individuals With Disabilities Education Act.* Washington, DC: U.S. Department of Education, Office of Special Education and Rehabilitative Services, Office of Special Education Programs.

Hunger, F., Twiss, R. M., Singer, M. J., & Lee, J. J. (1993). Brief for the United States as Amicus Curiae supporting appellees. *Sacramento City Unified School District, Board of Education v. Rachel Holland, by and through her guardian ad litem, Robert Holland, et al.,* No. 92–15608 (Ninth Circuit). Washington, DC: U.S. Department of Justice.

Idol, L. (1989). The Resource/consulting teacher: An integrated model of service delivery. *Remedial and Special Education, 10*, 38–48.

Idol, L., Nevin, A., & Paolucci-Whitcomb, P. (1994). *Collaborative Consultation* (2nd ed.). Austin, TX: PRO-ED.

Individuals With Disabilities Education Act (IDEA) Amendments of 1997. Washington, DC: U.S. Department of Education.

Jakupcak, J. (1993). Innovative classroom programs for full inclusion. In J. W. Putnam (Ed.), *Cooperative learning and strategies for inclusion: Celebrating diversity in the classroom* (pp. 163–179). Baltimore: Paul H. Brookes.

McGregor, G., & Vogelsberg, R. T. (1998). *Inclusive schooling practices: Pedagogical and research foundations: A synthesis of the literature that informs best practices about inclusive schooling.* Baltimore: Paul H. Brookes.

Morsink, C. V., Thomas, C. C., & Correa, V. I. (1991). *Interactive teaming: Consultation and collaboration in special programs.* New York: Macmillan.

Oberti v. Board of Education of Clementon, New Jersey, C.A. No. 91–2818, D.N.J. (August 17, 1992).

Roach, V. (1995). *Winning ways: Creating inclusive schools, classrooms and communities.* Alexandria, VA: National Association of State Boards of Education.

Sacramento City Unified School District v. Rachel Holland, No. 92–15608 (9th Cir. 1994).

Sharpe, M., York, J., & Knight, J. (1994). Effects of inclusion on the academic performance of students in general education classrooms: A preliminary study. *Remedial and Special Education, 15*(5), 281–287.

Smith, A. (1997). Systemic education reform and school inclusion: A view from a Washington office window. *Education and Treatment of Children, 20*(1), 7–22.

Udvari-Solner, A. (1996a). Examining teacher thinking: Constructing a process to design curricular adaptations. *Remedial and Special Education, 17*(4), 245–254.

Udvari-Solner, A. (1996b). Theoretical influences on the establishment of inclusive practices. *Cambridge Journal of Education, 26*(1), 101–119.

Udvari-Solner, A., & Frentz, J. (1996). A collaborative process for designing curricular adaptations. *Gateway, 1*(1), 8–9.

Udvari-Solner, A., & Thousand, J. (1995a). Effective organizational, instructional, and curricular practices in inclusive schools and classrooms. In C. Clark, A. Dyson, & A. Millward (Eds.), *Towards inclusive schools* (pp. 147–163). London, England: David Fulton.

Udvari-Solner, A., & Thousand, J. (1995b). Promising practices that foster inclusive education. In R. Villa & J. Thousand (Eds.), *Creating an inclusive school* (pp. 87–109). Alexandria, VA: Association for Supervision and Curriculum Development.

West, J. F., & Idol, L. (1993). The counselor as consultant in the collaborative school. *Journal of Counseling and Development, 71*(6), 678–683.

Will, M. (1986). *Educating students with learning problems—A shared responsibility.* Washington, DC: U.S. Department of Education, Office of Special Education and Rehabilitation Services.

CHAPTER 12

Including All Students in Statewide Educational Assessments

Harold L. Kleinert, Jacqueline Farmer Kearns, and Sarah Kennedy

One of the caveats of educational reform is the continually articulated need for rigorous outcomes for all students. A key to meeting the expectations is the requirement that all students be included in large-scale educational assessments. Yet current national estimates suggest that only about 50% to 60% of students with disabilities participate in statewide assessment programs (Vanderwood, McGrew, & Ysseldyke, 1998). Moreover, students with moderate and severe cognitive disabilities are typically excluded altogether (Elliott, Ysseldyke, Thurlow, & Erickson, 1998). Unfortunately, one effect of excluding specific groups of students from state and district educational performance measures can be a decreased concern for what those students are learning. Indeed, the disappointing lack of postschool success of students with disabilities across a range of follow-up studies (Blackorby & Wagner, 1996) is another indication that our efforts in special education have not been sufficiently focused on the "end-results" of our interventions but rather upon "getting in the schoolroom door" (Sage & Burello, 1994).

As earlier chapters have discussed, Congress recognized this underlying need by enacting Title II, National Education Reform *Leadership, Standards, and Assessments,* calling for the development of state assessment systems that fully include all students, as a major component of the 1994 Goals 2000: Educate America Act ("What is Goals 2000: The Educate America Act?", 1994). Goals 2000 requires each state to submit a State Improvement Plan to qualify for participating funds; an essential element of that improvement plan is the development of a reliable state-level assessment program providing the necessary accommodations for all students to participate.

Even more significant to the inclusion of students with disabilities in large-scale educational assessments are the 1997 Amendments to the Individuals With

Disabilities Education Act (IDEA). Under this act, all states will have to ensure that students with disabilities are fully included in both state and local district-wide educational assessments. Specifically, IDEA requires that children with disabilities be included in such assessments with "appropriate accommodations where necessary" [612 (a) (17) (A)]; and for those students who, even with accommodations, cannot participate in regular assessments, that states develop and implement alternate assessments "beginning not later than July 1, 2000" [612 (a) (17) (A) (i–ii)].

States must also report the performance of children participating in the alternate assessment [612 (a) (17) (B) (ii–iii)]; ensure that IEP teams individually address how students will participate in large-scale assessments (either via the general assessment, including any use of accommodations, or through an alternate assessment) [614 (d) (1) (A) (v)]; and consider the performance of students with disabilities in large-scale assessments, including those students participating in the alternate assessment, in the newly required State Improvement Plan performance goals and indicators [612 (a) (16) (D)].

Given the consistent and unambiguous language of these legislative mandates, there is clearly a national recognition that educational assessment measures should be inclusive of all students. Yet the fact that we *should* do something does not necessarily mean that we *know how* to. Indeed, we have some very substantial questions before us. Can we meaningfully include all students in large-scale educational assessments and, in the process, design performance measures that meet accepted standards of reliability and validity? In what sense can we even speak of rigorous expectations for students with the most severe cognitive disabilities? And at the most fundamental level, if there *are* rigorous expectations that apply to all students, what do those expectations look like, and what might be reasonable measures of their attainment? We cannot claim to have the final answers to these questions; however, we do have a grasp on the essential parameters that must be addressed, as well as direct experience with a number of the pitfalls that will unavoidably occur. In Kentucky, we have the results of 8 years of assessing *all* students, including students with severe, multiple disabilities, in the state's high-stakes assessment and accountability system.

This chapter describes the lessons we have learned from Kentucky's alternate assessment system for students with moderate and severe cognitive disabilities (the Alternate Portfolio). We briefly review the context of statewide educational reform (see also Chapter 5) in which Kentucky's alternate assessment system was developed, the history of its development, and its relationship to the regular assessment and accountability system. We detail the required Alternate Portfolio components (revised as of the 1998–1999 school year) and describe the evolving scoring standards.

The second part of this chapter discusses the value of portfolio assessment as a teaching tool for students with moderate and severe disabilities, especially for teaching higher-order skills (e.g., self-evaluation, self-direction) and for validating with parents and families the essential outcomes of their son's or daughter's education. In keeping with the general theme of this book, we consider how the alternate assessment can increase student learning ties to the family and to the community as a whole. We conclude the chapter with a discussion of systems issues in the development of alternate assessments as one small, though very integral piece, of school restructuring efforts for all students.

THE DEVELOPMENT OF KENTUCKY'S ALTERNATE ASSESSMENT SYSTEM

In 1990, Kentucky enacted the Kentucky Education Reform Act (KERA). That act established a required set of components for all schools that are described in Chapter 5. As noted in that chapter, a key component of KERA was the mandate for a comprehensive performance-based assessment and accountability system inclusive of all students. This statewide assessment would (a) be based on the key learner outcomes identified for all students, (b) be performance-based in that it would assess learning relevant to "real-life" demands and meaningful contexts, (c) drive school improvement through rewards for schools that improved their accountability scores and sanctions for schools that did not improve, and (d) exempt no student, unless medically necessary (Steffy, 1993). Although the jury is still very much out on the impact and effectiveness of the state's efforts to meet these four challenges, Kentucky is, nevertheless, the first state in the nation to include all students, even those with severe disabilities, in its mandatory performance-based assessment system (Elliott et al., 1998; National Center on Educational Outcomes, 1997). Within Kentucky's system, students with moderate and severe cognitive disabilities participate in the Alternate Portfolio Assessment. The score of a student in the state's alternate system is given equal weight with the score of any other student in determining school accountability. In this section we briefly describe the development of the alternate assessment. For a more detailed description of this process, the reader is referred to Kleinert, Kearns, and Kennedy (1997).

Kentucky's Regular Assessment and Accountability System

Through the 1997–1998 school year, Kentucky students in the fourth/fifth, seventh/eighth, and eleventh/twelfth grades have been assessed through writing portfolios; on-demand performance tasks in math, reading, social studies, science, practical arts, and the humanities; and transitional "NAEP (National Assessment of Educational Progress)-like" achievement tests. These cognitive indicators, along with noncognitive measures such as attendance, dropout and retention rates, and postschool outcomes, have been employed to calculate a performance index for each school, which is then used as the baseline value for determining future school rewards or sanctions (Steffy, 1993). For each 2-year accountability cycle, the overall performance index for that cycle becomes the baseline for the next cycle, and a new "threshold" level is calculated as the school's target for the subsequent biennium. Kentucky has since restructured its regular assessment to include more stan-

dardized test items (to allow for more precise national comparisons and to provide more accurate gauges of individual student growth over time) and has also
streamlined its portfolio requirements (e.g., fewer entries).

Alternate Portfolio Structure, Contents, and Entry Types

The Kentucky Alternate Portfolio Advisory Committee, as part of the initial development process, identified a set of key parameters for the alternate assessment.
First, each student's portfolio in the alternate system would be comprised of multiple entries, some of which would be required and some of which would be of the
student's own choosing. Second, the Alternate Portfolio would contain a sufficient
range of entries so as to comprise an accurate representation of both what the student had learned and the quality of the learning opportunities the school had provided the student. Among the components identified as essential for every Alternate Portfolio were:

The student's primary mode of communication. This is a critical component in
that a considerable number of students who meet the eligibility criteria for the
Alternate Portfolio cannot communicate verbally and thus need an alternative or
augmentative way of communicating, such as picture communication systems and/
or signing/gesturing. Indeed, in a statewide survey of teachers who were serving
students eligible for the Alternate Portfolio, Wheatley (1993) found that as many
as 50% of students eligible for the alternate assessment presently had (or needed)
an augmentative system. This portfolio requirement is founded on the fundamental assumption that a primary focus of education for all students should be to equip
them with an adequate means of communicating in their everyday environments.

The student's daily/weekly schedule. This schedule must be presented in the
form in which the student is learning to *use* it (e.g., a printed schedule for a student who can read, a picture schedule for a nonreader, or an object symbol shelf
for a student with deaf-blindness and multiple disabilities) and a description of
how the student uses that individualized schedule to initiate and monitor his or
her own activities throughout the day. *Performance data* on how the student is learning to use his or her daily schedule must be attached as well.

A student letter to the reviewer. This letter should indicate why the different
portfolio entries have been chosen, and it should identify the entry the student
would rate as his or her best or favorite. This letter can be written as a collaborative effort with typical peers, as long as the level of assistance provided the student
is clearly indicated.

Portfolio entries. To the maximum extent possible, each entry should involve
nondisabled peers and focus on one or more of the learner outcomes for all students. Students can include both individual and group projects, and are encouraged to work in heterogeneous, cooperative groups. Entries should incorporate clear
documentation of learned skills through the presentation of systematic instruc-

tional data and other tangible evidence (e.g., products, taped presentations, peer evaluations). The required and elective entries for each grade level are presented in Table 12.1. Beginning with the 1998–1999 school year, each of these entries must be linked to a core content area of the general curriculum.

A work resume for students in the 12th grade. This resume should indicate in-school and community job experiences, including employer evaluations, if available.

A letter from the student's parents or guardian. This letter should indicate their level of satisfaction with the student's portfolio entries and educational outcomes. This letter can be written or dictated by the parent(s) and also gives parents an opportunity to describe the extent to which their son or daughter is able to apply skills learned in school in family and community settings and activities.

Scoring Standards and Evaluation Criteria for Alternate Portfolios

The scoring standards for the Alternate Portfolio, developed by the Alternate Portfolio Advisory Committee in the summer of 1992 and since compressed into five essential components, include:

Standard 1: The student's ability to perform targeted skills and to plan, initiate, monitor, and evaluate his or her own performance on those targeted skills within and across entries.

Standard 2: The degree to which any needed assistance is provided via natural supports, such as peers in regular classes and coworkers in job sites (as opposed to evidence of assistance provided by paid staff only), and the use of adaptations and assistive technology to enhance independence.

Table 12.1. Alternate Portfolio Entry Requirements by Grade Level

Entry Types	*Fourth Grade*	*Eighth Grade*	*Twelfth Grade*
Language arts	X	X	X
Math	X	X	C
Science	X	C	C
Social studies	X	C	C
Arts & humanities	C	C	C
Health & PE	C	C	C
Vocational	N	X	X

Key: X = Required; C = Choice; N = Not required.

Standard 3: The presence of social relationships and mutual friendships with typical peers. Whereas the presence of multiple peer interactions is fairly easy to rate, one of the most challenging aspects in developing the alternate assessment scoring criteria was the determination of what constitutes clear documentation of mutual friendships. At the highest (Distinguished) level of performance, this standard states: "The student has sustained social interactions and is clearly a member of a social network of peers who choose to spend time together" (*Kentucky Alternate Portfolio Project, 1999,* p. 38).

Standard 4: Student outcomes evidenced across multiple school and community settings. For elementary-age students, emphasis is placed on performance in a wide variety of integrated or inclusive school settings. For older students, community-based performance is given increasing weight in conjunction with integrated school and class settings.

Standard 5: The use of age-appropriate activities and materials, and the systematic evidence of student choice-making throughout the school day, as evidenced both within and across portfolio entries. At the highest (Distinguished) level of performance, this standard states: "The student makes choices that have significant impact on student learning within and across all entries. All products are age appropriate" (*Kentucky Alternate Portfolio Project 1999,* p. 41).

Each of these standards is restated, in turn, to represent Kentucky's four performance levels for its regular assessment system: Novice, Apprentice, Proficient, and Distinguished.

For each standard and performance level, specific *scoring criteria* are identified through a benchmarking process. Each year since the inception of the alternate assessment, a statewide Benchmarking Committee (including members of the Alternate Portfolio Advisory Committee, additional teachers, local administrators, and university personnel) meet to identify "benchmark" portfolios representative of each of the four performance levels. These benchmark portfolios are selected from a sample of all the Alternate Portfolios developed. Benchmark portfolios represent clear-cut examples of performance for each level (e.g., the portfolio selected as the eighth "Apprentice Benchmark" scored at the Apprentice performance level in all or nearly all of the five individual standards). Benchmark portfolios are then used as standards or yardsticks in training teachers to score. For each of the accountability grade levels (fourth, eighth, and twelfth), a scoring manual has been developed that delineates overall scoring standards, clarifications, and scoring-decision rules at that grade level for each standard, as well as copies of the benchmark portfolios representative of each of the four performance levels for that grade. All teachers who have students in the alternate assessment then receive a full-day training on portfolio scoring each year in which they have a student with a portfolio due. An essential part of the continuing development of the Alternate Portfolio is the work of the Benchmarking Committee in identifying the best portfolio examples for training and clarifying scoring issues arising in the field.

For each of the five scoring standards, the student's portfolio is rated first on each standard individually. Each standard is evaluated holistically within the context of the entire portfolio (i.e., individual entries are not scored separately, but rather each standard is first scored across all entries). Based upon a "clustering" of these five individual ratings, a final holistic score of Novice, Apprentice, Proficient, or Distinguished is assigned to the student's portfolio, to be included in both the school and local district level accountability indices. For purposes of accountability, each student with an Alternate Portfolio contributes a weight equal to that of a student in Kentucky's regular assessment system. Thus a student with a severe disability whose Alternate Portfolio is rated Distinguished contributes a positive accountability effect and reward equivalent to that of a student rated Distinguished on all of the components in the regular assessment.

USING PORTFOLIOS TO TEACH HIGHER-ORDER SKILLS

A portfolio process in which students take the lead in selecting and evaluating their own entries and performances may provide a good way to enhance participation in daily classroom routines with typical peers, the development of important social supports, and the learning of self-evaluation and self-management skills (see Kearns, Kleinert, Clayton, Burdge, & Williams, 1998). At the same time, portfolios can increase learner links to both the community and the family.

Portfolios and Individual School Supports

The attributes of peer support, choice-making, and self-evaluation are clearly evidenced in the portfolio of *Leonard*, a 9-year-old student with severe, multiple disabilities. He included a videotaped "letter to the reviewer" illustrating the process he used to select his entries. The videotape showed two classmates holding up and describing the entries as Leonard used a gaze and smile to choose his favorite selections. The entry illustrated the communicative intent of his gaze and the level of assistance he needed from peers.

Craig, a middle school student with severe disabilities, used a videotaped portfolio entry to illustrate his use of a variety of assistive/adaptive devices. Craig's videotaped resume (see Light, Dumlao, & Stecker, 1993) illustrated his use of microswitches and adaptive devices to accomplish tasks in his school job. Another videotaped clip showed Craig giving a speech to his public speaking class and answering yes or no questions with the aid of an electronic communication device. An art entry evidenced not only the assistive/adaptive devices Craig used to communicate tool and color choices but also the actual art products themselves. These entries in Craig's portfolio provided valuable information about him in terms of his skills and abilities as well as the adaptations and supports necessary to enable his independent performance.

Portfolios as Tools for Transition

For students in their last years of school, the transition from school to work and integrated community living can be enhanced by portfolios that highlight their skills. *Janey*, a high school student with a moderate cognitive disability, included an entry that began with the question, "*What are the most important skills needed to keep a job?*" To answer this question, she developed, with the help of peer tutors, an employers' survey. Janey and her job coach then personally delivered the surveys to various employers. As the surveys were returned, she compiled the data and found that the employers felt that quality of work was the most important and appropriate dress the least important of the skills they were asked to rate. Assisted by peers, Janey typed the survey during computer lab and compiled the results during accounting class. We have enclosed her survey and tabulated results in Figure 12.1.

Janey's portfolio contained several other entries related to employment as well. Her resume indicated that she had work experiences at a local department store and a dry cleaner. Recommendation letters from her employers suggested that Janey gets along well with coworkers and works hard. In another entry, Janey explored careers related to teaching and child care. With help from peers (with the level of assistance provided described on the entry itself), she used the library to locate information about these careers and developed a written report.

Each entry in Janey's portfolio represented rich evidence of her skills and abilities. Specifically, targeted skills were evidenced in a variety of ways through student products, systematic instructional program data, and student and peer reflection across a variety of settings and activities.

Fostering Self-Management

Self-management includes all the things a person does to influence or structure his or her own behavior (Carter, 1993). We know that self-management (e.g., organizing our day, deciding how we will spend our money, what we will wear, etc.) is a critical skill for us all and represents an essential component of self-determination (King-Sears & Carpenter, 1997). Unfortunately, this is not a skill we have systematically taught to students with significant disabilities. A portfolio can serve as a valuable tool to facilitate self-management. Choosing one's best work for the portfolio provides a first step in self-evaluation, with specific entries serving as further evidence of student monitoring and self-evaluation. Examples of these include individualized daily schedules, exercise routine checklists, home chore schedules, and school job lists. In one portfolio entry, a student counted laps as she walked

Figure 12.1. Employer Survey Form and Survey Results

Employer Survey Form	*Survey Results*
I am doing a survey on skills that employers think are the most important. Please rate the following items as to their importance to you as an employer. Scoring/rating guide: Number 5 being the most important, number one the least important.	A. Dress appropriately 1 1 1 1 1 1 1 5 B. Regular attendance 4 2 4 3 3 4 2 5 C. On time to work 3 4 3 2 2 3 4 5 D. Quality of work 5 5 5 5 5 5 5 5 E. Gets along well with coworkers 2 3 2 4 4 2 3 5

A. Dresses appropriately _____

B. Regular attendance _____

C. On time to work _____

D. Quality of work _____

E. Gets along well with

workers _____

If there are any you think are more important and they are not listed, please feel free to list them.

_____

Name of Business or Organization

with friends to increase her physical activity. Five laps resulted in a star on her chart, which she maintained for one month. Another student kept a picture checklist of home chores. As a chore was completed, she checked off that chore from her list. Her mother followed up on this activity by signing the checklist when all the chores were completed. A third student used a checklist to remind her of the things she needed in order to shop for family grocery items, a part of her community-based instructional program. Her mother helped her complete the checklist after the student had brought all the items home and put them away, as shown in Figure 12.2.

Parent Perceptions of Their Children's Portfolios

Kentucky's Alternate Portfolio system requires that teachers obtain a *parent validation letter* for their students' portfolios. This gives parents a formal opportunity

Figure 12.2. Grocery Shopping Checklist and Evaluation Sheet

Grocery Shopping List

BEFORE I GO I NEED TO:

__ Decide correct time   __ Bring money $$$$

__ Make a shopping list   __ Get purse/ID card

Evaluation Sheet

GOT THE BASKET   PAID MONEY $$$$
__ I did great work   __ I did great work

__ I could have worked harder   __ I could have worked harder

GOT THE ITEMS ON THE LIST   PUT ITEMS AWAY AT HOME
__ I did great work   __ I did great work

__ I could have worked harder   __ I could have worked harder

to share their perceptions of their own child's work. In their validation letters, parents have written extensively about how the portfolio mirrors what their child has learned, and they have used this opportunity to reflect upon the importance of their son or daughter's educational experience to their child's present (and future) life. Although certainly not every validation letter includes *only* glowing remarks, in 8 years of statewide assessment with the Alternate Portfolio in Kentucky, the vast majority of these letters have been notably positive. Portfolio validation letters also give family members the opportunity to consider how the student has applied what he or she has learned at home and in community.

Issues and Lessons in the Development of Statewide Assessments

As states develop educational accountability systems that measure the learning of all students, there are a number of fundamental conceptual and methodological issues that must be addressed (see also Kleinert, Haigh, Kearns, & Kennedy, in press; Ysseldyke, Olsen, & Thurlow, 1997). Perhaps the most central issue is the question of *who* is being assessed. On the surface, this may seem to be a rather simple question with a perfectly obvious answer. It is, of course, the student who is being assessed! Yet we argue that the answer to this basic question is considerably more complex, if we want to develop educational accountability measures for students with significant cognitive disabilities that are truly fair, that do not automatically penalize students (and their schools) for the severity of their disabilities. If, in fact, we are measuring simple units of learning, we already know that students with moderate and severe cognitive disabilities, by definition, have significant impairments in both overall intellectual functioning and in measures of adaptive skills (American Association on Mental Retardation, 1992). By definition, those students with the most severe disabilities, including students with severe and profound disabilities, will score at lower levels of achievement on almost any objective measure of academic learning or adaptive behavior. Thus we argue that any alternate assessment system that is strictly tied to performance on specific tasks (no matter how functional or age-appropriate those tasks may be) will ultimately result in lower levels of independent performance for students with the most severe disabilities, even with the advantage of exemplary school programs.

Instead, we propose that the fundamental purpose of educational accountability systems is not "student accountability (i.e., the student proving what he or she has learned), but rather school accountability (i.e., the school documenting the best examples of what the student can do, in the context of the quality of the learning opportunities provided and the nature and characteristics of individualized supports)" (Kleinert et al., in press; see also Kleinert et al., 1997; and Ysseldyke & Olsen, 1999). We argue that the fundamental role of education in the lives of students with the most severe disabilities is not necessarily to establish independent performances across the broad range of typical activities and environments but rather "to both teach skills *and* foster supportive environments (including the development of meaningful social supports) to enable all students to fully participate in the lives of their community and school." Thus performance measures "ideally capture not only learned skills, but also the range of environments in which the student currently demonstrates those skills, as well as the social networks and quality of supports provided" (Kleinert et al., in press).

Within the context of school accountability, this position makes sense to us. A simple cataloging of student performances or a standardized measure of all learned skills would inevitably confine students with severe and profound disabilities to the "lowest" ranges of the accountability index. Recognition of the school's role in the development of supports and the quality of learning opportunities (and the assessment of those opportunities and supports as an integral part of the accountability process) puts the onus where it truly belongs—on the student's school—at the same time that it makes possible for students with even the most severe disabilities to evidence, in the language of Kentucky's assessment system, Distinguished levels of performance.

A second fundamental issue is *what* is being assessed—that is, the learning content of the alternate assessment. Kleinert and Kearns (1999) have noted that the "alternate assessment should be tied as closely as possible to the state's general education assessment. The same learner outcomes (or a subset of those outcomes) should form the basis for both the general and the alternate assessments, though students might have multiple ways for evidencing these same outcomes" (p. 109). This position is clearly consistent with IDEA's new requirement to reference each student's educational performance and IEP to the general curriculum for all students. To reflect this emphasis, in 1998 Kentucky changed the curriculum focus and required entries of the Alternate Portfolio from a functional domains-based model (i.e., personal management, vocational, recreation/leisure) to the state's general education curriculum model presented in Table 12.1.

A third major issue in implementing state-level alternate assessments is the need for vested ownership by teachers. This should be addressed in several ways, including developing and supporting a teacher-led, statewide training and technical assistance network for practitioners. Kentucky has developed a teacher training and assistance network for the Alternate Portfolio based on a similar regional network set up for the regular assessment. Veteran teachers serve as both regional and district leaders in providing assistance to new teachers. Similarly, teachers have played a pivotal role throughout the development of the alternate assessment, including identifying portfolio contents, scoring standards, benchmarking, and state policy-making. Teachers should always be invited to submit exemplary portfolio entries to use in portfolio training and to continuously improve the system.

The fourth systems challenge revolves around the logistical issues in setting up scoring (and rescoring) procedures, as well as recording and retaining scores for each school and local district's accountability index. Scoring and rescoring of portfolios requires considerable time; this time is very much a part of the real cost of the system. Kentucky relies on a regionalized network of trained scorers providing regular assistance. Scoring procedures must also be secure, with adequate backup systems, to prevent the accidental loss or even falsification of scores, especially in the context of "high-stakes" accountability. Finally, mathematical formulas must be worked out to ensure that the scores of students in the alternate assessment are weighted equally with the performance measures of students in the regular system; this is especially critical in multicomponent systems such as Kentucky's, in which all students may not be included in all assessment components.

A fifth issue is determining to *which* school student scores should be assigned for accountability purposes. Although at first glance it may appear obvious that the accountable school should in all instances be the school the student attends, in Kentucky this is not always the case. Kentucky tracks scores back to the school that the student would have attended if he or she did not have a disability (i.e., the student's *neighborhood* school). The rationale for this decision is that the neighborhood school is ultimately responsible for sending a student "out of district" (i.e., out of its attendance area), and thus that school still bears responsibility for the education of the student. It is not yet clear whether this policy has increased attendance for students with disabilities in neighborhood schools statewide. However, it does mean that separate schools for students with disabilities do *not* have account-ability indices in Kentucky (at present, the state has only one local-district, sepa-rate school for students with moderate and severe cognitive disabilities).

A sixth crucial systems issue is the involvement of higher education and teacher preparation programs in the development and implementation of the alternate assessment. Kentucky teacher educators have been involved at each step of the development of the Alternate Portfolio. Teacher educators need to have a firm grasp of the alternate assessment themselves, and they need to include key concepts (e.g., natural peer supports, self-monitoring and self-evaluation, academic expectations for all students) into course content for prospective teachers. Teacher *candidates* should also have the opportunity to attend the regional scoring trainings offered to current teachers throughout the state. Finally, the concept of portfolio assess-ment for all school-age students, including students with moderate and severe dis-abilities, can be reinforced by having teacher candidates develop their *own* portfo-lios to illustrate their competencies in working with learners with a wide range of needs. For a further discussion of systems issues, as well as "lessons learned," see Kleinert et al. (2000) and Kleinert and Kearns (1999).

CONCLUSION

In this chapter, we have sought to provide an overview of Kentucky's alternate assessment for students with moderate and severe cognitive disabilities, the Alter-nate Portfolio. We have discussed the development of the alternate assessment and the portfolio contents and scoring standards. We have noted that student portfo-lios can be used in a variety of ways: as an important teaching tool to enable stu-dents to evaluate their work and to organize their own learning; as an exciting ve-hicle for teachers and parents to communicate what students are learning; and, in Kentucky, as a part of the state's formal educational accountability system. We have briefly discussed how portfolio assessment can link students' learning to broader and essential contexts of valued social supports at school, in the community, and in the family. We have noted that children with severe disabilities in Kentucky are able to (and do) evidence exemplary scores in the state's accountability index. Most importantly, we have described an accountability system in which a school receives recognition and reward for a child with a severe disability who scores at the Dis-tinguished level on his or her Alternate Portfolio equal to that received for a child labeled gifted who scores Distinguished in the state's regular assessment. This fact alone sends a clear message to everyone—teachers, administrators, and, perhaps most important, families and students themselves—that the learning of all chil-dren fundamentally matters. Kentucky's educational assessment system has much room for improvement—but the underlying message should be at the very heart of education for all children who enter our schools.

NOTE

Portions of this chapter have been adapted from H. Kleinert, J. Kearns, and S. Kennedy, "Accountability for all students: Kentucky's Alternate Portfolio Assessment for students with moderate and severe disabilities," *Journal of the Association for Persons With Severe Handicaps, 22* (2), 1997, 88–101. This manuscript was supported, in part, by the U.S. Department of Education Office of Special Education and Rehabilitation Services (Grants No. H023F70004 and No. H086J20007). However, the opinions expressed do not necessarily reflect the position or policy of the U.S. Department of Education and no official endorsement should be inferred.

REFERENCES

American Association on Mental Retardation. (1992). *Mental retardation: Definition, classification, and system of supports* (9th ed.). Washington, DC: Author.

Blackorby, J., & Wagner, M. (1996). Longitudinal postschool outcomes of youth with disabilities: Findings from the National Longitudinal Transition Study. *Exceptional Children, 62*(5), 399–414.

Carter, J. F. (1993). Self-management: Education's ultimate goal. *Teaching Exceptional Children, 25,* 28–31.

Elliott, J., Ysseldyke, J., Thurlow, M., & Erickson, E. (1998). What about assessment and accountability? *Teaching Exceptional Children, 31*(1), 20–27.

Kearns, J., Kleinert, H., Clayton, J., Burdge, M., & Williams, R. (1998). Principal supports for inclusive assessment: A Kentucky story. *Teaching Exceptional Children 31*(2), 16–23.

Kentucky Alternate Portfolio Project. (1999). *Teacher's Guide.* Lexington: University of Kentucky, Interdisciplinary Human Development Institute.

King-Sears, M., & Carpenter, S. (1997). Teaching self-management to elementary students with developmental disabilities. *Innovations.* Washington, DC: American Association on Mental Retardation.

Kleinert, H., Haigh, J., Kearns, J., & Kennedy, S. (2000). Alternate assessments: Lessons learned and roads to be taken. *Exceptional Children, 67*(1), 51–66.

Kleinert, H., & Kearns, J. (1999). A validation study of the performance indicators and learner outcomes of Kentucky's alternate assessment for students with significant disabilities. *Journal of the Association for Persons With Severe Handicaps, 24*(2), 100–110.

Kleinert, H., Kearns, J., & Kennedy, S. (1997). Accountability for all students: Kentucky's Alternate Portfolio system for students with moderate and severe cognitive disabilities. *Journal of the Association for Persons With Severe Handicaps, 22*(2), 88–101.

Light, L., Dumlao, C., & Stecker, P. (1993). Video resume: An application of technology for persons with severe disabilities. *Teaching Exceptional Children, 25*(3), 58–62.

National Center on Educational Outcomes. (1997). *1997 special education outcomes: A report on state activities during educational reform.* Minneapolis: University of Minnesota, National Center on Educational Outcomes.

Sage, D., & Burrello, L. (1994). *Leadership in educational reform: An administrator's guide to changes in special education.* Baltimore: Paul H. Brookes.

Steffy, B. (1993). Top-down–bottom-up: Systemic change in Kentucky. *Educational Leadership, 51*(1), 42–44.

Vanderwood, M., McGrew, K., & Ysseldyke, J. (1998). Why we can't say much about the status of students with disabilities in education reform. *Exceptional Children, 64*(3), 359–370.

What is Goals 2000: The Educate America Act? (1994). *Teaching Exceptional Children, 27*(1), 78–80.

Wheatley, S. (1993). *Communication systems for students with intellectual disabilities: A statewide survey.* Unpublished manuscript, University of Kentucky at Lexington.

Ysseldyke, J., & Olsen, K. (1999). Putting alternate assessments into practice: What to measure and possible sources of data. *Exceptional Children 65*(2), 175–186.

Ysseldyke, J., Olsen, K., & Thurlow, M. (1997). *Issues and considerations in alternate assessments (Syn. Rep. No. 27).* Minneapolis: University of Minnesota, National Center on Educational Outcomes.

PART IV

Preparing for the Next Generation: New Systems for School Finance and Teacher Preparation

We set out in this book to examine the implications for inclusive education of the movement to bring schools and communities, including families, more closely together through school reform processes. In Part Four, we look to future solutions for two of the major barriers that have mitigated historically against inclusive educational practices: school finance models and personnel preparation.

In Chapter 13, Tom Parrish examines the trend of change in special education finance models at the state level, and the implication for inclusion. The relationship between special education fiscal policy and the least restrictive environment (LRE) and "continuum of services" requirements of the Individuals With Disabilities Education Act (IDEA) are explored. The chapter describes provisions found in the state models that create fiscal incentives for restrictive placements, provides examples, and discusses how and why these provisions must be removed. It urges that a conscious effort be made to consider the placement incentives associated with alternative fiscal policies and to develop fiscal provisions that support the LRE requirements of IDEA.

Finally, in Chapter 14, Jim Paul and his faculty colleagues at the University of South Florida take a careful look at the process of driving reform in higher education teacher training practices from the standpoint of evolving more collaborative policies arising from school/community partnerships. Faculty in the Department of Special Education at the University of South Florida are transforming their program to address the agendas of school reform and service integration. The chapter discusses the context in which reform in special education is occurring and describes how fundamental changes in the department's programs have been addressed. Specific examples of collaborative initiatives with local school districts, community agencies, and other departments in the university are presented along with some of the challenges that have arisen from such partnerships.

CHAPTER 13

Fiscal Policies in Support of Inclusive Education

Thomas B. Parrish

In this chapter we examine how fiscal policies interact with program goals in support of inclusive education. Fostering inclusive education as a federal policy goal has become a more clearly articulated objective through the 1997 reauthorization of the federal Individuals With Disabilities Education Act (IDEA). In addition, according to interviews with local officials, making inclusive education a top priority is also a primary rationale for change in many of the states that have engaged in special education finance reform (Parrish, 1997). The relationship between a range of program reforms related to the reduction of restrictive placement patterns and alternative provisions for financing these reforms is presented here. Provisions governing state and federal funding of special education can either foster or discourage inclusive education.

The reforms discussed in this chapter pertain to the provision of services for special education students in the least restrictive environment (LRE) and to greater integration of special education into other educational programs. Specifically, the chapter describes fiscal disincentives for serving students with special education needs in more inclusive settings, how these disincentives can be removed, and how limited educational resources can be used more efficiently to provide better coordination and articulation across educational programs. The chapter also argues that inclusive education should be considered from a fiscal and economic perspective. That is, beyond the need to remove fiscal barriers to the provision of inclusive special education services, arguments can be made in support of inclusive education from the perspective of educational cost-effectiveness and efficiency.

Finally, the chapter includes separate discussions of state and federal special education finance reform issues. State issues are discussed first, because states have the primary responsibility for special education services and provide substantially more support to these programs than does the federal government. A discussion of some of the most relevant provisions under reauthorized federal law follows.

Although it was federal legislation (IDEA) that originally ensured a free and appropriate education for all students with disabilities, it is estimated that about 12% of special education funding now comes from federal sources (from both IDEA and Medicaid sources).[1] This is despite the authorization, and what many consider the promise, of federal funding up to 40% of the average per pupil expenditure (APPE) for every special education student. In relation to this standard, which is different from the percentage of total special education expenditures funded by the federal government, Part B funding constitutes about 12.5% of the APPE.

Since IDEA was passed, special education costs and enrollments have grown considerably. The number of students receiving special education services nationally has grown from 7.4% of public school enrollments in 1976 to 12% in 1998. More than $19 billion in local, state, and federal funds were spent for special education and related services in 1987–1988 (the latest year for which such data are available). The best available estimate of this amount for 1998–1999 exceeds $45 billion. Of this amount, it is estimated that localities provide about 51%, the states about 37%, with a federal share of approximately 12% (Part B and Medicaid support combined). Although special education has represented a growing share of overall elementary and secondary school spending over the past two decades, in inflation-adjusted terms, federal aid per eligible student has shown little growth during this period, until the past few years. During the 1990s, federal special education aid per student showed a pattern of slight decline in inflation-adjusted dollars since peaking in 1991 (Parrish & Verstegen, 1994). However, this pattern was reversed in the allocation for fiscal year 1997, which returned the federal allocation for the school-age population to about 1991 levels in terms of inflation-adjusted dollars per student. Since 1997, substantial growth in the federal contribution has occurred.

The continuing growth in the number of students identified for special education services and the corresponding increases in cost have contributed to an unprecedented degree of public scrutiny regarding special education over the past few years.[2] In addition, there are growing concerns about the fiscal incentives for more restrictive, high-cost placements that are contained in some state special education funding formulas, and also about the lack of flexibility in the use of special education funds. Policy-makers are increasingly realizing that state and federal fiscal provisions may provide major stumbling blocks to program reform at the local level.

Each of the states and the federal government have different sets of policies and procedures for determining allocations of special education aid to local school districts. A great deal has been written and numerous typologies have been developed to categorize these alternative funding mechanisms (Hartman, 1992; Moore, Walker, & Holland, 1982; O'Reilly, 1993). Although this chapter discusses these alternatives and makes some policy recommendations, it does not endorse a single funding approach. Each alternative discussed has been designed to achieve different policy and program objectives. In choosing among competing fiscal policy options, each governmental entity must clearly define program objectives within its local policy context.

Nevertheless, the following set of general principles underlies this chapter: (a) Financing policy will influence local program provision; (b) incentives of one type or another are inherent in all financing systems; and (c) in developing fiscal policy, it is essential to develop provisions that will support, or at least not obstruct, program goals. Within the context of these principles, this chapter discusses the policy implications of alternative methods for encouraging inclusive placement options and presents methods for reducing the number of restrictive placements when this is a stated program objective.

DEFINING PROGRAM REFORM

Prior to considering the relationship between special education finance policies and inclusive education, it is necessary to develop some agreed upon definition of the specific reforms being pursued. From a fiscal perspective, such reforms generally foster placement of students in public rather than private schools, in neighborhood rather than specialized schools, and in inclusive rather than segregated classrooms and settings. Also relevant to finance policies are issues related to greater flexibility in the use of local resources, the creation of intervention systems for all students, and the preparation of special and general educators.

These issues are pertinent for several reasons. First, one way to avoid restrictiveness in the placement of students is to avoid fiscal incentives for identifying students for special education in the first place when alternative types of interventions are sufficient to meet their needs. For example, the removal of fiscal incentives to identify more special education students is a stated policy objective of special education finance reforms enacted in the states of Vermont, Pennsylvania, Massachusetts, and Montana, as well as for the reauthorized IDEA.

Another related objective for program reform is to provide a seamless set of services to meet the needs of all students, whether they have general, special, bilingual, or compensatory education requirements. (See McLaughlin [1995] and Miles & Darling-Hammond [1998].) These strategies attempt to reduce the barriers built around categorical programs, which result in the separation of associated programs and services. These barriers lead to the inefficient use of resources through the required maintenance of multiple administrative units, accounting structures, and facilities, and to the inefficient provision of services for students with multiple special needs. The separation of these services may also be seen as generally discouraging inclusive education.

RELATING FINANCE TO PROGRAM REFORM

The concept that appropriate instructional programs and related services cannot be provided without adequate financial support has long been recognized. A newer concept, but one that is becoming more widely recognized, is that the policies that underlie educational financing mechanisms may be as important in affecting program provision as the amounts allocated. Even the simplest funding systems contain incentives and disincentives that may directly influence the orientation, quantities, and types of services provided at the local level.

Unprecedented special education finance reform has occurred across the states and at the federal level over the past decade. Interviews with representatives of the 50 states revealed that this high level of activity is at least partly the result of the fiscal disincentives in many state funding formulas for the kinds of programmatic reform that states are attempting to foster. States increasingly realize that program policies, guidelines, training, and supports have little impact on program provision while appreciable fiscal disincentives to change practice remain in place. This is especially true in the current era of increasing fiscal constraint, in which local decision makers are hard pressed to pursue reform initiatives that will reduce the financial support they receive from state and federal sources. Furthermore, the policy messages from state and federal governments are clearly mixed. Local districts are sometimes asked to do one thing, while they receive financial encouragement to do just the opposite.

However, it is also clear that changes in fiscal policy alone are insufficient to result in program change. States reporting the most success in coordinating program and fiscal reform emphasize the need for financial incentives, or at least the removal of disincentives, as well as the provision of a comprehensive system of professional development and ongoing support to effect the desired changes.

SPECIAL EDUCATION FINANCE REFORM IN THE STATES

Over half the states have actively pursued special education finance reform over the past 5 years (Parrish, 1997). To fully appreciate this level of change requires an understanding of how difficult this type of reform can be for state policy-makers. Education is the largest single budget item in most states, and changes in the amount of state aid received by local districts inevitably create dissension. Given the strength of the advocacy groups associated with special education, funding can be among the most contentious issues that state policy-makers have to confront. The fact that over half the states have engaged in changing their special education funding formulas over the past 5 to 10 years provides strong evidence that a very powerful set of social conditions and reform issues is influencing these changes.

Factors Affecting Reform

In 1994–1995, the Center for Special Education Finance (CSEF) surveyed state directors of special education for the purpose of gathering information about special education funding systems and reforms under way at the state level (Parrish, 1997). These interviews indicated that the desire to remove fiscal incentives favoring more restrictive placements was among the major factors providing impetus for reform. This was not an issue in all states, however, because some states have formulas, like the federal formula under IDEA, that do not provide fiscal incentives for higher-cost placements. Other issues driving reform were rising costs and enrollments, and lack of flexibility in the local use of special education funds.

In states where fiscal incentives for utilizing segregated programs were a major issue, two principal, and often separate, elements of the funding provisions were motivating reform. These elements were (a) aid differentials within the public system that relate to type of placement and (b) differentials between the amounts of state aid received for private versus public special education placements.

Restrictiveness Resulting From Public Funding Mechanisms

States with public funding differentials favoring placements in separate classrooms, schools, or facilities tend to be those with resource-based systems or pupil-weighting systems that vary based on the primary setting in which students receive services. Both of these types of funding systems generally feature an array of primary service configurations, with state aid varying by type of placement. Because the funding differentials under these systems are directly related to the costs of alternative placements, both can be considered cost-based systems.

Historically, cost-based funding systems have been seen as strong bases for driving funding differentials. The concept underlying this type of system is that the amount of aid a district receives for a student with special needs should be directly related to the cost of providing services for the student. Since all categorical funding formulas have an underlying cost rationale, many school finance experts and policy-makers have preferred systems that differentiate funding amounts on actual differences in the cost of services.

Somewhat ironically, cost-based systems are now sometimes seen as problematic because they create fiscal incentives for higher-cost placements that are often provided in separate classrooms or facilities. An example of this type of problem is described in a feature article from *U.S. News and World Report*, "Texas pays local school districts ten times more for teaching special education students in separate classrooms. The result? Only 5 percent of special education students in Texas are taught in regular classrooms (Shapiro, Loeb, & Bowermaster, 1993, p. 47)."[3]

This type of perverse incentive, however, need not necessarily be found in cost-based funding systems. For example, New York has recently developed a new funding category for special education students who have been included in general education classrooms.

The Need for Other Cost-based Options

An important breakthrough in special education funding could be the development of a set of pupil funding weights that reflects alternative integrated modes of service with varying levels of support services for individual students. Such a system could allow a linkage between funding and service costs, while avoiding the fiscal incentives for more separate placements that have come to be associated with cost-based systems.

It is important to keep in mind that cost-based funding options were never designed to promote segregated or restrictive placements. Rather, they were designed to promote equity and efficiency in funding by linking state aid allocations to program costs. The fact that these systems have sometimes encouraged high cost, segregated placements in a number of states is an unintended consequence of a changing direction in program policy rather than a fatal flaw in the nature of cost-based systems.

Incentives for Private Placements

A second issue related to funding incentives for restrictive placements is the use of separate special education funding mechanisms for public and private special education schools. A quote describing this private schooling phenomenon also comes from *U.S. News and World Report*:

> Cities like New Haven [Connecticut] actually save money when they send students to out-of-district schools, even though these schools can cost the state more than $100,000 per student, because the state picks up the bulk of the cost. (Shapiro et al., 1993, p. 50)

Issues relating to fiscal incentives for private placements seem especially difficult for states to resolve. For example, in both Massachusetts and California, although major changes were made in the public special education funding systems, incentives for public schools to use private placements were retained. Similar concerns have been raised in New York, where a proposal to remove incentives to use private placements met considerable resistance. Use of private placements varies considerably across the states, however. Whereas New Jersey has over 5% of its special education students in private placements, Texas reports less than .01% and Utah 0% (U.S. Department of Education, 1998).

What seems important from a fiscal policy perspective is that state funding systems not favor private placements. Funding for high-cost students should follow students to local school districts, where decisions are best made concerning the appropriateness of private versus public school placements. This type of funding approach would remove any fiscal incentive for the use of private schools. Instead, their use would be based on children's needs and the merits and unique strengths of the programs and services these schools offer.

NEED FOR FLEXIBILITY AT THE LOCAL LEVEL

A lack of flexibility at the local level is also influencing state fiscal reform. An important concern in a number of states, as described above, is the lack of fiscal mechanisms to support more integrated services, thereby greatly restricting local flexibility in the design of appropriate services. A second concern relates to the inability to use special education funds, or the unavailability of other funds, to support certain types of instructional interventions outside of special education. Consequently, when special education is the only available source of funding for intervention services, there will be constant pressure on special education en-rollments and costs.

Interestingly, the majority of states do not require that special education funds be spent on special education services. This type of flexibility can, of course, have different implications. It may mean that special education funding is com-pletely rolled into the general state aid allocation and can be used for any pur-pose. In other states, these alternative uses may be limited to prereferral or other types of intervention or remedial services. In some states, it seems that this type of flexibility has always been available but has not been widely promoted or pub-licized. In other states, it has been granted more recently with the express pur-pose of promoting the development of some type of prereferral assessment and intervention system.

Flexibility in Reallocating Transportation Costs

Separate, categorical funding for transportation services is another important is-sue related to local flexibility in the use of funds, which may discourage inclu-sive education. As districts attempt to move students with disabilities back to neighborhood schools, they face start-up costs needed to make these schools fully accessible and to purchase multiple sets of specialized equipment, rather than just the one set that may be needed in a single specialized school. These costs may be largely offset through savings in transportation costs. Yet, in state fund-ing systems where transportation is categorically funded, dollars saved through reduced transportation services cannot be recouped for use in other ways (i.e., to support the start-up costs of more integrated programs in neighborhood schools).

Because transportation costs are ongoing, as opposed to what are often one-time costs associated with making schools more accessible, allowing flexibility in the reallocation of transportation costs could lead to better services for students and provide significant long-term savings to states and school districts. Clearly, funds being allocated for transportation services could be more advantageously used to enhance direct instructional services for students, when possible. To enhance inclusive education, it is important at both the state and district levels that special education funds be allowed to follow students as they move to more inclusive place-ments. In addition to transportation savings, the movement of students to neigh-borhood schools could also lead to other types of long-term savings. Separate special education schools generate additional costs in such areas as school administration and instructional support.

Better Program Coordination

Final issues relating to the need for increased flexibility in the use of funds at the local level are the perceived barriers to providing better articulated and coordinated sets of services across categorical program areas. General, special, compensatory, and limited-English-proficient (LEP) programs exist far too often in virtual isolation from one another in schools with high levels of special needs. Major concerns focus on inefficiencies that result from the need for multiple administrative and accountability structures, alternative forms of determining eligibility that tend to be cumbersome and costly, and the inevitable segregation that results from separated services.

The lack of integrated, well-articulated services can be especially disastrous for students with multiple needs. At the extreme, imagine the school day for a student designated as an English Language Learner (ELL), who receives compensatory instruction, and who receives special education services in a school in which all of these special programs are run separately from one another. Examples of more integrated and articulated services for schools are described in Miles and Darling-Hammond (1998). However, many local providers claim that important barriers to these types of change result from the limitations imposed on the use of state and federal funds. They attribute the types of segregated program options being provided in their schools to rules and regulations they believe preclude them from providing more integrated, well-articulated programs. Nevertheless, McLaughlin (1995) found that schools that were successfully implementing these reforms generally did not find that state and federal provisions posed a barrier to implementation. Similarly, federal officials in leadership positions report that nothing in the federal law precludes districts from exercising the kinds of flexibility needed to produce well-articulated and integrated schoolwide instructional programming (Verstegen, 1995).

Criteria for the Funding Formula

Given these concerns about state funding formulas that have provisions discouraging more inclusive services, what criteria should be used to evaluate state special education funding systems? Table 13.1 presents a set of criteria, or standards, that that may be used in considering alternative ways of allocating special education aid to local jurisdictions.

State policy-makers may find value in each of the criteria listed. However, in adopting state funding reform, it is essential to realize that although these criteria are not mutually exclusive, a major focus on one criterion may come at the expense of one or more others. For example, depending on how equity is defined, a highly equitable system might be one that is tightly linked to variations in local costs of providing special education services. Districts that spend more on special education services because their resource costs are higher, because they serve more students, or because they serve students with more severe needs, would receive more state aid in recognition of these cost differentials. On the other hand, such a system may also have a fairly substantial reporting burden, may lack flexibility, and may not be placement-neutral. Conversely, a system in which special education funds are allocated only on the basis of total district enrollment (e.g., as in California, Pennsylvania, Massachusetts, Montana, Pennsylvania, and Vermont) will be identification- and placement-neutral (i.e., no fiscal incentives to identify students for special education or to serve them in a particular type of placement). Yet such a system may also be perceived as quite inequitable because it fails to link aid allocations to local variations in pupil need. A system that is fully adequate and predictable may have problems related to cost control, and so on. Thus, in attempting to develop an ideal set of special education funding provisions for a given state, it is essential that policy-makers choose the criteria they wish to foster from among these alternatives and recognize that no system, no matter how simple, will be incentive free.

For example, the base federal special education funding system may be considered placement-neutral because the amount of funding per student is the same regardless of how the student is served. Although many may believe this to be a desirable attribute, this type of system does contain a fiscal incentive. Because the funding level will be the same regardless of the level of service provided, the fiscal incentive is to provide less service at a lower cost. Similarly, so-called identification-neutral systems, like those in Massachusetts, California, and Pennsylvania, actually contain fiscal incentives not to label students for special education, as districts will receive the same level of funding regardless of the number of students identified. Although this may be the policy objective in some of these states, it is essential to realize the incentives and disincentives embodied in alternative funding systems. As funding provisions will have a direct influence on program policies, decision makers must identify the policies they wish to promote and adopt a funding system that will foster them, or at least not inhibit them.

State Fiscal Policies That Foster Integrated Services

As discussed in the introductory section of this chapter, federal provisions under IDEA, bolstered through the reauthorization of this law in 1997, state that special education students should be served in the least restrictive environment. Given this policy objective, what types of fiscal policies can states adopt to foster more integrated special education services?

First, fiscal incentives favoring segregated and separate placements must be removed. Theoretically, this could be achieved under any type of special education funding system. For example, even systems that are driven by type of student placement could develop a weighting structure encouraging integration through the creation of larger weights for general education placements, as New York has done. Thus far, however, the states attempting to reduce the number of restrictive place-

Table 13.1. Criteria for Evaluating State Special Education Funding Formulas

UNDERSTANDABLE

- The funding system and its underlying policy objectives are understandable by all concerned parties (legislators, legislative staff, state department personnel, local administrators, and advocates).
- The concepts underlying the formula and the procedures to implement it are straightforward and "avoid unnecessary complexity."

EQUITABLE

- Student equity: Dollars are distributed to ensure comparable program quality regardless of district assignment.
- Wealth equity: Availability of overall funding is not correlated with local wealth.
- District-to-district fairness: All districts receive comparable resources for comparable students.

ADEQUATE

- Funding is sufficient for all districts to provide appropriate programs for special education students.

PREDICTABLE

- LEAs know allocations in time to plan for local services.
- The system produces predictable demands for state funding.
- SEA and LEAs can count on stable funding across years.

FLEXIBLE

- Local agencies are given latitude to deal with unique local conditions in an appropriate and cost-effective manner.
- Changes that affect programs and costs can be incorporated into the funding system with minimum disruption.
- Local agencies are given maximum latitude in use of resources in exchange for outcome accountability.

IDENTIFICATION NEUTRAL

- The number of students identified as eligible for special education is not the only, or primary, basis for determining the amount of special education funding to be received.
- Students do not have to be labeled "disabled" (or any other label) in order to receive services.

REASONABLE REPORTING BURDEN

- Costs to maintain the funding system are minimized at both local and state levels.
- Data requirements, record keeping, and reporting are kept at a reasonable level.

Table 13.1. (continued)

FISCAL ACCOUNTABILITY

- Conventional accounting procedures are followed to assure that special education funds are spent in an authorized manner.
- Procedures are included to contain excessive or inappropriate special education costs.

COST-BASED

- Funding received by districts for the provision of special education programs is linked to the costs they face in providing these programs.

COST CONTROL

- Patterns of growth in special education costs statewide are stabilized over time.
- Patterns of growth in special education identification rates statewide are stabilized over time.

PLACEMENT NEUTRAL

- District funding for special education is not based on type of educational placement.
- District funding for special education is not based on disability label.

OUTCOME ACCOUNTABILITY

- State monitoring of local agencies is based on various measures of student outcomes.
- A statewide system for demonstrating satisfactory progress for all students in all schools is developed.
- Schools showing positive results for students are given maximum program and fiscal latitude to continue producing them.

CONNECTION TO GENERAL EDUCATION FUNDING

- The special education funding formula should have a clear conceptual link to the general education finance system.
- Integration of funding will be likely to lead to integration of services.

POLITICAL ACCEPTABILITY

- Implementation avoids any major short-term loss of funds.
- Implementation involves no major disruption of existing services.

Adapted from *State Funding Models for Special Education* (Hartman, 1992).

ments have shown a greater inclination to move toward funding systems that do not differentiate funding based on student placement.

Second, states must make decisions about the extent to which they wish to encourage private special education placements. Some states may decide that private, as opposed to public, placements are more restrictive under any circumstance and may wish to create fiscal disincentives for their use. Other states may decide that private placements are an integral component of the continuum of available placements for their special education students and that these types of placements should be granted equal, but not preferential, funding in relation to public alternatives.

Third, the private schooling issue provides an example of the importance of developing funding systems in which dollars follow students as they move to less restrictive placements. Another example, as cited earlier, is the need for savings in transportation costs to follow special education students to their neighborhood schools to offset other types of costs associated with this type of move. This is an issue for states as they try to foster integrated program practices and for districts as they try to implement them.

Fourth, states reporting the most success in fostering more integrated service systems point to the need to support direct training for these types of program interventions. As fiscal disincentives favoring segregated services are removed, districts must be provided with training and assistance in overcoming the many practical difficulties associated with making changes of this type.

Fifth, states should fund and encourage intervention systems for all students. Students who are identified as eligible for special education because identification is the only way to provide them with remedial services have had their service options restricted. The spirit of greater program integration would seem to include retaining students in general education who do not require the additional protection and legal guarantees associated with special education. Accordingly, state funding systems that actively support alternative interventions for all students will be less likely to lead to program placements that are unnecessarily restrictive.

FINANCE PROVISIONS UNDER THE REAUTHORIZED FEDERAL LAW

The reauthorization hearings on IDEA in 1997 generated considerable discussion about special education finance at the federal level. A number of important provisions allowing greater latitude and flexibility in the provision of special education services were included under the reauthorized IDEA.

Census-based Funding

A new approach for distributing special education aid to the states was adopted. A simple description of "census-based" funding is that two states with identical school-age populations would receive the same amount of federal special education aid regardless of the number or percentage of special education students identified or served. This type of funding approach has also been adopted by several states as the basis for allocating state special education funds. It represents an important departure from prior special education fiscal policy because funding is unaffected by the number of identified special education students.

Proponents see it as an effective way to provide local jurisdictions with more discretion and flexibility, and as a way to break the linkage between special education identification and funding. States adopting this type of funding system credit such objectives with reducing administrative burden, increasing local flexibility, neutralizing incentives for identification and restrictive placements, and bringing rising special education costs under control. However, opponents sometimes express concerns that such a funding system is a retreat from the traditional governmental role of promoting special education.

Fiscal Disincentives for Least Restrictive Placements

States with funding formulas that distribute assistance to local education agencies (LEAs) based on the type of setting in which a child is served must have policies and procedures to assure that their funding provisions do not result in restrictive placements that violate the LRE requirement of IDEA. This new requirement could affect about one quarter of the states, whose special education funding systems are based primarily on placement, unless they can ensure that placements are not being made in violation of LRE requirements. It could affect additional states with subsidiary provisions based on placement, such as additional funding for students served in separate schools and institutions or categorical funding for special education transportation services, if those provisions are resulting in placements that violate the LRE requirements.

More Permissive Use of Federal Funds

Another change allows nondisabled students to receive benefits from special education services provided for children with disabilities. This provision encourages LEAs to meet an important intent of the law—that children with disabilities are educated to the maximum extent possible with children without disabilities—without having to fear audit exceptions under the excess costs or commingling of funds requirements.

CONCLUSION

Issues related to blended funding and service provision are at the heart of the education reform movement and are central to the current special education finance debate (McLaughlin, 1995; Miles and Darling-Hammond, 1998; Verstegen, 1995).

A critical question that confronts the development of future fiscal policy in special education is whether funding should retain its purely categorical nature. There is a natural tension between separate, highly categorical funding streams and overall education reform objectives favoring more "unified" schooling systems (McLaughlin & Warren, 1992). In "unified" systems, the strict barriers between categorical programs begin to disappear and are replaced by a more seamless set of educational programs and services designed to meet the special needs of all students.

At the federal level, this type of blended funding is permitted under Title I of the revised Elementary and Secondary Education Act for high-poverty schools. Currently, schools with 50% enrollments of students in poverty are allowed to blend funds from a variety of federal sources to make schoolwide changes for the benefit of all students. Under the reauthorized IDEA, federal special education funds may be included under these provisions.

Fiscal provisions of this type allowing greater integration can enhance program reforms like more inclusive education. However, changes in fiscal policy alone are not likely to be sufficient to bring about substantial changes. These types of fiscal reforms also must be accompanied by a set of specific program reform goals as well as technical assistance and training.

Inclusive education can be fostered within the context of any basic funding model. Whether this actually occurs, however, will depend on specific implementation details and will require a careful definition of the exact practices to be fostered under the proposed set of program reforms. For example, is the policy goal limited to reducing the number of restrictive placements for special education students, or is there also a desire to foster inclusive education? Beyond this, is there a related policy goal to provide more integrated services across all categorical programs at the school level? These policy objectives differ and will require somewhat differing fiscal policies. In shaping appropriate fiscal policy, it is important to identify the related program reform objectives as precisely as possible. Given the strong link between fiscal and program policy, program objectives must be well considered and carefully defined prior to any serious consideration of fiscal reform. If inclusive education and cross program coordination are goals, the program provisions underlying these general objectives will have to be clearly defined with supporting fiscal provisions crafted accordingly.

NOTES

1. The estimates contained in this section are based on responses from 25 states to a survey on special education spending conducted by the National Association of State Directors of Special Education (NASDSE) with assistance from the national Center for Special Education Finance (CSEF).

2. Recent examples of this interest include major articles regarding special education programs and costs in *U.S. News and World Report* (December 13, 1993) and the *New York Times* (April 6, 7, and 8, 1994).

3. Although this quote from *U.S. News and World Report* provides a good example of the types of problematic fiscal provisions found in many states, the author has discussed it with Texas officials who question whether such a tenfold differential ever was in place in the state. Regardless, the Texas special education funding system subsequently has been changed.

REFERENCES

Hartman, W. T. (1992). State funding models for special education. *Remedial and Special Education, 13*(6), 47–58.

McLaughlin, M. J. (1995). *Consolidated special education funding and services: A local perspective* (Policy Paper No. 5). Palo Alto, CA: Center for Special Education Finance, American Institutes for Research.

McLaughlin, M. J., & Warren, S. H. (1992). *Issues and options in restructuring schools and special education programs.* College Park: University of Maryland.

Miles, K. H., & Darling-Hammond, L. (1998). Rethinking the allocation of teaching resources: Some lessons from high performing schools. *Educational Evaluation and Policy Analysis, 21*(1), 9–21.

Moore, M. T., Walker, L. J., & Holland, R. P. (1982). *Fine-tuning special education finance: A guide for state policymakers.* Princeton, NJ: Educational Testing Service, Education Policy Research Institute.

O'Reilly, F. (1993). *State special education finance systems, 1992–93.* Palo Alto, CA: Center for Special Education Finance, American Institutes for Research.

Parrish, T. (1997). Fiscal issues relating to special education inclusion. In D. Lipsky & A. Gartner (Eds.), *Inclusion and school reform* (pp. 275–298). Baltimore: Paul H. Brookes.

Parrish, T. B., & Verstegen, D. A. (1994). *Fiscal provisions of the Individuals With Disabilities Education Act: Policy issues and alternatives* (Policy Paper No. 3). Palo Alto, CA: Center for Special Education Finance, American Institutes for Research.

Shapiro, J., Loeb, P., & Bowermaster, D. (1993, December 13). Separate and unequal. *U.S. News and World Report,* pp. 46–51.

U.S. Department of Education. (1998). *Twentieth annual report to Congress on the implementation of the Individuals with Disabilities Education Act.* Washington, DC: Author.

Verstegen, D. A. (1995). *Consolidated special education funding and services: A federal perspective* (Policy Paper No. 6). Palo Alto, CA: Center for Special Education Finance, American Institutes for Research.

CHAPTER 14

Developing and Nurturing a Collaborative Culture for Change: Implications for Higher Education

James Paul, Betty Epanchin, Hilda Rosselli,
Al Duchnowski, and Ann Cranston-Gingras

During the last decade the widespread emphasis on school reform has challenged the vision, philosophy, content, and practices of traditional teacher education programs in colleges and universities. On one hand, changes in our understanding of knowledge and learning have forced critical attention to the nature of educational research and the foundations of pedagogy. Similarly, changes in organizational theory and decision making have stimulated alternative visions of schooling, policy development, and collaborative work, notwithstanding the relationship between university-based teacher education programs and schools. On the other hand, political and economic forces have pressed for emphasis on accountability for educational outcomes, which has created a serious public policy debate regarding the purpose of education. In particular, the social agenda of schools since the 1960s has focused on equity, and an ethic of care for the social welfare of all children, dramatically illustrated in the debate about inclusion, has been challenged on both economic and moral grounds. That is, there is not enough money to provide social support for all children and, even if there were, the policy commitment to do so undermines the traditional role of the family. The moral and religious construction of this debate has generated a great deal of controversy and anger. At issue are the roles of basic social institutions, such as the family and schools, and ethical principles, such as those having to do with duty, justice, care, privacy, and community.

This dynamic social, political, economic, and moral ecology of education has been characterized more by the conflicting forces of change and resistance than by any consensus between or among business, political, and professional communities on how children should be educated for the 21st century. It is in this context that teacher educators have been seeking to establish models that better connect universities and schools, pedagogy that is more reflective and critical, and research that accommodates the paradigm change that is occurring.

Changes in the preparation of special educators are shaped generally by this larger ecology, and more specifically by the restructuring movement in general education and the inclusion movement in special education that have only recently begun to converge. Teachers of special education have, therefore, focused on relationships with their colleagues in general education as well as relationships with public schools in rethinking the knowledge bases for education and the forms of practice (Paul et al., 1995). In this chapter, the focus is on the experiences of faculty in the Department of Special Education at the University of South Florida over the past several years, and the lessons we learned from transforming our work to address the agendas of school reform and services integration. We begin with a discussion of the contexts in which reform in special education is occurring, followed by a description of how we approached fundamental changes in our programs. Specific examples of collaborative initiatives with local school districts, community agencies, and other departments in the university are presented along with some of the challenges that have arisen from such partnerships.

CONTEXTS FOR REFORM OF TEACHER EDUCATION

With an incendiary portrait of education in *A Nation at Risk* (National Commission on Excellence in Education, 1983), the White House launched an attack on public education in America. Since then, the media have flooded the public with studies, technical analyses, and endless commentaries about the poor state of affairs. Concerns have centered on a reported decline in student achievement in the primary grades, poor performance of college students in science and math when compared with students in other countries, poor return on dollars invested in student achievement, and young adults entering the work force unprepared and forcing the private business community to spend large sums of money on basic and remedial education. The general argument has been that schools are staffed by unqualified teachers, and parents are unhappy with the education their children receive. Pundits have crafted an image of public education as a bureaucratically controlled institution that wastes resources and defeats the professional and moral interests of teachers. In many instances, teachers and administrators have been characterized as inept, if not lacking in intelligence and knowledge.

Lengthy analyses and debates focused considerable attention on factors contributing to the presumed decline in public education. These factors, or causes of the decline, became targets for reform. A great deal of blame has been placed on parents, who do not send their children to school ready to learn, and on poorly prepared teachers and curricula that neither challenge nor inspire students. As a result, there has been an emphasis on working with parents and on improving teacher education. The focus on teacher education, as a central feature of the education reform movement, has produced considerable innovation in teacher education programs in response to the charge (Epanchin & Wooley-Brown, 1993; Evans, Harris, Adeigbola, Houston, & Argott, 1993; Paul et al., 1995; Paul, Duchnowski, & Danforth, 1983; Paul, Rosselli, & Evans, 1995; Rosselli, Perez, Piersall, & Pantridge, 1993).

CHANGING A SPECIAL EDUCATION TEACHER EDUCATION PROGRAM

When we started thinking about the nature of our teacher education program and how to determine what changes we needed to make to respond to the school reform movement, one of our first challenges was to understand the context in which we were working. We, like others in our situation, were faced with changing our teacher preparation program to serve the interests of our students who we knew would be teaching in schools that were being restructured. What would a teacher need to know and be able to do in a restructured school? In the absence of a coherent philosophy of education guiding the restructuring of schools, what philosophy should ground the teacher education program? With strong differences existing among schools and among diverse professional and parent constituencies regarding the inclusion of children with disabilities, what kind of educational environment should be used for internship placements? How should we assist students preparing to be teachers in understanding the complex issues associated with assessment and instruction when professionals are so deeply divided on fundamental issues? Attempting to respond to these and other similarly basic questions shaped our early discussions.

Several assumptions guided our early efforts. First, if anything was clear in the reform of education, it was and is that we have not come to terms with the diversity of interests now represented in schools. Ethnicity, gender, ability, behavior, ideology—all are constructed in the vision of the majority culture and understood, often exclusively, in the moral and epistemological image of the modern world. The education of teachers, no less than the education of the students they teach, has reflected the traditional insensitivity to diversity. We considered our commitment to diversity to be a test of the fidelity of the mission we had set for ourselves in restructuring our program.

A diversity agenda was implemented in two ways. First, we recruited, employed, and have retained an ethnically diverse faculty. Six of the first eight new faculty employed are African American; four of the six are female, joining a predominantly male faculty. Second, we developed a methodologically pluralistic research training program. This involved recruiting the participation of qualitative and interpretive researchers from other departments throughout the university to work with our doctoral students and faculty in order to complement the almost exclusive quantitative research training program that was in place.

The second assumption involved the development of community. In most research universities one expects to find individual faculty competing for limited resources and for students to assist in their research. We believed that revisioning and restructuring our program should be a synergistic product of a collective effort to rethink our work. We came up with several strategies to facilitate community development. Perhaps the most successful strategy was the development of collaborative research groups (CRG). These groups included faculty and doctoral students who chose to pursue a particular area of research. The groups agreed to meet for 2 hours each week and to give the meeting the same priority one gives to meeting a class. The CRGs served the purpose of building community and creating a research culture in which constructivism is valued.

A third assumption had to do with our relationship with schools and our view of ourselves as faculty members in a university. We believed that the future of our work as teacher educators depended on our ability to establish authentic collegial linkages with schools where we could share in the learning about restructuring and its implications for teacher education. Difficulties with the traditional role of experts, assigned to go in to assist schools, were described frequently in the literature. One difficulty, we found, is that the role of expert suggests that that person has special knowledge that is needed and valued. The literature during the past decade has been helpful in distinguishing "craft," or teacher knowledge, from the knowledge generated by systematic research. It has become increasingly clear that the theory/practice schism—the view held by many teachers that faculty research is irrelevant, on the one hand, and the view held by many faculty that teachers are not interested in research, on the other—is a function of the different kinds of knowledge being developed/constructed and discussed. Another difficulty is that the role of expert tends to establish a hierarchical and privileged relationship between the one who's an expert and the one who isn't. The status issue can keep relationships distant and prevent the development of trust where real stories are told and real concerns are shared. The task is to be relevant and of value while learning, not to sabotage the relationship with the trappings of the expert role. Our strategies for establishing authentic collegial linkages with schools included developing professional development schools and consortia between the university and school district programs.

Gaining Support for a Change Agenda

As is well documented in the literature, change is difficult for programs, and one of the most challenging aspects of changing a program has to do with developing motivation to change. When change is mandated, questions loom: Why change? What's wrong with the way we are doing things? How is this going to affect me? Am I going to lose something I really like? Addressing these concerns in a fair and supportive manner is essential if people are to buy into a change agenda.

In our situation, these issues have been addressed over time and through numerous discussions as part of the work of the Teacher Education Committee, a group composed of all faculty and staff who teach and work with the teacher education program, both undergraduate and graduate. This group is charged with establishing and implementing the curriculum, creating policy that supports the program(s), and monitoring the quality of the program(s). These charges have been broadly defined to include issues related to educational experiences both at the university and in the field. The restructuring agenda was first introduced when this group was formed. Initially, much of the group's work had to do with student petitions and requests for exceptions to existing program guidelines. These requests served as a vehicle through which faculty voiced their beliefs and gradually reached consensus on specific solutions. Over time, most of the faculty came to trust the process, and these discussions provided a means of reaching consensus on some basic issues.

From student petitions, the committee moved to curriculum revision and revision of field experiences. The categorical master's level programs were revised to reduce the overlap across areas and to maximize class enrollment and monitoring of students' experiences. When the process first began, attendance was sporadic and one of the greatest irritants for some faculty was repeating content discussed at previous meetings for faculty who had missed meetings. Currently, the teacher education committee (TEC) meets less frequently, moving from weekly to biweekly to monthly, but attendance is predictably high and the group appears committed to the process.

Advocating for Policy and Procedural Changes Within the State and University Structures

When our department began its restructuring efforts, we did so within a context that voiced support and encouragement for our efforts at both the state and college level; however, at all these levels, policies existed that posed problems for our restructuring. In order to be able to have input into the decision making surrounding these issues, our faculty got involved in a number of policy-making groups such as the State Advisory Council, the state Comprehensive System of Personnel Development (CSPD) Oversight Committee, committees that were reviewing standards and certification requirements, and committees charged with reviewing and credentialing other teacher education programs within the state. When we began our efforts, the state was rigidly categorical in its approach to certification and openly critical of efforts to place more decision making at the university level. Now the state has a committee to recommend certification modifications, and the Commissioner of Education is recommending that more decision-making authority be given to local schools and universities.

Similarly, from the beginning of our efforts to change, guidance and support were sought at the College of Education level from the chairpersons of the committees charged with reviewing programs and approving program changes. Whenever a forum was available, information about our efforts was shared. As other programs expressed interest or shared similar efforts, alliances were formed and cooperative efforts across departments were begun. Over time a coalition of faculty committed to transforming teaching education has emerged and become an influential voice within the college. This group of faculty is now seeking status within the college as a standing committee that has as its overarching purpose the reform and renewal of teacher education.

Experimental Programs

Because our program is a large one, a change in practice can be quite complicated and disruptive. Although experimentation is the means through which we learn, it is difficult to do on a program level. We have therefore developed several pilot projects through which we are testing ideas before we attempt to revise our entire program. Each of these projects grew out of a concern or question about an issue; thus the projects are discussed in relation to the concern they addressed.

How do we prepare teachers who are culturally sensitive and informed? We wanted to prepare teachers who have the skills and knowledge to work with diverse children and families, but how to do this was a question we began discussing early in our reform efforts. The PILOT (Preparing Innovative Leaders of Tomorrow) program was a funded project developed in an effort to address this question. Over a 3-year period, PILOT admitted 30 African American men who were majoring in behavior disorders to our undergraduate program. PILOT students changed the ethnic and gender composition of our undergraduate classes significantly in a very short period of time. PILOT students were carefully selected on the basis of their potential to be school-based leaders, and their leadership potential was immediately evident in our classrooms. Some of the questions and concerns raised had not previously been voiced in our classes. By virtue of the students' presence, faculty and the majority of our undergraduates were exposed to greater diversity of thought and opinion.

The presence of students from diverse backgrounds, however, is not sufficient for preparing teachers who are culturally sensitive and informed. Content is also needed, as are diverse teaching strategies. Faculty began discussing the infusion of content related to diversity and taking faculty development courses to learn teaching strategies that meet diverse students needs.

How do we collaborate with schools in order to prepare teachers who have the skills and knowledge needed for school reform? There have been several projects designed to address this question. The STEP (School-based Teacher Education Partnership) program was a federally funded personnel preparation project designed to address a number of concerns that school districts were expressing: high numbers of out-of-field teachers, attrition of teachers, university schedules that were inconvenient and cumbersome, and university courses that were repetitious and irrelevant.

STEP features an alternative schedule of classes, an accelerated curriculum, an adult learning model, and a performance-based assessment system. This project grew out of our realization that most of our master's-level students are full-time teachers with responsibilities to family and community. Although they are conscientious students, their perspectives are rarely changed by classes that meet one night a week. More important, their practices are rarely altered. In full-time programs, students typically are immersed in their studies along with a group of their peers who are studying and experiencing many of the same things. Collegial discussion and peer feedback develop naturally during the course of the educational experience.

Because faculty believed in the value of immersion in one's educational studies and in working with a peer group, program models used by other disciplines were explored in an effort to find a way to institute the valued practices while also enabling students to keep their teaching jobs. This led to the creation of a master's track that used an alternative calendar and an accelerated curriculum featuring reformatted courses that fit into a 2-week, 5-day-a-week format. With this schedule, it was possible for students to take more classes during the summer months when they were not teaching. Class time in these reformatted courses was designed for student participation. Class activities, in combination with the readings and required private reflections (students kept reflective journals that faculty responded to on a regular basis) were intended to stimulate critical thought about the ethical, political, and pedagogical challenges teachers face daily. Faculty used the journals to learn about students' reactions so they could alter activities or address individual student's concerns. During these intensive courses, debates, role plays, and large- or small-group discussions were used frequently to simulate or analyze complex teaching situations. Most activities were carried out collaboratively with more experienced teachers helping students who were just entering the field. Feedback from faculty and students has been very positive to date, and the program retention and completion rates are significantly higher for STEP students than for traditional students.

To ensure that students also acquire specific skills and knowledge expected by professional and accrediting bodies, students are required to complete a portfolio that demonstrates their mastery of competencies set forth by the Florida Department of Education and the Council for Exceptional Children. These competencies are subsumed under five major headings: Assessment, Behavior Management, Instruction, Collaboration, and Systematic Inquiry. Mastery is demonstrated through a reflective essay about the student's activities and work in each of these areas, documentation of work in these activities, and an action research project carried out in their classrooms or schools in each of these areas. Projects are completed during the academic year with assistance and support from doctoral students in teacher education and departmental faculty.

This combined approach of group activities and individualized work provides students with multiple opportunities to construct knowledge and have a voice in determining the direction of their educational program. Students progress through the entire program with the same cohort, leading to the formation of close, lifelong professional bonds. Because of the intensity of the program, students report that course work is a dominant factor in their lives while in the program, and faculty note important shifts in thinking and attitudes as students progress through the program. Although this project was designed in response to school district needs, it is not collaboratively managed. School district personnel serve on an advisory board and have actively supported the program, whereas the design, implementation, and staffing of the project have remained at the university. Subsequent projects, developed collaboratively with the school districts, have enabled us to experiment with shared responsibility for implementation and staffing.

The *USF/Polk County Teacher Preparation Program for Paraprofessionals* was an undergraduate program collaboratively developed with Polk County special education personnel in response to the critical need for qualified special education teachers in Polk County. The purpose of this project was to "home-grow" special education teachers, particularly those from minority backgrounds. In planning the project, features valued by the Department of Special Education were incorporated with those valued by the Polk County personnel. Together, the school district and university personnel planned, implemented, and shared responsibility for staffing the project. It was federally funded for 7 years, during which time more than 50 students graduated from the project and Polk County's teacher shortages were significantly reduced.

The *Inquiry-based Teacher Education Project* also was a federally funded project that piloted the use of school-based master teachers who assumed responsibility for supervising practicum students assigned to their schools. In this project, clusters of students were placed at a school where a site-based coordinator (a master teacher) was given the responsibility for students' placements and well-being at the school. The site coordinators made a point of learning about the courses students took so they could assist them in a manner consistent with the on-campus program when the students needed help. When a problem arose, the site coordinator contacted the university and together they developed a plan for dealing with it. Each semester, the site coordinators met with the Teacher Education Coordinator to discuss how the collaboration could be improved. When the project was funded, the site coordinators assumed supervisory responsibility for action research projects that the students were assigned. These additional duties provided the coordinators with more input and instructional responsibility. This shared responsibility for the preparation of teachers improved the alignment of content and field practice.

Evolving Vision as a Result of Our Restructuring Efforts

Unlike the ideal of a planned and orderly change process, we are creating our future as we learn and develop together. When we began this process, we held a few firm but unstructured beliefs: that we should work in partnership with the public schools as equal collaborators, not as the outside experts; that we were committed to the concept of affirming differences; that a quality teacher education program should be a transformative experience; and that teachers should be prepared not only to fit into the schools of today but also to be the change agents in creating better, more inclusive schools for the future. To accomplish these goals we actively recruited diverse faculty and students, and together we have worked to forge better programs for children with special needs. Through our experiences implementing and administering our program and through our Teacher Education Committee discussions, we have endorsed a constructivist, collaborative approach to teacher education, and we now are also endorsing the following values and practices:

1. *Stable training teams or cohorts* so that students progress through their program of study with essentially the same people, thereby having a group of peers who are facing the same learning challenges and with whom learning can be shared.
2. *Mentoring relationships* through which students can learn clinical skills and strategies for dealing with the complex political and ethical challenges that teachers face.
3. *Ample opportunities to test and practice* emerging skills and knowledge in ecologically valid settings without fear of reprisal.
4. *Guided practice in thinking about complex teaching dilemmas* through the use of teaching cases and vignettes.
5. *Reflection upon daily practice* and a forum to share these reflections, when desired.

All of these practices provide opportunities for students to construct knowledge about teaching and the collaborative practice of special education. All of our students are on teams and some of our faculty stay with a team for several semesters, teaching them several core courses. This continuity between a faculty member and a team promotes and supports mentoring relationships. Each semester students spend time in the schools with students who have disabilities, and field supervisors also function as mentors.

School/University Partnerships

Spending 2 to 3 days a week in schools, faculty are able to witness the frenetic working pace of teachers who never have enough time to reflect on the myriad of daily decisions made in the classroom. In our experience, a new level of respect was reached as one faculty member considered the differences between the abstract and distanced participation that usually characterizes the lives of professors at work in the university and the daily responsibilities that face educators in schools. The reality of unmotivated students, late buses, the cycle of incomplete homework, the continual interruptions and schedule changes all can have a sobering impact on one's vision of school and the potential for reform initiatives to really make a difference.

The very nature of the school reality made genuine conversation more challenging. In the reality of schools, conversations that held promise for the genuine sharing of ideas and collaborative problem solving were often interrupted by, "I need to get back . . . the bell is going to ring," or, "I've got bus duty, got to go." The same scenario was often true for school administrators as well. The ever-present walkie-talkie clearly linked the administrator to the immediate needs and functioning of a school. In the ideal school, there would be dedicated time, perhaps during the summer months, to support the type of spontaneous collaboration that grows out of a shared cup of coffee (Christensen et al., 1996).

This adjustment to time and pace was so noticeable that upon returning to the university environment, one professor found that the urgency and immediacy of the school world made long meetings at the university less acceptable and subsequent lack of prompt action more intolerable. She couldn't help but think, "Don't they (the university) realize it's a war zone out there? We don't have time to sit back and contemplate the nature of a crisis while we're witnesses to increasing casualties." (The use of the term "them" to describe one's part-time colleagues appears to be characteristic of the behavior of "boundary spanners.")

Even when reform at the school level was well supported by district and school policy changes, another conundrum of school reality was witnessed when change had still not filtered into the daily world of the classroom. When block scheduling was established at a school, for example, teachers were encouraged to use time more creatively for either single discipline or integrated experiences. Yet seldom was this opportunity fully maximized. The bells still ran the schedule even when permission was granted to ignore them. This type of school reality presents a dilemma for those who write about reform and teacher empowerment because invisible barriers still exist that can impact the implementation of school improvement efforts. Perhaps the remembered experiences of teachers as students still heavily influence their reluctance to experiment with new ideas. Or perhaps the sense of orderliness often favored by teachers, which also serves as a stabilizer in the fragmented world of teaching, still overpowers an embracing of innovation. Or perhaps change is still seen as new ideas imposed from outside and therefore to be deflected (Barth, 1990).

Responding to School Realities

This insider view of schooling eventually led to several initiatives redesigned to take into consideration the reality of schools while supporting the university's and school's shared visions for reform and restructuring. Perhaps, as Barth (1990) suggests, the university can best assist by "helping professionals clarify and reveal their own rich thinking about good schools" (p. 110). To help encourage a commitment to inquiry and continued professional development (Holmes Group, 1995), one faculty meeting per month was dedicated to Faculty Focus Groups at a school with which we work closely. A process was used to identify questions or issues of interest to faculty, who were then encouraged to group themselves according to their interests. These focus groups were then supplied with reference materials located by the university faculty member and doctoral students. Teachers were encouraged to decide how this knowledge could be utilized to improve classroom or school practice. Some showed an interest in systematically documenting the level of impact, whereas others were more content simply to acquire ideas that could be used in the future. This focus on improvement-oriented inquiry may be the long bridge toward what has often been described as teacher-initiated research. In our case, teachers were not always eager and willing to start researching their own practice, which may have been a remnant of the fear that the university "would tell us what we're doing wrong." Then again, it may have been simply a response to an already full plate onto which was being placed one more expectation.

Not surprisingly, the focus groups supported an enhanced and later unified voice for "special" educators in the school. The needs of migrant students, students in dropout prevention programs, ESOL students, nonreaders, students receiving free or reduced-price lunch, and gifted and ethnically diverse students were all represented in discussions that first acknowledged the legitimate needs of each special population, followed later by a recognition that an inclusive approach to education demands a greater responsibility from all general educators for these students' outcomes. Once the complexity of the school's composition had been honestly acknowledged, some teachers found themselves wondering if there really were any general education students anymore.

Another mechanism modeled after Barth's (1990) "halfway houses" was created to support professional development for both interns and cooperating teachers: Intern Support Group meetings. In lieu of individual Senior Seminars for which each intern was expected to return to the university, these groups brought together all of the interns at the school to discuss challenging issues typically faced during internship. After topics were identified, a continuum of participation was offered to faculty, ranging from simply attending the meetings to cofacilitating them. Sometimes teachers contributed their favorite article or list of tips and strategies as part of their involvement. The benefit to the university's student teachers was the exposure to a larger number of the school faculty, many of whom shared their own frustrations and solutions to the same problems encountered by the interns. The benefit to school faculty may have been the realization that their craft knowledge has as much legitimacy as the empirical research taught in the university's training program. The demand of teachers for workshops that prepare them for Monday may indeed be a call in disguise for more informal sharing of ideas, that work for somebody somewhere. Universities wishing to be supportive of school reform may do well to design more deliberate opportunities for informal conversation and the sharing of ideas, as mirrored in recent staff development literature (Sparks & Hirsch, 1997).

Linking Schools and Universities: A Reality Check for Collaboration

When the faculty met during a summer retreat to reflect on their experiences in a school, a priority issue was how the school could be made to feel more a part of the university. What was still lacking was the two-way level of reciprocity sought as an integral part in any partnership. According to Dixon and Ishler (1992), this type of "organic collaboration," a term coined by Whitford, Schlechty, and Shelor (1987), occurs when both parties become equally vested and power and control issues dissipate.

One solution often sought is to appoint school faculty to joint positions at both the district and university levels. In our case a faculty member coordinated the university's special education practicum placements and taught an undergraduate course for the university onsite at a school. One reason this arrangement worked so well is that the teacher's role as a mainstream consulting teacher and coteacher made it easier to attend meetings and handle responsibilities associated with the school. This approach, however, requires a different type of job appointment, a modification that may require both district and union support, a discussion of differential job assignments, and perhaps waivers for certain district policies.

Policy issues seem to surface frequently as a result of university/school partnerships. The perception that one or two schools are intensely involved with the university conjures up questions of equity and fairness within a district. We encountered issues of equity involving the placement of student teachers, selection of cooperating teachers, and professional development opportunities. The university may rightly feel a need to have a voice in these decisions so as to ensure continuity and congruence with the teacher education program. However, the resolution of these dilemmas will need to consider policies and perspectives beyond just those at partnership sites.

School/university partnerships are also intended to eliminate the incongruence that occurs when student teachers are taught "novel, cutting-edge" teaching techniques at the university but then regress to more traditional means of teaching as modeled by their supervising teachers (Murray, 1995). In our case, the innovative practice at the school level was sometimes outstripping the teacher education program. Teams of content area teachers and at least one special education teacher were expecting the university student teachers to jump right in and show proficiency in the skills of collaboration and shared problem solving. Unfortunately, their training programs had not prepared them for working with others outside their specialty disciplines. Teachers who were expected to design curriculum around major themes or big concepts discovered that student teachers were unfamiliar with some of the natural but abstract connections between disciplines. Also, the perceptions that student teachers held of their responsibilities as professionals were often still very traditional and narrow. For example, when special education student teachers were placed in regular classroom settings to work with and support special education students included in the regular classroom, they often complained, asking, "When can I spend time in a special education classroom?"

Clearly, as universities become more involved in the daily workings of schools, they will be better able to redefine the role of higher education in the restructuring and reform of education. As more and more boundary spanners develop a sense of how to work effectively in two worlds, the "tourist-visa" mentality that Barth

(1990) describes will fade away in favor of a more symbiotic partnership, one in which authentic collaboration can and will be the norm influencing ways in which special and general education can work together.

Expanding the Vision: Collaboration Across Colleges

Another example of the restructuring and change in the department is our work in the area of improving programs for children who have emotional and behavioral disabilities and their families. This area of exceptionality was the focus of teaching and research for several faculty members in the department; consequently, it easily became another vehicle for our changing values and orientation to teacher education. Holding to the philosophy described above, we began to pursue approaches that would integrate local and generalizable knowledge into a holistic vision. This vision would facilitate decision making about effective program implementation and contribute to our continued examination of local, craft, and contextual influences on teacher knowledge.

We are learning about decision making and parent involvement in the context of developing interventions for children who have serious emotional and behavioral disabilities. Just as we examine site-based versus top-down processes in school governance and decision making, we are exploring similar strategies for developing special education placement and individualized educational planning. In this case the traditional approach consists of a multidisciplinary team that conveys its assessment of a student's deficits to the parents and recommends an intervention plan. In the participatory model, parents are viewed as equal decision-making partners with valid expertise in understanding their child. The focus of intervention is strengths-based, and the expertise of the professionals lies in their knowledge of the array of available service and interventions. Professionals facilitate access to service for the family, employing a mutually developed plan that respects the families' strengths and their status as equal members of the team.

The implementation of these values and skills into our teacher education program is a formidable task. We are aware that much of what we propose is counter to prevailing perceptions of parents who have children with disabilities as well as to prevailing views of the role of professionals. Furthermore, the data supporting such models are sparse. Our task is twofold: We need to develop a training program to produce a new generation of teachers and related professionals who have the skills necessary to implement family friendly interventions; and we need to conduct research demonstrating the efficacy of such models.

A major strategy that we are employing to achieve these goals is collaboration with several components of the university. The collaboration described thus far has been primarily between the Department of Special Education, other departments in the College of Education, and the public schools. In addition to these initiatives, we have developed fruitful relationships with several other departments in various colleges across the campus. These include the Departments of Anthropology, Community Health, Sociology, the School of Social Work, and the Florida Mental Health Institute (FMHI). For example, we have developed a joint doctorate with the Department of Anthropology, enabling students to develop a deeper level of proficiency with ethnographic and oral history methods to be used in special education research. Recently, our first student completed this program and did an oral history of children of migrant farm workers who are at risk for needing special education services. In the Department of Community Health, which is in the College of Public Health, one project in its beginning stages is an attempt to assess the current status of AIDS education for special education students and to develop information and guidelines for policy-makers.

Perhaps our most productive relationship is that with the Department of Child and Family Studies at FMHI. Briefly, FMHI has been established at USF with the broad mission of improving Florida's mental health system through an integrated series of research, training, and service activities. The Department of Child and Family Studies has developed an extensive program of activities that focuses on children who have serious emotional disabilities and their families. Assisted by a federal grant from the Office of Special Education and Rehabilitative Services and the Center for Mental Health Services, the research and training activities have expanded to include issues with a national scope as well as those that concern Florida.

In a sense, the collaboration between FMHI and the Department of Special Education was almost inevitable. As the department engaged in activities to restructure the teacher education program in special education, results from FMHI's studies and those of other researchers indicated the relatively poor outcomes for children served in special education programs, particularly for those children identified as having emotional disabilities (Duchnowski, Johnson, Hall, Kutash, & Friedman, 1993).

The search for improvement in these outcomes began to focus on systemic factors. There was clearly a need for new working relationships between schools and social service and health care agencies. The role of families in the education and treatment of their children was undergoing a dramatic change from passive recipient of information to active decision-making partner (Duchnowski, Dunlap, Berg, & Adeigbola, 1994). It was proposed that there would be changing roles for teachers and the other professionals who work with children who have disabilities and their families. Traditional unidimensional interventions and traditional professional training were in need of a reconceptualization to accommodate the data supporting holistic, multidisciplinary approaches that stressed family involvement and cultural competency. These were some of the same values guiding the reform activities in the Department of Special Education at USF (Paul et al., 1993).

Several faculty from FMHI received joint appointments in the Department of Special Education and served as research mentors for students, coinvestigators with department faculty, active members of the CRGs, and instructors in courses. There are two projects that illustrate the success of the collaboration in contributing to reform in both public education and the preparation of teachers of children who have disabilities. These projects focus on children who are at-risk, or who already display serious behavioral and emotional problems, and the families of these children.

Child and Adolescent Service System Local Project

The Child and Adolescent Service System Program (CASSP) is a federal initiative that has the broad goal of improving the service delivery system for children who have serious emotional disabilities and the families of these children (Day & Roberts, 1991). Federal grants were awarded at the state level to improve the collaboration between the major child-serving agencies, that is, mental health, special education, child welfare, and juvenile justice. In the second wave of funding, states competed for grants to fund projects at the local level that would exemplify the value of collaboration and thereby improve services for children and their families. Florida was successful in this competition and located a project in a middle school, which was a PDS described earlier. In the application, the relationship between the school, the community, and the University of South Florida was stressed as a very positive factor that could contribute to the success of the project. Again, there was confluence of vision and values. The school set as goals improved family involvement, the recognition of cultural diversity and the need for cultural competency, and improved outcomes for children with emotional and behavioral disabilities. The university placed these goals very high in its developing teacher education program, and community-based social service agencies sought to implement a program with these CASSP values.

As a result, the program was implemented with a doctoral student in special education serving as the project coordinator. Other students who were doing internships at this school also benefited from the CASSP project. The evaluation of the initiative is serving as a dissertation topic for another doctoral student. More important, we can see the results of the broad based collaboration. Service providers are now implementing school-based interventions to better serve the children and their families, the school has formed a student and family assistance team in which teachers and others have taken on new roles because they feel they have to in order to do what needs to be done, and student teachers will be increasingly exposed to this model intervention. The federal funding has ended, but the program will continue. Although no one has adequate resources, all of the members of the partnership recognize the cost-effectiveness of such a program. The school district and the provider agencies will continue an economic commitment, and the department will assign an advanced doctoral student to serve as program coordinator and at least one first-year student will experience an on-site practicum, gain valuable experience, and ultimately assume a leadership role.

The Child and Family Policy Program

There have been many studies documenting the need for leadership personnel to administer, evaluate, and continue developing the innovative program models that employ the holistic, collaborative, multidisciplinary approach (Duchnowski, Kutash, & Knitzer, 1997). Although this need certainly exists at both the undergraduate and graduate levels, the department decided to take its first step with the development of a specialty track in the special education doctoral program. A faculty team was joined by family members, public school representatives, and service providers to develop this program. It consists of a core curriculum in special education and a series of seminars and field placements that are multidisciplinary in nature and guided by the values of the department in restructuring teacher education. The overarching goal is to produce leaders who will inform public policy in the implementation of programs that are both cost-effective and efficacious in improving outcomes for children with emotional and behavioral disabilities and their families.

In 1993, the department and FMHI each agreed to support a doctoral student through 3 years of training. In 1994, the department was awarded a training grant from the Office of Special Education Programs to support 15 students through their doctoral training. The field placements for these students were in schools that engaged in reform/restructuring activities aimed at improving outcomes for all children and increasing the role of families in all aspects of the education of their children. Students accepted into this program had a strong experience base in one of the child-serving disciplines and possessed a master's degree. They typically conducted their research at one of the school-based sites.

With these two projects we made substantial progress toward our goals of developing the new generation of professionals and of contributing to the emerging research base supporting the new models of delivering special education services to children and their families. Although our initial focus has been at the doctoral level, we are now examining how to infuse these concepts into the master's and undergraduate degree programs.

CONCLUSION

In responding to the challenge for our program to become more relevant to the changing needs of future teachers, we have been guided by a commitment to diversity, interdisciplinary programming, multiple research methods, and an emphasis on care and competence. We have been influenced by the overall context of school reform, inclusion, and human services integration. Throughout this process of change, we have been following a constructivist approach, with new initiatives evolving from what we learn from children and their families, from our students at the university, and from each other. Michael Fullan (1993) uses an apt analogy in suggesting that the reform of schools is guided more by a compass than a map. Our experience at the University of South Florida is that our persistent and collective sense of the direction of change we are pursuing is usually clearer than our specific objectives. The vision that guides our work has helped shape the beginnings of a moral community, one in which core values are care, learning, diversity, hard work, and investment in building and maintaining the social capital of the learning communities inclusive of school and university members.

The difficult changes effected by the school reform movement and services integration are felt by individual faculty members, who are expected to change their concept of themselves as experts, the content and methods of teaching courses they have taught routinely for many years, and the way they work with their faculty colleagues. They are expected to teach in ways that amplify the role of the person behind the pedagogy, to work more collegially with teachers and other leaders in schools, and to learn new ways of understanding inquiry. Teacher educators who have taught many teachers to teach children with disabilities, and have earned positive student evaluations of their teaching, are having to learn ways of thinking about teaching and learning that are different from and may be in conflict with the education they received in preparing for their role as teacher educators.

We have come to believe that the process of individual change should be embedded in the context of a learning community in which the redefinition of one's ways of thinking and working is expected and supported. The welfare of the community and the culture that sustains it, then, is central to the process of change and must become a shared responsibility of all members. Changes in curricula, course delivery, program policies, and relationships are part of a complex process of building a culture in which individuals also must change and grow with the community. It is not easy. It is deeply rewarding. The experiences shared in this chapter should be understood as a part of a continuing journey.

REFERENCES

Barth, R. (1990). *Improving schools from within*. San Francisco: Jossey-Bass.

Christensen, L., Epanchin, B., Harris, D., Rosselli, H., Smith, L., & Stoddard, K. (1996). Anatomy of six public school–university partnerships. *Teacher Education and Special Education, 19*(2), 169–179.

Day, C., & Roberts, M. (1991). Activities of the child and Adolescent Service System program for improving mental health services for children and their families. *Journal of Clinical Child Psychology, 20*, 340–350.

Dixon, P., & Ishler, R. (1992). Professional development schools: Stages in collaboration. *Journal of Teacher Education, 43*(1), 28–34.

Duchnowski, A. J., Dunlap, G., Berg, K., & Adeigbola, M. (1994). Rethinking the role of families in the education of their children: Policy and clinical issues. In J. Paul, H. Rosselli, & D. Evans (Eds.), *Integrating school restructuring and special education reform*. Ft. Worth, TX: Harcourt Brace.

Duchnowski, A. J., Johnson, M. K., Hall, K. S., Kutash, K., & Friedman, R. M. (1993). The alternatives to residential treatment study: Initial findings. *Journal of Emotional and Behavioral Disorders, 1*, 17–26.

Duchnowski, A. J., Kutash, K., & Knitzer, J. (1997). Integrative and collaborative community services in exceptional student education. In J. L. Paul, M. Churton, W. Morse, A. Duchnowski, B. Epanchin, P. Osnes, & I. Smith (Eds.), *Special education practice: Applying the knowledge, affirming the values and creating the future* (pp. 171–187). Belmont, CA: Brooks/Cole.

Epanchin, B., & Wooley-Brown, C. (1993). A university–school district collaborative project for preparing paraprofessionals to become special educators. *Teacher Education in Special Education, 16*(2), 110–123.

Evans, D., Harris, D., Adeigbola, M., Houston, D., & Argott, L. (1993). Restructuring special education services. *Teacher Education in Special Education, 16*(2), 137–145.

Fullan, M. G. (1993). *Change forces*. New York: Falmer Press.

Holmes Group. (1995). *Tomorrow's schools of education*. East Lansing, MI: Author.

Murray, F. B. (1995). Design principles and criteria for professional development schools. In H. G. Petrie (Ed.), *Professionalization, partnership, and power: Building professional development schools* (pp. 23–38). Albany: State University of New York Press.

National Commission on Excellence in Education. (1983). *A nation at risk: The imperative for educational reform*. Washington, DC: U.S. Government Printing Office.

Paul, J., Duchnowski, A., & Danforth, S. (1993). Changing the way we do our business: One department's story of collaboration with public schools. *Teacher Education in Special Education, 16*(2), 95–109.

Paul, J., Epanchin, B., Rosselli, H., Townsend, B., Cranston-Gingras, A., & Thomas, D. (1995). Addressing the inevitable conflicts in reforming teacher education: One department's story. *Journal of Learning Disabilities, 28*(10), 646–655.

Paul, J., Rosselli, H., & Evans, D. (1995). *Integrating school restructuring and special education*. Ft. Worth, TX: Harcourt Brace.

Rosselli, H., Perez, S., Piersall, K., & Pantridge, O. (1993). Evolution of a professional development school: The story of a partnership. *Teacher Education in Special Education, 16*(2), 124–136.

Sparks, D., & Hirsch, S. (1997). *A new vision for staff development*. Alexandria, VA: Association for Supervision and Curriculum Development.

Whitford, B. L., Schlechty, P. C., & Shelor, L. G. (1987). Sustaining action research through collaboration: Inquiries for invention. *Peabody Journal of Education, 64*, 151–169.

About the Contributors

Editor's Note: The editor wishes to thank Carmen Collins for her hard work and valuable editorial skills in assisting with the preparation of this volume.

Lou Brown, Ph.D., is Professor of Rehabilitation Psychology and Special Education at the University of Wisconsin, Madison, Wisconsin.

Ann Cranston-Gingras, Ph.D., is Associate Professor in the Department of Special Education at the College of Education, University of South Florida, Tampa, Florida.

Al Duchnowski, Ph.D., is Professor in the Department of Special Education at the College of Education, and Florida Mental Health Institute, University of South Florida, Tampa, Florida.

Betty Epanchin, Ed.D., is Professor in the Department of Special Education at the College of Education, University of South Florida, Tampa, Florida.

Rebecca Farmer, M.S., is Teacher Consultant, Fayette County Public School, Lexington, Kentucky.

Dianne L. Ferguson, Ph.D., is Professor and Senior Research Associate with Educational and Community Supports at the College of Education, University of Oregon, Eugene, Oregon.

Karen Symms Gallagher, Ph.D., is Emery Stoops and Joyce King-Stoops Dean of the Rossier School, and Professor, Division of Education Policy and Administration at the University of Southern California, Los Angeles, California.

R. J. (Pat) Gallagher, Ph.D., is Professor in the Department of Special Education at the College of Education, California State University, Northridge, California.

Kathy Gee, Ph.D., is Associate Professor in the Special Education Program at the School of Education, St. Mary's College of California, Moraga, California.

Martin Gerry, J.D., is Director of the Center for the Study of Family, Neighborhood and Community Policy at the University of Kansas, Lawrence, Kansas.

Jack Jorgensen, Ph.D., is Director of Pupil Services in the Madison Metropolitan School District, Madison, Wisconsin.

Jacqueline Farmer Kearns, Ed.D., is Associate Director of the Inclusive Large-Scale Standards and Assessment Project (ISSLA) at the Interdisciplinary Human Development Institute, University of Kentucky, Lexington, Kentucky.

Sarah Kennedy is an Alternate Assessment Consultant with the Inclusive Large-Scale Standards and Assessment Project (ISSLA), Louisville, Kentucky.

Harold L. Kleinert, Ph.D., is Executive Director of the Interdisciplinary Human Development Institute at the University of Kentucky, Lexington, Kentucky.

Patricia J. Kleinhammer-Tramill, Ph.D., is Associate Research Professor at the Institute for Educational Research and Public Service, and the Department of Special Education at the School of Education, University of Kansas, Lawrence, Kansas.

Paula Kluth, Ph.D., is Assistant Professor in the Teaching and Leadership Department at the School of Education, Syracuse University, Syracuse, New York.

Robi Kronberg, Ph.D., is a consultant in Littleton, Colorado.

Hal Lawson, Ph.D., is Professor of Education and of Social Welfare, as well as Special Assistant to the Executive Vice President for Academic Affairs, in addition to being Provost at the University of Albany, State University of New York, Albany, New York.

Beth McKeown, M.S., is a trainer with Networks for Training and Development, Inc., in Philadelphia, Pennsylvania.

Laura Owens-Johnson, Ph.D., is Assistant Professor in the Department of Exceptional Education at the University of Wisconsin, Milwaukee, Wisconsin.

Thomas B. Parrish, Ed.D., is Director and Managing Research Scientist at the Center for Special Education Finance at the American Institutes for Research (AIR), Palo Alto, California.

James Paul, Ed.D., is Professor in the Department of Special Education at the College of Education, University of South Florida, Tampa, Florida.

Ginevra Ralph, Ph.D., is Research Assistant and Instructor at Educational and Community Supports at the College of Education, University of Oregon, Eugene, Oregon.

Charlotte Ross, Ph.D., is Director of Faculty Mentoring at the School of Education, Illinois Benedictine University, Lisle, Illinois.

Hilda Rosselli, Ph.D., is Associate Dean at the College of Education, University of South Florida, Tampa, Florida.

Wayne Sailor, Ph.D., is Professor in the Department of Special Education at the School of Education, and Senior Scientist at the Beach Center for Families and Disability, Life Span Institute, University of Kansas, Lawrence, Kansas.

Nadia Katul Sampson, M.A., is Research Assistant and Project Specialist at Educational and Community Supports at the College of Education, University of Oregon, Eugene, Oregon.

Joanne Suomi, Ph.D., is an Adapted Physical Education Teacher in the Stevens Point School District, Stevens Point, Wisconsin.

Jacqueline B. Temple, Ph.D., is Assistant Professor at the Graduate School of Education in the Department of Curriculum and Instruction, Portland State University, Portland, Oregon.

James Tramill, Ph.D., is a researcher at the Institute for Educational Research and Public Service at the School of Education, University of Kansas, Lawrence, Kansas.

Kenneth R. Warlick, Ph.D., is the Director of the Inclusive Large-Scale Standards and Assessment Project (ISSLA) at the Interdisciplinary Human Development Institute, University of Kentucky, Lexington, Kentucky.

Jennifer York-Barr, Ph.D., is Associate Professor of Educational Policy and Administration at the University of Minnesota, Minneapolis, Minnesota.

Nancy Zollers, Ph.D., is Adjunct Professor in the Department of Education at Tufts University, Medford, Massachusetts.

Index

NAMES

SUBJECTS